LIVERPOOL MONOGRAPHS IN HISPANIC STUDIES

6 VISION AND THE VISUAL ARTS IN GALDOS

PETER A. BLY

A STUDY OF THE NOVELS AND NEWSPAPER ARTICLES

X
FRANCIS CAIRNS

Published by Francis Cairns (Publications) Ltd

c/o The University, P.O. Box 147, Liverpool L69 3BX
Great Britain

First published 1986

British Library Cataloguing in Publication Data

Bly, Peter A.
Vision and the visual arts in Galdós: a study of the
novels and newspaper articles.—(Liverpool
monographs in hispanic studies, ISSN 0261-1538; v.6)
1. Pérez Galdós, Benito—Criticism and interpretation
I. Title   II. Series
863´.5   PQ6555.Z5

ISBN 0-905205-30-8

Printed in Great Britain by
Redwood Burn Ltd, Trowbridge, Wiltshire

For Siobhain

"He who sees life clearly must perchance see it darkly and few see it more clearly than Galdós."

CONTENTS

ACKNOWLEDGEMENTS

This study was made possible through the generosity of the Social Sciences and Humanities Research Council of Canada. A Research Grant allowed me to gather material in Las Palmas and Madrid, whilst a Released Time Stipend enabled me to write up my ideas sooner than I could have otherwise expected. I am deeply indebted to the Council.

I am also grateful to Associate Dean John Beal, School of Graduate Studies and Research, Queen's University, for providing me with funds to complete the revised draft of this study.

The staff of the Interlibrary Loan Office, Douglas Library, Queen's University, spent many hours locating and obtaining books across North America, whilst Mrs. Paulette Bark, heroically deciphering a typescript that was more a quilt of longhand corrections, completed the typing of this manuscript with impressive speed and accuracy. My parents, wife and children gave me support and encouragement when they were needed most. To all I am extremely grateful.

P. A. Bly

Kingston, January-July, 1983

Abbreviations of Editions of Galdós' Work

AN   *Los artículos de Galdós en "La Nación", 1865-1866, 1868*, ed. William H. Shoemaker (Madrid: Insula, 1972)

CP   *Las cartas desconocidas de Galdós en "La Prensa" de Buenos Aires*, ed. William H. Shoemaker (Madrid: Cultura Hispánica, 1973)

E   *Benito Pérez Galdós: ensayos de crítica literaria*, ed. Laureano Bonet (Barcelona: Península, 1972)

ENI   *Episodios nacionales*, edición ilustrada de Arturo Mélida *et al.*, 10 vols. (Madrid: La Guirnalda, 1881-85)

OC   *Obras completas*, ed. F. C. Sainz de Robles, 6 vols. (Madrid: Aguilar, 1961-69)

OI   *Obras inéditas*, ed. Alberto Ghiraldo, 11 vols. (Madrid: Renacimiento, 1923-31)

P   *Los prólogos de Galdós*, ed. William H. Shoemaker (Mexico City: Andrea and Univ. of Illinois Press, 1962)

RMIE *Benito Pérez Galdós y la Revista del Movimiento Intelectual de Europa, Madrid, 1865-1867*, ed. Leo J. Hoar Jr. (Madrid: Insula, 1968)

All references to these editions will be followed by the appropriate abbreviation, volume number (where necessary) and page number. I have translated all non-English quotations in the hope that the book may interest students of other literatures as well as Hispanists and Galdosistas.

Abbreviations of Periodicals

AE   *Arte Español*

AEA *Anuario de Estudios Atlánticos*

AG   *Anales Galdosianos*

BHS *Bulletin of Hispanic Studies*

CHA *Cuadernos Hispanoamericanos*

HR   *Hispanic Review*

JAAC *Journal of Aesthetics and Art Criticism*

KRQ *Kentucky Romance Quarterly*

LL   *La Lectura*

NLH *New Literary History*

RCEH *Revista Canadiense de Estudios Hispánicos*

RE   *Revista de España*

TLS   *Times Literary Supplement*

INTRODUCTION

The origins of literature's frequent association with the visual arts, in particular with painting, are generally traced back, firstly, to the reported saying of the Greek poet Simonides that "painting is mute poetry and poetry a speaking picture" and, secondly, to the widely misinterpreted dictum of the Roman poet Horace, "ut pictura poesis" (poetry is like painting).[1] The statement of Cervantes in his *Los trabajos de Persiles y Sigismunda* (1617) is typical of many made by literary theorists in the Renaissance and Baroque periods: "History, Poetry and Painting ... are so much alike that when you write History, you are painting, and when you are painting, you are composing verse."[2] Hildebrand Jacob, to give another example from another literature, makes the same point over a century later: "The nearer the *Poet* approaches to the *Painter*, the more perfect he is; the more perfect the *Painter*, the more he imitates the *Poet*."[3] In practice, however, this purported parallelism merely amounted to the poet using pictorial description of physical shapes and the painter

---

[1] The phrase, taken from the *De arte poetica*, line 361 (see *The Complete Works of Horace*, ed. Casper J. Kramer [New York: Modern Library, 1936], p. 409), properly stated that some poems, like some paintings, repay repeated scrutiny, while others do not. See Jean H. Hagstrum, *The Sister Arts: The Tradition of Literary Pictorialism in English Poetry from Dryden to Gray* (Chicago: Univ. of Chicago Press, 1958), p. 9.

[2] *Obras completas*, ed. Angel Valbuena Prat (Madrid: Aguilar, 1967), p. 1668; for other examples see E.C. Riley, *Cervantes's Theory of the Novel* (Oxford: Clarendon Press, 1964), p. 57.

[3] Quoted by Jean Hagstrum, "The sister arts: from neoclassic to romantic", in *Comparatists at Work*, ed. Stephen G. Nicholls, Jr., and Richard B. Vowles (Waltham, Massachusetts: Blaisdell, 1968), pp. 169-94. See Roy Park, "Painting and poetry", in his *Hazlitt and the Spirit of the Age: Abstraction and Critical Theory* (Oxford: Clarendon Press, 1971), pp. 115-37.

taking his subject-matter from poetry, with the consequent neglect of other considerations.[4] As each art could avail itself so readily of the other, whether in the form of textual illustrations or literary subjects for canvases, the intercommunion of the two sister arts could always appear to be quite natural and automatic. But Lessing's famous attack on the whole convention in his *Laocoön* was based on the belief that painting should concern itself with the depiction of space, and poetry with the question of time, and that the properties of the two arts cannot be mixed. Far from destroying the tradition, Lessing's treatise only served to initiate a polemic that is still unresolved. In the nineteenth century, with poetry now having given way to the novel as the pre-eminent literary form, and painting more concerned with the contemporary world and Nature than with literary models, Henry James, on the one hand, could still claim a fundamental and complete parallelism between a novelist and a painter: they had the same inspiration and the same processes (if different vehicles) and embraced the same causes.[5] On the other hand, Degas, the French painter, was as obstinate as Lessing in his opposition to this affinity, declaring that the respective Muses performed their tasks independently of each other.[6] Modern critics have allied themselves with one or the other viewpoint: whilst Jean Laude adamantly insists that the two arts have to be separated,[7] Helmut Hatzfeld maintains that a comparison of both arts in a particular period is mutually illuminating.[8]

Those who doubt or caution against the wisdom of interart correspondence show an awareness that the terminology of the visual arts when transcribed to literature and vice versa produces a certain impressionistic vagueness that fails to express fully the reality of the written text or the art object, even after due allowances have been made. Words like "metaphor", "image", "icon", and even "colour" do not necessarily mean the same thing in each art. The common vocabulary can and does prove more of a stumbling block than an

[4] See M.H. Abrams, *The Mirror and the Lamp* (New York: Oxford Univ. Press, 1953), p. 34.

[5] *The Art of Fiction and Other Essays*, ed. Morris Roberts (New York: Oxford Univ. Press, 1948), p. 5.

[6] See Jean Seznec, "Art and literature: a plea for humility", *NLH*, 3 (1972), 569-74.

[7] "On the analysis of poems and paintings", *NLH*, 3 (1972), 471-86. Jean-Paul Sartre, "What is writing?", *Partisan Review*, 15 (1948), 9-31, is of the same opinion.

[8] "Literary criticism through art and art criticism through literature", *JAAC*, 6 (1947-48), 1-21.

aid.[9] For René Wellek, the perception of a parallel between literature and art is essentially a subjective experience, the result of a mood or an impression that depends on the ability of the individual reader or viewer to make free associations, when not directed to do so by the artist or writer.[10] Lessing had made the same point in his *Laocoön*: "The first who likened painting and poetry to each other *must have been a man of delicate perception, who found that both arts affected him in a similar manner.* Both, he realized, present to us appearances as reality, absent things as present; *both deceive and the deceit of either is pleasing*" (my italics).[11] Indeed, this sensible reminder of the basic deceit, both visual and verbal, of the sister arts will receive a surprising reformulation in the writings of Benito Pérez Galdós, the main topic of this study.

★   ★   ★

One of the unfortunate results of this centuries-old polemic has been the excessive concentration on the first and most frequent type of interart parallel, the acknowledged verbal reproduction of a famous

---

[9] See Amado Alonso and Raimundo Lida, "El concepto lingüístico de impresionismo", in their *El impresionismo en el lenguaje* (Buenos Aires: Univ. de Buenos Aires, 1936), pp. 121-249; Svetlana and Paul Alpers, "*Ut pictura noesis*?: criticism in literary studies and art history", *NLH*, 3 (1972), 433-58; G. Giovannini, "Method in the study of literature in its relations to the other fine arts", *JAAC*, 8 (1949-50), 185-95; Oleg Grabar, "History of art and history of literature: some random thoughts", *NLH*, 3 (1972), 559-68; Alastair Fowler, "Periodization and interart analogies", *Ibid.*, 487-509; Edmund L. King, *Gustavo Adolfo Bécquer: From Painter to Poet. Together with a Concordance of the "Rimas"* (Mexico City: Porrúa, 1953), p. 43; Sigmund Skard, "The use of colour in literature", *Proceedings of the American Philosophical Society*, 90 (1946), 163-249. Mario Praz, *Mnemosyne: the Parallels Between Literature and the Visual Arts* (Princeton: Princeton Univ. Press, 1970), p. 40, believes that the work of writers who are also artists should offer the best test of the theory of a parallel between the arts. Henry Krawitz, *Writers on Painting: a Study of the Theory and Criticism of the Visual Arts in Zola, Wilde, James and Proust and Its Relevance to Their Fiction* (Ann Arbor: Xerox University Microfilms, 1980), also finds that a writer's familiarity with the technique of painting through his own or others' experience is an aid.

[10] "The parallelism between literature and the arts", *English Institute Annual for 1941* (New York: Columbia Univ. Press, 1942), pp. 29-63; see also Joseph Frank, "Spatial form in modern literature", in his *The Widening Gyre: Crisis and Mastery in Modern Literature* (New Brunswick, New Jersey: Rutgers Univ. Press, 1963), pp. 3-62; James D. Merriman, "The parallel of the arts: some misgivings and a faint affirmation", *JAAC*, 31 (1972-73), 153-64, 309-21; Guillermo de Torre, "'Ut pictura poesis'", *Papeles de Son Armadans*, 82 (1963), 9-44.

[11] *Laocoön*, ed. William A. Steel (London: Dent, 1949), p. 3.

art object, like that of Holbein's "Christ in the Tomb" in Dos-
toevsky's *The Idiot*.[12] This concentration really ignores a whole range
of other approaches that might be equally effective in suggesting
correspondences between the sister arts. For example, the mere
mention of an art object's title or author might be sufficient for the
reader to recall the work in question. Or, conversely, the novelist
might, in a mood of playful teasing, describe a famous canvas in great
detail and then withhold the identity of the artist or the title. This is
what happens in Zola's *L'Oeuvre*, where the painter-protagonist,
Claude Lantier, paints a naked female bather sitting beside a clothed
gentleman. For his contemporary readers there would be no doubt
that Zola is recalling the sensational study by Edouard Manet.[13]
Obviously, in this instance, Lantier's profession and the historical
circumstances contribute to the identification. In other cases,
however, these aids may not exist and the identification of art sources
will depend both on the reader's knowledge and the novelist's
willingness to offer clues. For example, the author may refer to a
woman's smile as that familiar to visitors to the Louvre. It would be
an easy deduction to say that the author was thinking specifically of
Leonardo Da Vinci's "Mona Lisa". Yet, whether the verbal
description is extended, concise or concealed, the reader is being
asked in the first moment to identify from his or her memory a
known, historical art object.

   Now this is not the only function discharged by these sorts of
interart parallels, as we shall see shortly, but it is one which
distinguishes them from our second kind of verbal parallel: those
that relate to non-historical or imaginary works of the visual arts.
Here the reader is not being asked to recall or identify a real work of
art, but to construct an imaginary art object from the words of the
author. These may be extensive and describe in detail an art object, or
amount to only very brief allusions to the techniques or vocabulary
of the visual arts. For example, a novelist might refer to the colours
and spatial dimensions of a landscape, as if they were immobilized on
a canvas frame. The unfortunate problem here, of course, is that the
lexicon of the visual arts has been employed so frequently in
literature that some terms have become clichés.[14] Can we be sure, in

---

[12] See Jeffrey Meyers, *Painting and the Novel* (New York: Barnes and Noble, 1975), p. 141.

[13] See Emile Zola, *Oeuvres complètes* (Paris: Fasquelle, 1967), V, 538.

[14] Such seems to be Balzac's use of art in his novels, according to Pierre Laubriet, *L'Intelligence de l'art chez Balzac* (Paris: Didier, 1961), p. 437.

fact, that the novelist really intends an interart parallel when he chooses this vocabulary?[15] And even if he has no such purpose, cannot the reader, on his or her own accord, accept the parallel as valid and meaningful?

In the last analysis, though, one might wonder whether the inclusion of visual art terms, however brief or extended, intended or hackneyed, is absolutely necessary for the establishment of correspondences between the arts. Surely any verbal transcription of a scene, panorama or character appearance demands that the writer's retina and then his mind's eye first immobilize their features as if they were components in a painting or any type of art surface. In turn, the reader will reproduce the process, but in reverse: as the eye scans the words on the printed page, the mind's eye will re-create the stasis of the original tableau. Clearly, though, to examine all instances of this basic pictorial description in Galdós' fiction would be a Herculean task. For the purpose of this study, I have limited discussion to those textual passages in which the vocabulary of the visual arts, however stereotyped, appears. In this regard, it is further desirable to widen our terms of reference; the visual arts are so often confined to the higher forms of painting, sculpture and architecture that such popular, low-brow forms as silhouettes, figurines, photographs, mural graffiti, panoramas and magic lanterns (to cite only a few examples) tend to be unjustly ignored.

Nevertheless, interart parallels in novels can only constitute one dimension of a complex pattern of heterogeneous materials. If they are not to intrude embarrassingly in the development of the fiction as pleasant but irrelevant displays of erudition, then they must be integrated into the theme of the novels and serve as significant guides for the reader. Jean Hagstrum insisted that this was perhaps the most effective role the visual arts could discharge in a work of literature.[16] Certainly, in Aldous Huxley's novel, *After Many a Summer*, for example, the Vermeer canvas in Stoyte's elevator, with its emphasis on the power of reason, forms a highly memorable contrast to Stoyte's animalistic behaviour as he rushes up and down the stairs in

---

[15] Kenneth Clark, in *Aldous Huxley, 1894-1963: a Memorial Volume*, ed. Julian Huxley (London: Chatto and Windus, 1965), p. 15, criticizes the ability of writers to reproduce a portrait or painting: "Men of letters are by no means always safe guides to painting ... they do not distinguish between the subject of a picture and the way in which that subject has recreated itself pictorially in the artist's imagination."

[16] *The Sister Arts*, p. xx; see also Hugh Witemeyer, *George Eliot and the Visual Arts* (New Haven: Yale Univ. Press, 1979), p. 7.

search of his enemy.[17] One might add that when the novelist has also practised the plastic arts, written reviews or studies on them, and maintained close contacts with the artistic community, then the importance of the interart parallels in his or her fiction will be all the greater and worthier of study.[18] Such is the case of the subject of our book, Benito Pérez Galdós.

★   ★   ★

Our brief historical and theoretical survey has been necessary because of the lack of such a foundation in the existing studies on this aspect of the work of Benito Pérez Galdós (1843-1920), Spain's greatest novelist after Cervantes. This deficiency has also been compounded by the rather fragmentary and sparse nature of the studies that do exist. The thirty-one contemporary social novels of "the first epoch" (1870-79) and "the contemporary series" (1881-1915) upon which his reputation rests, have received only superficial attention. The studies of J. J. Alfieri[19] and Joaquín Gimeno Casalduero[20] are really pioneer compilations of references to the visual arts. Only Geraldine Scanlon has focused attention on this topic in one particular novel, *Angel Guerra*.[21] As for the forty-six historical novels or *Episodios nacionales* (*National Episodes*) (1873-79; 1898-1912), Hans Hinterhäuser has made some general observations.[22] Even more lamentable is the total absence of any

---

[17] See Peter Bowering, " 'The sources of light': pictorial imagery and symbolism in *Point Counter Point*", *Studies in the Novel*, 9 (1977), 389-405.

[18] See Mary Gaither, "Literature and the arts", in *Comparative Literature: Method and Perspective*, ed. Newton P. Stallknecht and Horst Frenz, 2nd ed. (Carbondale: Southern Illinois Univ. Press, 1971), p. 184; H.P.H. Teesing, "Literature and the other arts: some remarks", *Yearbook of Comparative and General Literature*, 12 (1963), 27-35; Ulrich Weisstein, "Comparing literature and art: current trends and prospects in critical theory and methodology", in *Proceedings of the IXth Congress of the International Comparative Literature Association, Innsbruck, 1979*, ed. Zoran Konstantinović, Steven P. Scher and Ulrich Weisstein (Innsbruck: Vlg des Inst. Für Sprachwissenschaft der Univ. Innsbruck, 1981), III, 23.

[19] "El arte pictórico en las novelas de Galdós", *AG*, 3 (1968), 79-86, and "Images of the 'Sacra Familia' in Galdós' novels", *Hispanófila*, 74 (1982), 25-40.

[20] "La caracterización plástica del personaje en la obra de Pérez Galdós: del tipo al individuo", *AG*, 7 (1972), 19-25.

[21] "Religion and art in *Angel Guerra*", *AG*, 8 (1973), 99-105.

[22] "Pintura de historia y literatura", in his *Los "Episodios nacionales" de Benito Pérez Galdós*, trans. José Escobar (Madrid: Gredos, 1963), pp. 356-69.

analysis of Galdós' art criticism for the Madrid newspapers, *La Nación* (1865-68), *La Revista del Movimiento Intelectual de Europa* (1865-67), *Revista de España* (1870-76), and *La Prensa* of Buenos Aires (1884-1901). Even Galdós' friendships with leading contemporary painters like Aureliano de Beruete, Sala, Sorolla and Arredondo remain largely veiled in mystery.[23]

The only area that has been examined by the critics in some depth is that of Galdós' own efforts in the visual arts. During his early years in Las Palmas and for a short while after his move to Madrid in 1862, Galdós made a hundred or so private pencil sketches of people he knew (especially his lifelong friend León y Castillo) or events he had witnessed (like the local controversy over the siting of a new theatre by the waterfront in the Canary Island capital). Gathered together in four albums, they reveal Galdós' early penchant for cartoons and caricatures, to be continued later in his literary career in the margins of books he read or the manuscripts and proofs of his novels. At the same time, however, in the pencil drawings of ships he saw in Las Palmas harbour, in the water-colour of the main city square or later sketches of churches, he also displays a keen eye for the regular lines, angles and contours of stone, wooden or metal structures. His youthful endeavours, aided by lessons in drawing at the Las Palmas Academy of Don Silvestre Bello, were publicly recognized in the 1862 Provincial Art Exhibition when two drawings received honourable mentions. He also showed skill in the construction of the maquette of a medieval city, remarkably reminiscent of Toledo, and in the carving of wooden statuettes and ships. During summer holidays later in Santander, he would make frequent trips to the countryside with his friend, the politician Antonio Maura, to paint landscapes in oils. This notable production in the visual arts, though intended for personal enjoyment and not

---

[23] Gregorio Marañón, "Galdós en Toledo", in his *Obras completas* (Madrid: Espasa-Calpe, 1968), IV, 349-53, has described how the Toledo painter Arredondo accompanied Galdós on his research trips around the old imperial city during the composition of *Angel Guerra*. Of other friendships there are only tantalizingly brief glimpses. The Valencian novelist, Vicente Blasco Ibánez, reminds Galdós in a letter of a beautiful Chilean woman he had seen in the studio of Sorolla, in *Cartas del archivo de Galdós*, ed. Sebastián de la Nuez and José Schraibman (Madrid: Taurus, 1967), p. 134. Alfieri, "El arte pictórico", p. 81, quotes a source to the effect that Galdós became acquainted with some female models at the studio of Sala. Finally, in an interview with the journalists Luis Antón del Olmet and Arturo García Carrafa, *Los grandes españoles: Galdós* (Madrid: Alrededor del Mundo, 1912), p. 66, Galdós recalled that during his early years in Madrid he became a friend of the painters Rosales and Cruzada Villaamil when he attended sessions at the Ateneo club.

for public scrutiny, offers a number of contacts with Galdós' literary work, especially in the distortion of human features or the minute depiction of architectural details.[24] Some critics have gone so far as to claim that the Las Palmas cartoons represent Galdós' first attempt at a comic novel.[25] However, such claims can only be tentative so long as Galdós' art work remains for the most part dispersed and inaccessible.

★   ★   ★

The aim of the present study is to correct some, though not all, of the lacunae noted above. I have concentrated discussion on the newspaper articles and novels, although excluding the three dialogued novels of "the contemporary series", *Realidad, La loca de la casa* and *El abuelo*. I have not attempted to catalogue every allusion to painters or works of art. My main concern has been to examine the

---

[24] For details and reproductions of Galdós' art work, see the following studies: Carmen Bravo-Villasante, *Galdós visto por sí mismo* (Madrid: Magisterio Español, 1970); H. Chonon Berkowitz, *Pérez Galdós: Spanish Liberal Crusader* (Madison: Univ. of Wisconsin Press, 1948); Jacques Beyrie, *Galdós et son mythe* (Lille: Université de Lille III, 1980); Marcos Guimerá Peraza, *Maura y Galdós* (Las Palmas: Excmo Cabildo Insular, 1967); Benito Madariaga, *Pérez Galdós: biografía santanderina* (Santander: Institución Cultural de Cantabria and Instituto de Literatura José María de Pereda, 1979); Rafael de Mesa, "Galdós, dibujante", *Hispania* (Buenos Aires), 11 (1943), 18-19; Luis and Agustín Millares Cubas, "Don Benito Pérez Galdós: recuerdos de su infancia en Las Palmas", *LL*, 20 (1920), 333-52; C. Palencia Tubau, "Galdós, dibujante, pintor y crítico", *Ibid.*, 29-40, 134-45; José Pérez Vidal, "Galdós, caricaturista", in his *Canarias en Galdós* (Las Palmas: Excmo Cabildo Insular, 1979), pp. 227-50, and "Pérez Galdós y la noche de San Daniel", *Revista Hispánica Moderna*, 17 (1951), 94-110; Francisco Rodríguez Batllori, "La adolescencia de Galdós: su afición al dibujo, y sus primeras obras literarias", *Semana*, 610 (30 October 1951), and *Galdós y su tiempo: estampas de una vida*, 2nd ed. (Madrid: Augustinus, 1969); Enrique Ruiz de la Serna and Sebastián Cruz Quintana, *Prehistoria y protohistoria de Benito Pérez Galdós: contribución a una biografía* (Las Palmas: Excmo Cabildo Insular, 1973); José Vega, "Galdós, dibujante", *ABC* (20 December 1955).
As a literary celebrity, Galdós was, appropriately, the subject of a number of visual art homages in his own lifetime and after his death: busts (by Daniel Vázquez Díaz and Bañul); oil paintings (by Sorolla and Massieu); statues (by Victorio Macho and Pablo Segura); and caricatures (by Bagaría, Santana Bonilla and Fresno) as well as countless photographs. For reproductions of some of these visual art forms, see José López Rubio *et al*, *Benito Pérez Galdós* (Madrid: Prensa Española, 1972).
Galdós was also the recipient of canvases presented to him by his artist friends: Sala, Fenollera, Beruete, Lhardy, Arredondo, Hispaleto and Fillol; see Emilia Pardo Bazán, "El estudio de Galdós en Madrid", in her *Obras completas*, ed. Harry L. Kirby, Jr. (Madrid: Aguilar, 1973), III, 1123-26, and Luis Bello, *Ensayos e imaginaciones sobre Madrid* (Madrid: Calleja, 1919), pp. 95-129.

[25] Berkowitz, *Pérez Galdós*, p. 32, and Millares, "Don Benito", p. 349.

nature of the art references in order to ascertain whether there is any common preoccupation running through the journalism and the novels, a concern that is of crucial significance for the proper interpretation of Galdós' work. To present my findings with more immediate clarity, I have avoided a chronological discussion of the relevant material, preferring instead to treat all the journalism first and then to consider the fiction by special groupings. In other words, in my attempt to cover all those areas of Galdós' writings which involve an intercommunication of the sister arts, I have started from the most external point – Galdós' public comments on this inter-relationship – and then slowly moved to the heart of the matter: the thematic relevance of the interart parallels in his great series of contemporary social novels.

PART I

GALDOS AS CRITIC OF THE VISUAL ARTS

HIS NEWSPAPER ARTICLES

CHAPTER 1

SMALL BEGINNINGS

La Nación (1865-68) and La Revista del Movimiento Intelectual de Europa (1865-67)

Galdós' first successful literary endeavours in Madrid were regular columns for a number of newspapers including *La Nación* and *La Revista del Movimiento Intelectual de Europa*. The visual arts were just one of several topics that Galdós treated. After only two years in the capital he obviously felt competent to cast judgement on the art treasures he was discovering. His preparation for this task had started in Las Palmas with his perusal of such illustrated magazines as *El Museo de las Familias* and *El Semanario Pintoresco Español* to which his family subscribed.[1] Once in Madrid, the process of self-instruction increased apace with frequent trips to museums and exhibitions and with the acquisition of studies on art.[2] Viardot's guide to the Prado collection, found in Galdós' library, contains numerous marginal annotations referring to what must have been the canvas numbers in the Prado. At times Galdós feels knowledgeable enough to correct errors made by the Frenchman, as for

---

[1] See Josette Blanquat, "Les Annotations marginales des livres de Galdós", in *Etudes ibériques et latino-américaines* (Paris: Presses Universitaires de France, 1968), pp. 23-43. The eighteen well-annotated volumes of *El Semanario Pintoresco* cover the years 1833-1852. Later Galdós would cut out various illustrations from such magazines as *El Mundo Ilustrado* and *La Ilustración Española y Americana* and paste them into scrapbooks, thirteen in all, according to Rodolfo Cardona, as cited by Alfieri, "El arte pictórico", p. 79.

[2] F.M. Tubino, *El arte y los artistas contemporáneos en la península* (Madrid: Durán, 1871) and Louis Viardot, *Les Musées d'Espagne* (Paris: Hachette, 1860) are listed in H. Chonon Berkowitz, *La biblioteca de Benito Pérez Galdós* (Las Palmas: El Museo Canario, 1951).

example, when he substitutes the name of Velázquez for that of Murillo as the author of one particular painting.[3] Galdós must also have read treatises on aesthetics like those by Hegel and Taine, although there is no evidence that he possessed these works in his library.[4] The only allusion, and then a very cryptic one, to his possible theoretical readings at this time is the reference to P. J. Proudhon's "extraordinary *Philosophy of Art*" (*RMIE*, 107).[5] Probably those most responsible for the development of Galdós' appreciation of the visual arts were his friends in the Madrid circle of artists and art critics. In later years Galdós was to acknowledge the special debt he owed the satirist and art critic, Federico Balart, whose opinions, Galdós wrote in 1894, "were dogmatic: his ideas about everything seemed to me incontrovertible. In matters of art and literature I can truly say that he implanted in me ideas which took root for ever ... Our chats never ended; the ancient and modern, the forms inherited from past ages and the attempts of ours to express beauty, occupied us for long hours, with him teaching me, and me learning what I could from his great genius and the example of his exquisite taste" (*CP*, 521-22).[6]

La Nación

For an old friend and fellow Canarian in Madrid in the late 1860s, León y Castillo, Galdós' "qualities as an art critic, above all, seemed to us extraordinary".[7] This is perhaps an overgenerous statement, if one thinks in terms of quantity, for Galdós' art reviews in *La Nación* amount to little more than three full-length features, out of a total of one hundred and thirty-one articles, with occasional comments

---

[3] Viardot, *Les Musées*, p. 141.

[4] See Berkowitz, *La biblioteca*, pp. 27-32 for those books on art that he did possess. Curiously, many, including John Ruskin's *The Seven Lamps of Architecture*, trans. Carmen Burgos, and J. Bacon's *Theory of Colouring*, 13th ed., were left unopened by Galdós.

[5] Galdós was probably referring to P.J. Proudhon's *Du Principe de l'Art et de sa destination sociale* (Paris: Garnier, 1865).

[6] Balart was also responsible for arousing Galdós' important interest in Dickens. Art and literature had many analogies for Balart: see *Impresiones: literatura y arte* (Madrid: Librería de Fernando Fe, 1894), p. 71. Balart was also the subject of a portrait in Galdós' series "Galería de figuras de cera" for *La Nación* on 22 March 1868 (*AN*, 467-68).

[7] As reported by Luis Doreste Silva in Las Palmas, 10 May 1935; translated by William H. Shoemaker, *The Novelistic Art of Galdós* (Valencia: Albatros/Hispanófila, 1980), p. 24.

dispersed in others. Nevertheless, his remarks on the visual arts are always pertinent; in particular, one notices a certain preoccupation with the irregular appearances of art works or the conditions which affect their viewing. One of his earliest laments was for the absence of a permanent gallery for exhibiting new work, hitherto relegated to positions on the staircase of the Academy of San Fernando or the convent of Las Trinitarias. The practice of Prado officials of hanging works belonging to different schools in one area instead of allocating one room per school, and of positioning small canvases near the ceiling with huge canvases below elicited his indignation (*AN*, 134; *RMIE*, 172). Criticizing the same fault in the hanging of the Spanish exhibits at the 1867 Paris World Fair, Galdós reveals that his concern is not an idiosyncrasy or snobbish prissiness, but rather a serious desire to gain the best possible view of an art object. The exhibits in Paris were housed in such a narrow, poorly-lit area that the perspective was distorted and colours appeared in false hues.

This "classical" obsession with the proper distances between viewer and art object[8] should not obscure the fact that Galdós was attracted even at this early stage by irregular features in art works, as is very evident from his comments on three famous female portraits that he studied in the Louvre in the summer of 1867. Standing before Leonardo Da Vinci's "Mona Lisa", Sarto's "Lucrezia del Fede" and Van Dyck's "The Duchess of Oxford", Galdós felt he was confronted by living women and yet the respective features of the three faces did not correspond to the classical precepts: the Mona Lisa's mouth was half an inch too wide; Lucrezia's nose slightly flattened, and the Duchess of Oxford, whilst not slender, had a forehead that was somewhat narrow. The attraction of all three portraits lay, in fact, in their deviation from classical norms: "... the secret of painting is to incarnate in the deviation of a line, a protuberance, a depression, the features and movements of the great physiognomy of the spirit" (*AN*, 520).

On the other hand, an *excessive* deviation from the classical proportions is particularly reprehensible, especially in ecclesiastical architecture, the topic of his most accomplished article on the visual arts in these early years. The style of the newly erected church of The

[8] See Emilio Orozco Díaz, "El concepto y la palabra 'barroco' en los novelistas españoles del siglo XIX: unas notas sueltas centradas en Alarcón, Galdós y Clarín", in *Homenaje a Gonzalo Torrente Ballester* (Salamanca: Biblioteca de la Caja de Ahorros y Monte de Piedad, 1981), pp. 583-613.

Happy Outcome in the Madrid suburb of Pozas is discussed within the historical context of the architecture of other Madrid churches. Galdós has only words of harsh criticism for the grotesque Greco-Roman style favoured by Madrid's architects over the ages. Lacking the grandiose perspective and elegant lines of the classical models, their grotesque external ornamentation reveals only too clearly that the architects did not know how to fashion "the spirit of art, the mysterious language of its lines" (*AN*, 47). In short, Madrid ecclesiastical architecture lacked a guiding idea, which for Galdós and for his mentor, Federico Balart, was the axiomatic principle governing all the visual arts.[9] The only exception, prior to the erection of The Happy Outcome church, was the old church of St. John Lateran, otherwise known as the Bishop's Chapel. Here the architecture made a positive contribution to the religious experience: the majestically simple design of the interior was surpassed only by the arrangement of the lines or veins of the Gothic pilasters stretching from the floor to the roof where they formed symmetrical angles. Although the pattern may have been capricious, the overall effect was one of aesthetic harmony. This will be one of the fundamental principles of Galdós' appreciation of the visual arts: there must be some pattern of lines and angles whose initial visual complication, like some optical puzzle, can be unravelled by the intelligent eye.[10]

This is the design exhibited by The Happy Outcome church: its classical proportions and the slenderness of the façade make it the most beautiful church in Madrid with its pure horizontal and vertical lines triumphing over Churrigueresque sinuosities. The spire is like some proud minaret standing out in the morning light against the tumbledown roofs and black chimneys of the Madrid skyline. Even the lay-out of the buildings and plots of land in the vicinity of the church achieves a harmonious compromise of regular and irregular lines and angles, so different from the monotonous regularity of row houses in the city centre: "The variety of the constructions, the

---

[9] "Our painters have an excessive preference for execution over conception, for process over idea" (Balart, *Impresiones*, p. 6).

[10] The same challenge is presented by a moving art object like the religious floats paraded in Holy Week: the candles illuminating the statues create a magic lantern effect, a "piece of architecture carved in light, a symmetrical conflagration, a geometric burst of flame" (*RMIE*, 182). For Barbara J. Bucknall, "Vision and the visual arts", in *The Religion of Art in Proust* (Urbana: Univ. of Illinois Press, 1970), p. 48, the magic lantern, consisting of scenes painted onto individual slides rotated in turn, is an art object that lies "half-way between an optical toy and a picture".

interspersing of gardens and houses, the original shape of the cupolas, the gateways and the railings, all produce a richly varied whole, *which, without impairing the symmetry, offers a special enjoyment to the eye"* (my italics; *AN*, 478). Galdós' criterion is clear enough: art displays may overwhelm the visual senses, but they must at all times embody a logical, rational idea. Yet at the same time his own words betray his lack of assurance that this is always the case: "without impairing the symmetry" suggests that he is indeed very conscious of the possibility that the eye might delight solely in the artistic form. It is only a momentary hesitation, however, for when he proceeds to indicate the major artistic defect of the church, he once more strongly reasserts the classical norm of an underlying idea. As a result of plaster being used to cover walls and columns, the outlines of the volutes are broken, rose-windows appear like huge medallions and the points of the crests are like pyramids of marzipan. All the normal lines of architectural joins have been exaggerated or distorted and there is none of the magic chiaroscuro effects usually associated with stone buildings (*AN*, 480-81).[11]

As an antidote to all this cerebral appreciation of art Galdós could at times turn to the irregular forms of more popular art works. For instance, in an article of 3 May 1868 he encourages the readers of *La Nación* to inspect the water-colour caricatures of the cartoonist Llovera currently on display in the window of Scropp's shop: they are as good as, if not better than, the massive canvases on historical topics that are purchased by Government departments only to decorate some attic. Three years earlier, Galdós had described the poor-quality reproductions of saints that were being sold on street stalls. With the large blobs of bright colours giving the appearance of some magnificent French pavilion, the paintings were really parodies of the style popularized by Ribera. Nonetheless, despite their low commercial value, they are superior to the originals found in the Prado and which are "condemned to hear the wearisome disquisitions of the tourist, or to see fixed on their lines and colours the

---

[11] Surely Pedro Ortiz Armengol, "El convento de las Micaelas en *Fortunata y Jacinta"*, *Estafeta Literaria*, 550 (1974), 4-7, is wrong when he declares that Galdós "celebrates" the plaster work of The Happy Outcome church. Pedro Navascués Palacio, *Arquitectura y arquitectos madrileños del siglo XIX* (Madrid: Instituto de Estudios Madrileños, 1973), pp. 239-40, notes that the internal style of the church was not intended by its architect, Ortiz de Villajos, to be a historical reconstruction. Juan Antonio Gaya Nuño, in *Arte del siglo XIX*, Vol. XIX of *Ars Hispaniae: historia universal del arte hispánico*, (Madrid: Plus Ultra, 1966), p. 286, is extremely critical of the building.

motionless lens of some incredulous pupil of Apelles" (*AN*, 156).[12]
The reason for this apparently paradoxical rejection of serious art is
that these cheap, gaudy reproductions have been silent witnesses to
all sorts of social conditions and human emotions in their constant
transfer from one owner to another. Galdós accepts their grotesque-
ness because it does not pretend to be otherwise, unlike the French
exhibits he was so ready to condemn at the 1867 Paris World Fair.
Channel's "Original Sin" contained a wax-like Venus emerging from
a mass of water that had the appearance of a foaming bath rather
than the sea. Furthermore, the figure of God resembles Jupiter
reciting poetry (*AN*, 418-19). In these studies and some genre
paintings, also on display, the distortions are obviously not intended
and therefore Galdós has to condemn them. On the other hand, the
fantastic shapes favoured by Gustave Doré in his illustrations of the
Bible, *Don Quixote* and the *Divine Comedy* have to be recognized as
the work of a revolutionary genius (*RMIE*, 113). In short, Galdós'
comments on the visual arts in these early newspaper articles, though
not extensive, show that from an early stage in his career as a writer
he was preoccupied by the whole question of the regular or irregular
shapes of art objects and their retinal reflections. The role of the
human eye in alliance with the intelligence of the mind is crucial in
determining the correct appreciation of the art form whose construction must be founded on a governing idea.

[12] The contemporary critic and feminist, Concepción Arenal, "El realismo y la
realidad en las bellas artes y la poesía: IV: la pintura", *RE*, 74 (13 June 1880), 304-21,
insists on the same universality of painting, but without going so far as Galdós does
here.

CHAPTER 2

MATURE ART CRITICISM

La Prensa (1884-1901)

The most developed art criticism Galdós wrote went unappreciated by his regular Spanish readers until after his death in 1920. Ghiraldo's collection of a great majority of the articles written for *La Prensa* of Buenos Aires (*OI*) and Shoemaker's later definitive collection (*CP*) revealed the extent to which the visual arts had occupied Galdós' attention and elicited mature response at a time when he was also heavily engaged in the writing of his most accomplished fiction. Broadly speaking, the *La Prensa* articles dealing with the visual arts fall into two groups: first, his reviews of the triennial exhibitions held in Madrid in 1884, 1887 and 1890; and second, his accounts of gallery visits and architectural sights on his frequent trips abroad in the 1880s (to Portugal in 1885, to France and Germany in 1886, to Germany, Holland and Denmark in 1887 and to Italy in 1888).[1] A few miscellaneous comments are sprinkled through other articles. Both groups reveal Galdós' considerable knowledge of visual arts in contemporary Spain and a creditable knowledge of world art history. The interest of the articles, however, lies in more than a display of knowledge: running through most of them is the thread of a serious preoccupation with the lines of composition (colouring is a secondary concern), particularly if they deviate in any

---

[1] Curiously enough, despite a number of journeys to England, he never gave an account of its art treasures to his Argentinian readers. In his semi-fictionalized autobiography, *Memorias de un desmemoriado*, there is only a passing reference to the National Gallery (*OC*, VI, 1709).

way from the classical norms, thereby raising questions about the correspondence with the reality of life. The subjects of the compositions are also scrutinized now from this standpoint.

The Madrid Exhibitions

Originally held every two years after the inaugural exhibition of 1856, the expositions of new paintings, lithographs, architectural models and other minor visual art objects had become by the 1880s, after the political upheavals of the previous decade, a three-year event.[2] Enormously popular with the public, these exhibitions had made a great contribution to the renaissance of the visual arts in Spain, so that now only the German school was a worthy rival in painting. This pre-eminence had been achieved despite the tragic loss of such masters as Rosales, Fortuny and Casado del Alisal. Chauvinism may have been a factor in Galdós' ranking of the Spanish exhibits over the French canvases at the 1867 Paris World Fair, but by the time of his 1884 articles for *La Prensa* he had every justification for lauding the amazing fecundity of Spanish artists. Even so, he was not remiss in calling attention to some of their weaknesses, especially their inability to draw line compositions. Luna's mural for the Senate Chamber on the "Battle of Lepanto" and Muñoz Degraín's famous "The Lovers of Teruel" were only two of a multitude guilty of this shortcoming. When a canvas stood out because of its linear composition, like Villodas' "Naumachia" in the 1887 exhibition, then Galdós duly and loudly applauded, for he recognized the difficulty of acquiring this skill: "The line is rebellious and escapes the persecution of the artist trying to fix on canvas its elegant projections. The feeling for colour is easier to cultivate than that for line, because the latter demands long practice, which present-day impatient youth is not usually prepared to do" (*CP*, 244-45). Nevertheless, despite this somewhat classicist pontificating, Galdós was forced on occasion to recognize that in some exceptional studies the defect of line drawing was not a drawback at all. In Checa's "The Entry of the Barbarians into Rome" at the 1887 exhibition, some of the barbarians' horses are given impossible stances, but the canvas was still a great success. Sorolla's version of "The Burial of Christ" at

---

[2] See Aureliano de Beruete y Moret, *Historia de la pintura española en el siglo XIX: elementos nacionales y extranjeros que han influido en ella* (Madrid: Ruiz Hermanos, 1926), p. 91.

the same exhibition differs radically from the tradition established by Titian, Van Dyck and others: the figures are excessively sober and silhouettish, especially those on the periphery; there is also a certain exaggeration in the execution of the forms, and yet the viewer is convinced of its merit. Benlliure's giant canvas, "The Vision of the Coliseum", is a marvellous work of fantasy showing the souls of martyred Christians meeting with St. Telemachus at the Roman Circus before ascending to Heaven in a cloud: it is, Galdós says, "a falsification of reality by our imagination, but ecstasy and delirium have a real value in the workings of the mind" (*CP*, 247). Earlier he had disclaimed any personal taste for this genre: "I say of the fantastic what I said of the archaeological: it's fine and all very well, but it does not convince me. However, in these matters you have to leave personal preferences aside and accept each artist as he is, with his abilities as well as his defects. In art you cannot deny anything, nor raise the flag of an exclusive, intolerant criterion" (*CP*, 246). Galdós the realist has to admit, then, that not every canvas will follow the classical rules of linear composition, and more seriously, that even a breaking of the rules may produce an acceptable work of art. The implications of this double standard will also be important in the assessment of the attitude Galdós shows towards the visual arts in the fiction he composed at the same time.

Deviation from observable reality, albeit on a different level, is also an important criterion in Galdós' consideration of the subjects of these giant canvases. Taken from national and international history, they are, naturally, examples of the most immediate manifestation of the "ut pictura poesis" tradition. These studies had dominated the Madrid exhibitions from the 1860s, but by 1890, much to Galdós' joy, the tide had turned and now the historical paintings had given way to genre studies. Galdós' strictures against the historical pictures (well-known and accepted as accurate by modern scholars)[3] are directed against two aspects. First, the enormous size

---

[3] See Gaya Nuño, *Ars Hispaniae*, p. 36, and the Marquess of Lozoya, *Historia del arte hispánico* (Barcelona: Salvat, 1949), V, 429. Beruete, *Historia*, p. 90, notes that, for the public of Galdós' time, only those who painted historical subjects were considered painters. Pedro A. Berenguer in *La guerra y el arte* (Barcelona: Revista Científico-Militar, 1890), p. 161, an autographed copy of which Galdós possessed in his library, conjectures that the preference for the historical canvas might be due to the character and education of the Spanish people. Francisco de Mendoza, *Manual del pintor de historia* (Madrid: Fortanet, 1870), p. 477, recommends that a painter choose as his subject-matter any event of history, whatever its importance. Luis Alfonso, "La pintura contemporánea", *RE*, 29 (28 November 1872), 169-86, maintains that a historical canvas will always have more value than a genre painting.

of the compositions, which, because of the length of time expended upon them, can only be purchased by Government departments. Secondly, Galdós is opposed to the fundamental artificiality of the studies, which are encouraged by the academies of art. Too much attention is devoted to the minute portrayal of the archaeological paraphernalia of history, like dress, weapons and insignia. Moreover, the models for the figures in historical canvases betray only too easily their modern mien beneath the period costume. The great painters of history in previous ages, like Velázquez, Raphael, Murillo, Van Dyck and Rembrandt, had succeeded in harmonizing dress and model and in ignoring the tyranny of archaeological detail. In fact, Galdós is not opposed in principle to historical painting, but he believes that painters should select their subjects from contemporary history, with which they are more directly familiar:

> So-called historical painting is acceptable when it represents some important event or other contemporaneous with the painter's life and is represented with people and dress of his own time; otherwise, it is just impossible ... The artist has been given his inspiration in order to interpret beautiful reality, not to illustrate History by adding picturesque documents to the treasures of the archives. Turn your back on supposed or induced reality and look at the reality that you can see and feel before you. (*OI*, I, 22)

In most cases (Mariano Fortuny was an exception)[4] the artists themselves were to blame for slavishly following the Academy's precepts, for it was all a question of insight or mental vision: "The artists *do not want* to comprehend ... that the public will only enthuse over those subjects whose authenticity is easily verifiable" (my italics; *CP*, 245). On the other hand, Fortuny, "who *had deep insight* (in Spanish "que veía mucho"), never fell into the puerile temptations of painting the Cid or the Catholic Monarchs" (my italics; *CP*, 98). Admitting to being only a layman in art matters, Galdós feels that on this point, however, he perceives the reality of the needs of modern Spanish painting more correctly than the artists themselves. They may be able to represent pictorial perspective correctly, but in the area of subject selection they demonstrate a lack of percipience. And yet Galdós knew how difficult such a task was, since the past appealed so strongly to the vivid imagination of Spanish artists. So, once again, as in the distortion of linear

---

[4] Galdós saw the Catalan as the most original modern painter, a worthy successor to Goya (*CP*, 51; see also *AN*, 420).

arrangements, fantasy or escapism replaces logic and reason. Galdós is consistent, then, in his awareness of the gap, so dangerous at times, between the initial visual appreciation afforded by the optical organ and the subsequent rational evaluation by the mind (when not subverted by its own internal eye, the imagination).

The European Travelogues

Galdós' frequent trips abroad in the 1880s, besides providing ample and varied material for his regular columns in *La Prensa*, also enabled him to share with his Argentinian readers his impressions of some of the great works of world art and architecture, hitherto only known to him through often imperfect lithographic reproductions in illustrated journals, as he admitted on several occasions (e.g. *CP*, 260). There are many passages chronicling general facts and details about painters, their work and their position in the history of art, of which his assessment of the Bologna school is a typical example: "It is a mannerist school whose artists do not lack, however, brilliant qualities. The first defect with which to charge this artistic family is its lack of inventiveness, for almost always it treats the same subjects exhaustively illustrated by its predecessors. But it is undeniable that it broadened the field of composition and maintained the fine principles of design" (*OC*, VI, 1653). Such doses of erudition did not satisfy Chantal Cologne who – incredibly – accused Galdós of not discussing Italian painting as extensively as he could have done, because "his interest in the plastic arts is not essential and because he knows that the majority of his readers are hardly interested in them".[5] Had Cologne probed deeper into the art passages, she would have noted that many articles focus interest on exceptional and irregular forms. Even the eagerly awaited confrontation with Rembrandt's masterpiece, "The Night Watch", the reason for his trip to Holland in 1887, provoked anguished reflections on the master's misuse of light; Galdós found it unrealistic: "Certainly the light effect is wonderful; but for it *to fit reality* you have to assume that the scene is illuminated by a blaze and that was not the artist's intention. Rembrandt decided to paint an effect of midday light and

---

[5] "Les Voyageurs espagnols du XIXème siècle et la peinture", in *Naturalisme et cosmopolitisme dans les littératures ibériques au XIXème siècle* (Lille: Université de Lille III, 1975), p. 95.

nowhere does the sun produce the chiaroscuro or the enormous contrasts that are the delight of 'The Night Watch'" (my italics; *CP*, 260). Second only to Velázquez in portraying reality, Rembrandt overwhelms the viewer with this particular distortion: "... we admire the majestic skill with which he falsifies nature" (*CP*, 261). Once more, Galdós is forced into an ambivalent position: on the one hand, he has to recognize this distortion of reality; on the other, the distortion has to be accepted because of its marvellous execution. In Italy this lesson is thrust repeatedly before his eyes. Like all geniuses, Titian and Tintoretto with their fantastic use of colour appeal to the viewer precisely because they have broken the traditional rules. Similarly, Michelangelo's "Final Judgement" is a radical interpretation of a traditional subject: the artist has challenged Nature and changed its laws according to his own whim; yet in the process he has succeeded in creating a work of artistic beauty.

Galdós' appreciation of architecture evinces the same pattern. The fine, adapted Gothic architecture of the Belem monastery in Lisbon exhibits a "fantasy, independence and a desire for originality that at times borders on extravagance ...". In the cloisters there are Baroque artistical whims which, with their "exuberance of broken lines and the novelty of their geometrical combinations" (*OC*, VI, 1621), recall Russian architecture. In St. Mark's Cathedral in Venice it is not so much the shape of lines and angles that pleases his eye, as that of light and shade: "The gold and marble glitter strangely in the vaults of the roof, forming fantastic patterns of light and shade" (*CP*, 329).

Galdós' preferences in statuary are again for the exceptional. The great Danish sculptor, Thorwaldsen, whose work he went to Copenhagen expressly to see in 1887, re-created Greek nudes with an unequalled flair, "interpreting the form in extraordinary conditions" (*CP*, 279). Michelangelo's figures broke all the rules: his "David" had a number of irregularities but all go unnoticed because of the extreme animation of the sculpture. His most famous piece, the figure of Moses in a Rome church, is of monstrous proportions, but in the semi-obscurity of the religious building, it has all the appearance of a real person: "That marble is alive, that head is thinking, those hands are going to move and that huge, disproportionate body is going to get up from its seat. And when it does stand up, it will surely touch the roof of the church with its head, because it is simply huge and the greatness that it expresses will also increase its colossal proportions" (*OC*, VI, 1635). In contrast,

Michelangelo's disciples (apart from Bandinelli in Italy and Berruguete in Spain) can only reproduce the exaggerated dimensions of their master's originals, without capturing their basic concepts. The contorted postures in Bernini's statues around Rome bear witness to this failure to turn unusual shapes into great works of art. Thus, Galdós overlooks imperfections of line or colour so long as the artist is able to convince the viewer that there is an underlying concept behind the exaggeration. If it is an exaggeration for exaggeration's sake, without any "ideación elevada" or "lofty concept" (*OC*, VI, 1636), then he rejects the art work.

Madrid Architecture and Statuary

Public monuments in the nation's capital were generally of such poor quality that it was with some relief that Galdós announced, in an article of 4 June 1884, that the new composition by the Catalan sculptor Manuel Oms, "Isabel the Catholic", appeared to mark a welcome renaissance in public monuments to perpetuate the country's noble heritage, for again the art form embodied well conceived ideas of spatial relationships. The group had a dramatic quality that might not earn the approval of academic purists, but really the movement was so measured, "the placing of the figures so discreet, the effects and interplays of light so perfect, the lines so beautiful" that even the traditionalists would admire the work because it was based on "lofty ideas" and showed mastery of form (*CP*, 50).

Concern over the probable shapes and dimensions of future constructions of steel, the new material used for public buildings, dominates an article written in 1890 on Madrid architecture. Galdós bravely prophesies: "The lightness of the material and its boundless resistance allow enormous sizes, combinations of more varied planes and a greater movement in all forms. Hence there will be different outlines *that will embody the aesthetic sense*. What outlines are they, or rather, what will they be like?" (my italics; *CP*, 433). Yet his judgement of existing steel structures, like a neo-gothic church in the Philippines, or the Eiffel Tower, are not all that complimentary, although he does admit that the Tower's arches and arrangement of lines, especially when illuminated at night, are graceful and harmonious to the eye. The age of steel will come, but in the meantime Spanish architects should follow the example of his good friend, Arturo Mélida, who in his restoration of the Toledo church of St.

John of the Kings was adapting old Spanish styles to modern needs, instead of slavishly imitating foreign models like his colleagues, the architects of Madrid mansions. Artificiality, inauthenticity and unreality are the criteria by which Galdós judges works of architecture and art: contemporary reality must dictate the artistic shapes and patterns. Any aberration, as in the art work of previous ages, must be the inspiration of a genius who will establish new norms with the boldness of his original concepts.

★   ★   ★

As in the earlier *La Nación* articles Galdós shows the occasional sign of lassitude with the welter of art treasures he encounters on his European travels: "... one does not travel just to admire museums, look at wonderful façades and praise architects" (*CP*, 274), he remarks rather testily in an article from Germany in 1887 and again in an article from France in 1889. For relief from the sublime, he would resort to some popular art-viewing, like that of the panoramas, tableaux of images folded around a cylindrical surface and then unrolled for the viewer.[6] The examples on the battle of Sedan during the Franco-Prussian War of 1870 that he had seen in Berlin in 1887 were far superior to those he had seen in other European cities. Of even greater realism were the battle scenes of the dioramas with the foreground details modelled in the round so as to join imperceptibly with the more distant parts painted in perspective on a vertical panel and viewed through an aperture in a screen.[7] Common people can readily appreciate their beauty because the illusion of the visual reality is complete: art reproduces an experienced or easily imaginable reality.

The conditions for viewing works of art are again instrumental in the correct appraisal or otherwise of art objects. Painting, like history, has to be viewed from a proper distance, otherwise colours and linear perspective suffer. Goya's famous "The Death of St. Joseph of Calasanz",[8] which hangs in the chapel of the Escolapios'

---

[6] See *The Oxford Companion to Art*, ed. Harold Osborne (Oxford: Clarendon Press, 1970), p. 810.

[7] *Ibid.*, pp. 315-16.

[8] The title is really "The Last Communion of St. Joseph Calasanz", according to Pierre Gassier and Juliet Wilson, *Goya: His Life and Work* (London: Thames and Hudson, 1971), p. 329.

college in Madrid, is shrouded in darkness, with the result that the torrents of light Goya poured onto the canvas seem like a sunbeam enclosed in a sheath of obscurity. Moreover, one visit to an art gallery is not sufficient to form an opinion of the merit of a work. Only by making frequent visits does the spectator succeed in approximating to an accurate assessment: "In art you have to proceed with a *great deal of serenity and to think a lot before giving an opinion* on a matter so serious as an artist's work. It is necessary to put your first impressions in quarantine and then subject them to a purifying process" (my italics; *CP*, 243). Both in the fabrication and the appreciation of the visual art object, then, there must be a pattern of ideas that can be decoded by the spectator's mind if he is not to be overpowered completely by the assault on his visual senses.

CHAPTER 3

ART CRITICISM AND LANDSCAPE DESCRIPTION WITH A LITERARY FORM

Revista de España (1870-76)

Descriptions of picturesque landscape employing the vocabulary of the visual arts had fittingly complemented some passages of art criticism in the *La Prensa* articles. Galdós had waxed lyrical over the wonderful panoramic view of Florence from the tower of San Miniato which he recognized from fifteenth-century Florentine paintings. The view of Naples from the slopes of Mount Vesuvius was so magnificent that it defied verbal expression and demanded, he implied, a plastic art form. The bright colours and reflections of the vessels moored alongside the canals of Rotterdam reminded him of their frequent appearance in Flemish landscape paintings. By and large, however, these passages are few and infrequent in the *La Prensa* articles, where a more factual style is preferred for topographical description. In fact, there had been greater scope for picturesque landscaping within the context of art criticism in two articles he had penned a decade earlier for another Madrid publication, the prestigious *Revista de España*.[1] His treatment of visual art material in both articles foreshadows the approach in his fiction, a correspondence that is made even more interesting and pertinent by

---

[1] "Las generaciones artísticas en la ciudad de Toledo", *RE*, 13 (1870), 209-39 and 15 (1870), 62-93; and "Cuarenta leguas por Cantabria (bosquejo descriptivo)", *RE*, 53 (1876), 198-211, 495-508.

the selection of the same locales (Toledo and the Cantabrian coast) for the setting of some of his novels (*El audaz, Angel Guerra,* and *Gloria, Marianela,* respectively).

"Las generaciones artísticas en la ciudad de Toledo" (1870)

Galdós' enthusiasm for Toledo, aroused soon after his arrival on the mainland by his mentor Federico Balart, manifested itself in frequent weekend visits in the company of other writers and artists. He enlightened his Argentinian readers in a letter of 1884: "It is very pleasant to go to that untouched theatre of past episodes, so picturesque, so beautiful in every way, and decorated by the most brilliant arts of the Middle Ages and Renaissance. It is a theatre made all the more interesting by the august silence that invades it and the delightful solitude that fills everything" (*CP*, 79-80; see also *CP*, 349). An impressive and earlier testimonial to his affection for Toledo had been the publication of "Las generaciones artísticas" in 1870. Palencia Tubau rates the piece as Galdós' best art criticism for a number of reasons: clarity and simplicity of style, a correct appreciation of the various stages in the artistic development of the city's buildings; the choice inclusion of local legends; the well-balanced descriptions of architecture and paintings; and, above all, the great admiration he shows for the old city.[2] Unfortunately, Palencia failed to recognize the great debt Galdós owed to the authorative study of Toledo made nearly thirty years earlier by Amador de los Ríos, a heavily annotated copy of which is to be found in Galdós' library.[3] For a more recent critic, Josette Blanquat, the debt is exceedingly great and she accuses Galdós of all sorts of flagrant borrowings.[4] Whilst it is true that Galdós used the book as a mine of information, he also clearly went out of his way not to imitate his source in a slavish manner. For example, whereas Amador's guide opens with an account of Toledo cathedral, in Galdós' article this key architectural treasure is reserved for the climax of the city tour. Moreover, Galdós' style is decidedly more literary than that exhibited in Amador's listing.

Blanquat's second major contention was that Galdós followed

---

[2] "Galdós, dibujante", p. 143.

[3] See *Toledo pintoresca, o descripción de sus más célebres monumentos* (Madrid: Ignacio Boix, 1845).

[4] "Les Annotations marginales", p. 28.

Amador in propagating a romantic vision of the Imperial City. That this is patently untrue is proven by Galdós' very laconic opening where he offers a very unflattering view of the city from the railway station, a scene that anticipates the opening shot of Orbajosa in *Doña Perfecta*, written six years later. The traveller alighting from the train coach is confronted by a steep rock on the left, a flat plain on the right and some miserable-looking houses in the centre. The narrator ruefully comments that this is what "through a somewhat ridiculous tradition" is known as the Imperial City (*OC*, VI, 1582). After this initial shock the visitor is relieved to catch sight of the more customary picturesque panorama of Toledo: the majestic perspective of the beautiful Alcántara bridge and the architectural group of the Visagra Gate and the turrets of the city walls. However, more discordant notes are sounded: Toledo is a dead city, not made for modern man, who in the age of democracy and universal freedom prefers to live on flat ground. Only antique-lovers and archaeologists will find pleasure in climbing Toledo's steep streets. Furthermore, given the present shabby appearance of the structures in the main square, the Zocodover, it is amazing that the city was once the political and cultural capital of Spain. In this extensive picture of the physical lay-out of the modern city Galdós regularly oscillates, then, between the artistically beautiful (the imposing vistas of the Tagus and the castle of San Servando on the hills opposite the city, for example) and the ugly (the dizzy angles of houses, walls and roofs, the sad silence of the empty narrow streets). Why should the young Galdós have gone out of his way to serve up this disconcertingly ambivalent picture of what for his source author had been a Romantically appealing paradise? It certainly was a challengingly unorthodox view of the city. The answer has to be sought in the technique Galdós has adopted for describing the military and artistic history of Toledo: he regards each new civilization as a fresh artistic layer added to those already there, and in order to re-create the Toledo of each civilization, whether it be Visigothic, Moorish or Christian, he has to peel off this accretion of layers imposed by succeeding ages. The point of his insistent inclusion of rickety, unaesthetic modern structures throughout the city is to remind the reader in strongly visual terms how some of the architectural treasures of past ages he is describing have been lost or replaced by unaesthetic buildings. Very conscious of the modern appearance of the city, the reader should then resist the temptation, so strong in Amador de los Ríos' book, of superimposing a timeless artistic fabrication upon a prosaic contemporary reality. For example, in order to visualize the Palace of the Goths, he or she has to erase mentally the current structures of La Concepción, Santa Fe and the Mendoza hospital as well as a collection of dirty hovels and yards inhabited by chickens and mules. The mental effort that is required of the reader should be, in itself, a sufficient guarantee against any Romantic escapism. Thus, it has to be remembered that Galdós' guide to the art treasures of the Imperial City, for the most part authoritatively factual and straightforward, is held within a literary frame that stresses the impermanence of the works and ultimately calls into question the nature of that artistic world that Romantic minds can, it seems, so firmly imagine.

This questioning is continued by Galdós' tendency to dwell, as in his other journalistic reports, on unusual art structures or effects that seem to deviate from standard classical canons of design. A good example is his picture of the Moorish style of the church of Christ of the Light. In fact, Galdós' own marginal drawings on the relevant page in Amador's study demonstrate very clearly the young writer's fascination with the complicated structure of the interconnecting arches of the domes in the ceiling. This interest is not to be found in Amador's account and is even superior to that of the Romantic poet and essayist, Gustavo Adolfo Bécquer, in his *Historia de los templos de España*:[5]

> How beautiful that small area is; it is divided into nine spaces by arches and windows which transmit the light, fragmented and tempered by the brightness and variety of such colourful ornaments. That interior is a cage where geometrical exactness, together with the combinations of the decoration, would form a spectacle of enchanting confusion like that caused by those linear figures of their wonderful titles. *It is truly an enchanted area, a small labyrinth extended in three dimensions, a kind of jigsaw, an ingenious toy to torture the mind, a very simple shape which becomes, through the combinations of its lines, the most complicated and manifold structure.* (my italics; *OC*, VI, 1590)

To the physical eye the domes first appear as a chaotic maze of shapes: only when the viewer's reason is able to disentangle the lines does the artistic puzzle make any sense. A mathematical game for the intelligent viewer, it is nothing less than a dizzy kaleidoscope for the undiscerning gazer. In the case of the carvings in the Cathedral choir

---

[5] *Obras completas* (Madrid: Aguilar, 1966), pp. 964-65. Bécquer is more factual, less lyrical in his description of this architectural item.

there is no such rational explanation, but, nonetheless, Galdós still finds their shapes appealing, especially that of the dragon-cum-sybil figure that hovers above these carvings. He is decidedly more at ease with the decoration on the arches in the Cathedral's cloisters: here the imported Gothic forms have been adapted to Spain's tradition with the result that the carved foliage is very realistic and also creates a chiaroscuro effect because the sunlight can penetrate around the figures which are carved in relief. Art and religion fuse in this part of the Cathedral, for while the eye is pleased by the shapes it gazes at, the mind can meditate at ease on spiritual matters. Later, however, Galdós expressed some uneasiness about such lavish art works in temples of worship where humility should reign supreme.

Discussing other historical buildings in the city, Galdós criticizes Egas' portico for the Santa Cruz hospital because of its confusing mixture of Gothic and Greco-Roman styles: the columns, the cornice, the attic and archivolt all resist the pure arrangement of vertical and horizontal lines, seeking unsuccessfully the incorrect, disproportionate, sinuous forms of the Gothic. In contrast, the façade of the Alcázar displays a harmonious regularity of windows that matches the elegance of the patio and famous staircase.

Galdós' failure to appreciate the more revolutionary aspects of El Greco's second period was a surprising blind spot when his fascination for other irregular shapes was already obvious. He could praise El Greco's "great facility for composition, steady hand for drawing and the often exact and right use of colour and tone" (*OC*, VI, 1616) during his first period; but the squalid, emaciated, yellow figures of the second period (apart from those in "The Burial of the Count of Orgaz") did not strike an appreciative response in Galdós until a few years later when, after frequent conversations with two friends, Francisco Giner de los Ríos and Manuel B. Cossío, the leading Krausist teachers at the independent Free Institution of Education in Madrid, he came to accept El Greco's "mental aberrations" as yet another example, like that of Michelangelo, of an artistic genius revolutionizing art and setting new patterns.[6]

Throughout the article, then, a number of tensions are at work. Firstly, there is the conflict between Galdós' fascination for the visual arts and his awareness at the same time of their exposure to decay and destruction over the years. Secondly, there is a discernible pull between what might be termed his classical notions of design and

[6] Marañón, "Galdós en Toledo", p. 563.

dimension, and those that lie outside the norm. Sometimes these extremes are revolutionary and daring in their originality, but can be delightfully experienced by the viewer's mind because his reason can decode the visual messages. At other times, Galdós surrenders all aesthetic criteria to the pure, unadulterated pull of the visual senses by works that, by the accepted norms, are grotesque or repellent. This absorbing plurality of responses will be codified to some extent, as we shall see later, in a coherent use of the visual arts in his fictional works.

"Cuarenta leguas por Cantabria"

Six years later, again for the *Revista de España*, Galdós wrote a travel guide on another part of the country he had also come to know intimately since his arrival in the Peninsula: the countryside and coastline around Santander. About half the length of his article on Toledo, "Cuarenta leguas" contains the same mixture of topographical painting and commentary on art and architecture, though now the respective proportions seem inverted. Galdós' doubts and hesitations (unfounded) about the artistic coherence of the piece are glimpsed in some of the letters to his great Santander friend, the novelist Pereda, written during the composition of the article. In one letter, dated 28 November 1876, he confides: "You can imagine what I have suffered, unsuccessfully, to give the article an acceptable shape. At first I thought of giving it some novelesque form, introducing passages and episodes to make this kind of literature feasible ...; when it is totally descriptive, it is unbearable."[7] However, he did subsequently remove the novelistic passages and was ashamed of the final result, fit, he considered, only for tourists to the region. Pereda's opinion, after reviewing the draft of the article, correcting place names and excising some infelicitous references to nuns, was far more positive. He even went as far as to say that the first part was the most scintillating piece of writing Galdós had ever produced.[8] Be that as it may, of greater significance for our study is the reappearance of Galdós' ambiguous appreciation and representation of visual art works and picturesque landscapes.

---

[7] Reproduced in Carmen Bravo-Villasante, "28 cartas de Galdós a Pereda", *CHA*, 84 (1970-71), p. 10.

[8] Reproduced in Soledad Ortega, *Cartas a Galdós* (Madrid: Revista de Occidente, 1964), p. 44. The same difference of opinion is reflected in a subsequent exchange of letters.

His first description, of the old historic town of Santillana del Mar, is typical in this respect. Though praised by modern authorities on the region as an accurate account,[9] the piece was attacked for its pejorative tone by a local resident, the Marquess of Casana, and it is not difficult to see why.[10] In a manner reminiscent of the de-romanticizing introduction of "Las generaciones artísticas" Galdós notes that the misnamed town is isolated from the main coastal road, even bypassed by the modern telegraph poles. Indeed, and very pertinently for our thesis, it is a place that is difficult for the human eye to capture in a correct focus: the visitor only sees the town (previously hidden by hills) when he is inside it. Once he leaves, it disappears from view. Only the nuns of the local convent enjoy some kind of panoramic view of the luscious green countryside in the surrounding area, and then only from an upstairs window. The houses are either very small, with roofs that seem to be within the reach of the traveller's hand, or are very large and stretch upwards to the sky. Some hide their ugliness in a corner, others, large and tumbledown, supported by rotting beams, seem to obstruct those people who pass by in the street. The main ecclesiastical building of the town, the Colegiata, is simply depressing: the capitals of the portal have been ruined, the figures of the Apostles mutilated, and on the inside, whatever sculptured forms the Romanesque temple once possessed have now been covered over with plaster, with effects that, as in the church of The Happy Outcome in Madrid, nauseate Galdós.

The area of the church that receives most attention is that of the cloister and charnel house, at the entrance to which Galdós is met by the chilling sight of a skeleton propped up against the socle. Pertinently, Galdós emphasizes the eye contact between living person and dead skeleton: the first thing on which the visitor's eye fixes are the empty sockets staring at everyone who enters the cloister. We are insistently reminded, therefore, of the finality of human eyesight and existence, and then, as the visitor peers at the charnel house and cemetery, of man-made art as well: "Man and art, the Christian sentiment that built the cloister and the egoism that allowed it to be lost, will fall into the same ruin, into the same mass of mud, whose dominion will be shared by bracken and bugs; everything will turn to dust and no one will even remain to feel proud

<hr/>

[9] Enrique Lafuente Ferrari, *El libro de Santillana* (Santander: Diputación Provincial, 1955), p. 22.

[10] According to Galdós in a letter to Pereda of 27 March 1877; see Bravo-Villasante, "28 cartas", p. 21.

of that dross" (*OC*, VI, 1447).[11] Far bleaker than his momentary doubt in "Las generaciones artísticas" about the propriety of art treasures in places of worship, this vision of the ultimate destiny of man and his art works is the most nihilistic passage in all Galdós' writings: an awareness of the temporality, both of the art work and the perceiving eye that appraises it, adds a deeper dimension to Galdós' attitude towards art. Consequently, it is appropriate that this dramatically pessimistic picture of Santillana del Mar (the restored palace of the Casa-Mena family with its beautiful library is the only exception) should be compared by Pereda to a visual art item: the magnificently sombre caricatures which the famous engraver Gustave Doré drew for an edition of Balzac's *Les Contes drolatiques*.[12]

By way of contrast Galdós now paints, as best he can in words, pictures of the beautiful Cantabrian coastline at Comellas, the next stop on his trip. He pays particular attention to the depth and line of the panorama before him: the horizon is almost invisible as the blue of the sea merges into that of the sky. The trail of black smoke from the transatlantic liners forms a nice horizontal accompaniment to the vertical masts and white sails of fishing boats in the foreground. Yet this picture-postcard view is really an exception in his Cantabrian tourist guide. More typical, surprisingly, is the marshy wasteland of La Rabia. His examination of the town of San Vicente de la Barquera, just beyond Torrelavega, combines both types of landscape: on the one hand, the beautiful artistic impression; on the other, the ugly physical reality. Viewed from the road, the town, which is situated at the end of a wide valley with a majestic backdrop of high mountains and two bridges in the foreground, presents one of the most delightful artistic panoramas that any traveller could hope to confront. Indeed, the huge size of everything (land, sky, mountains, meadows, rivers), even the picturesque reflections of the city in the water, produces in the spectator an effect of a "marvellous phantasmagoria" (*OC*, VI, 1451). Dazzled by the artistic beauty of the landscape and also by the geometrical patterns of rivulets and mud patches on the outskirts of the town, Galdós would prefer to remain looking at this canvas: "So beautiful is all this that it really is a

[11] It is interesting to note that, in a prologue he wrote thirteen years before his death for José María Salaverría's *Vieja España* (Madrid: Sucesores de Hernando, 1907), Galdós claimed that, whereas his friend saw in the darkened chapels of Burgos Cathedral the symbols of death, he could only view the sculptures and interplay of light as symbols of life's joys and delights (*P*, 81-82).

[12] Ortega, *Cartas*, p. 44.

pity to see that after the distant view of San Vicente, we come to San Vicente itself" (*OC*, VI, 1451). For the reality offered by the town is in stark contrast to the artistic impressionism of its landscape setting. Far from being a Spanish Glasgow, the city is a collection of dark old houses, ugly shops, grubby iron balconies, and a church that looks like a fishing hut. The town is even more depressing than Santillana del Mar, for it is devoid of life, reduced to nothing but skeletal form. Galdós seems to be experiencing a perverse delight in juxtaposing these contrasting visions of the town.

The picture (eagerly awaited by Pereda) of the giant rock formations of Las Gargantas at the end of the Deva valley is another example of Galdós' sharp eye for strange shapes and their resemblance to art forms. The masses of rock hanging threateningly over the traveller's head as he moves along the narrow defile are like towers, minarets and spires, far superior to the "richest and most varied architecture" (*OC*, VI, 1455). Furthermore, the spectator's eye is so impressed by their irregularity that he comes to believe that the vision is the product of his own imagination, "a large and stormy phantasmagoria of struggling masses like those that twirl around in the painful caverns of a nightmare" (*OC*, VI, 1455). Once more the emphasized architectural abnormalities of the rocks induce in the viewer moments of cosmic disorientation when the regular dimensions of assumed reality appear perilously subject to confusion.

In what appear at first sight to be routine tourist guides to the city of Toledo and the Cantabrian coastline, Galdós goes out of his way to focus attention on the abnormal, the grotesque and the irregular, both in natural landscape and art objects. It is almost as if he feels the need to balance the visual attractions of artistic splendours with the reverse picture which stresses the existence of unaesthetic forms and ideas. Is it not that Galdós is trying to warn his readers against letting themselves be seduced by the attractive appearances of art objects or scenes? Surely the frequency with which he refers to the human eye's fascination with intricate artistic shapes, his awareness of the attractiveness of the grotesque and irregular, and then of the finality of all arts, together with his unconventional pictures of both regions, all seem to indicate that his aims in the two articles were far more ambitious and profound than the mere cataloguing of tourist beauty spots. Even at this early stage in his literary career he was clearly interested in the disturbing misperceptions and misinterpretations to which the human eye was liable when viewing art objects or picturesque landscapes.

PART II

THE HISTORICAL NOVELS AND THE VISUAL ARTS

CHAPTER 4

THE ILLUSTRATED EDITION OF THE FIRST TWO SERIES OF THE *EPISODIOS NACIONALES* (1881-85)

By 1873 Galdós' literary apprenticeship on Madrid newspapers had been well served and he was feeling ready to devote himself entirely to literature. He had already published two historical novels, *La Fontana de Oro* (1870) and *El audaz* (1871), as well as the novelette, *La sombra* (1871). He was now ready to embark on the composition of two series of interconnected novels, covering the political and social history of Spain between 1805 and 1834.[1] The 1881-85 illustrated edition of these twenty *episodios nacionales* constitutes Galdós' only attempt to combine the visual arts and the novel in that most obvious intersection between the sister arts, the illustration of the printed text. This aim had been in Galdós' mind right from the beginning, as he admitted in the prologue to the first of the illustrated volumes in 1881: "Before these twenty novels became a reality, when the first of them was not written, nor even well thought out ... I felt and decided that the *Episodios nacionales* should be, sooner or later, an illustrated work" (*P*, 52). He felt that the illustrators' pens would provide "all the vigour, accent and soul" needed to fulfil the task of pleasing the reader. He recognized that not every novel benefited from illustrations, but felt that the *Episodios* did because they added delights that could not be acquired from a simple reading of the printed text. Galdós was insistent that the illustrations are an integral part of the *Episodios*: the "graphic text" of the illustrated edition is "in my opinion an almost intrinsic condition of the *Episodios*

[1] See Brian J. Dendle, "A note on the genesis of the *Episodios nacionales*", *AG*, 15 (1980), 137-40, for a review of Galdós' changes in the temporal scope of the two series.

nacionales" (*P*, 52). In fact, he says that with the drawings of the Mélida brothers his printed words have received "an interpretation superior to the printed letters themselves" (*P*, 52). Obviously, the twenty novels could and did, first of all, exist without the graphic additions; but with them a whole new dimension of meaning could be furnished for the greater benefit of the reader, whatever his social condition.

In this support for the advantages to be derived from an interart co-operation, Galdós was, of course, repeating a point made many years earlier in Spain by Mesonero Romanos, another great mentor of his, who in the 1836 prospectus for his new magazine, the *Semanario Pintoresco Español*, noted that the English editors of the *Penny Magazine* had used woodcuts in the middle of their texts to make "more perceptible the purpose of the article".[2] The illustration complemented or balanced the printed text; it was, though, a delicate balance that required, according to the critic Francisco Esteve Botey, a close collaboration between illustrator and novelist.[3] This correlation of the two media is seen at its best in the close positioning, especially during the Romantic period, of the illustration and the corresponding sentence or paragraph.[4] However, because of the ability of the human eye to encompass with greater rapidity the graphic material on the book page, it is not surprising that at times, especially in newspaper or magazine articles on local customs or dress, as Margarita Ucelay Da Cal has shown, the pictures soon became the dominant partner, with the printed text often reduced to a minimum.[5] In illustrated novels, of course, the dissociation could not be so extreme, but obviously a dangerous tension between the two partners was always a distinct possibility. It was this danger that worried a contemporary of Mesonero, Francisco Pérez de Anaya,

[2] "Prospecto" to *Semanario Pintoresco Español* (Madrid, 1836), p. 4.
[3] *El grabado en la ilustración del libro* (Madrid: Consejo Superior de Investigaciones Científicas, 1948), p. 203.
[4] María Carmen de Artigas-Sanz, *El libro romántico en España* (Madrid: Consejo Superior de Investigaciones Científicas, 1953), p. 50. Galdós' own ability in this regard is seen not only in the editorship of the illustrated edition of the *Episodios*, but also, albeit on a much smaller scale, in the letter he wrote over a decade later to be published alongside the lithographic reproduction of Aureliano de Beruete's painting of Orbajosa for the Madrid newspaper *Apuntes* on 5 April 1896; see Leo J. Hoar, Jr., "Galdós y Aureliano de Beruete: visión renovada de Orbajosa", *AEA*, 20 (1974), 693-707, and Robert J. Weber, "Galdós y Orbajosa", *HR*, 31 (1963), 348-49.
[5] "Relaciones entre el texto y los grabados", in her *Los españoles pintados por sí mismos (1843-1844): estudio de un género costumbrista* (Mexico City: El Colegio de México, 1951), pp. 130-35; see also J. R. Harvey, *Victorian Novelists and Their Illustrators* (New York: New York Univ. Press, 1971), p. 169.

who made a scathing attack on the fashion for novels to have illustrations on every page.[6] In English literature, George Eliot, in a letter to Leighton, the illustrator of her novel *Romola*, expressed some of the misgivings an author can have over this partnership with another artist: "But I am quite convinced that illustrations can only form a sort of overture to the text. The artist who uses the pencil must otherwise be tormented to misery by the deficiencies or requirements of the one who uses the pen, and the writer, on the other hand, must die of impossible expectations."[7]

Galdós clearly did not belong to this school of doubters. By 1885, when the last of the ten volumes of the illustrated edition had appeared, his enthusiasm for the work of his illustrators, now increased from the two Mélida brothers to a band of a dozen or so, had far from waned. Indeed, he claimed that the joint venture was a landmark in illustrated book production in Spain, "a true museum of the plastic arts applied to printing" (*P*, 59). Zinc engravings had been preferred to woodcuts because of their more attractive, more faithful reproduction of the artist's original drawing; but the state of Spanish printing technology, not so advanced as that of France or Britain, had not permitted him to realize the art work he had wanted.[8] However, despite these technological setbacks, the considerable time and energy he spent on co-ordinating contributions or corresponding with his collaborators[9] and his worries about the marketability of the ten volumes,[10] Galdós was fully satisfied with the more than twelve

[6] "Estado que presenta la industria tipográfica; causas que impiden sus progresos con perjuicio de los operarios, ruina de considerables capitales, y medios que pueden emplearse para que se ponga al nivel de los países más adelantados", *Revista de España, de Indias y del Extranjero*, 13 (1848), 5-15, 113-37; see Lee Fontanella, "The fashion and styles of Spain's 'costumbrismo'", *RCEH*, 6 (1982), 175-89, for a full discussion of these different approaches to textual illustration.

[7] Quoted by Witemeyer, *George Eliot*, p. 160. Thackeray, the sole major Victorian novelist to illustrate his own work, did not experience such misgivings: see Stephen Canham, "Art and the illustrations of *Vanity Fair* and *The Newcomes*", *Modern Language Quarterly*, 43 (1982), 43-66. John Bayley, "The art of Russianness", *TLS*, 3 December 1982, p. 1329, notes that Tolstoy was dissatisfied with the illustrators of his novels until he met Leonid Pasternak.

[8] Enrique Mélida reported to Galdós in a letter of 7 June 1880 (housed in the Casa-Museo Pérez Galdós) on the advantages of the "tintograma", a process of photographic reproduction, specimens of which he had just received.

[9] See Julia Mélida, *Biografía de Arturo Mélida* (unpublished manuscript, to be found in the Casa-Museo Pérez Galdós), p. 8.

[10] See the correspondence between Galdós and Mesonero Romanos in E. Varela Hervías, *Cartas de Pérez Galdós a Mesonero Romanos* (Madrid: Excmo Ayuntamiento de Madrid, 1943), p. 57; Galdós and Pereda, in Ortega, *Cartas*, p. 79, and Bravo-Villasante, "28 cartas", p. 32; Galdós and José Ortega Munilla, in La Nuez and Schraibman, *Cartas*, p. 194; Galdós and Ramón Pérez de Ayala, in Ortega, *Cartas*, p. 444.

hundred illustrations.[11] The question now has to be asked: was this satisfaction of Galdós misplaced or unfounded? Did the illustrations really complement or add a further dimension of meaning to the written text, as he claimed?

Some guidance in answering these questions can be obtained from an examination of Galdós' own signed illustrations in the two series. By also appearing as an illustrator of his own printed words, Galdós was enabling readers to evaluate his contribution to this most immediate of interart parallels. Three in number, the illustrations appeared in the sixth *episodio* of the first series, *Zaragoza*, and are similar in that they all depict architectural structures: Saragossa Cathedral with a partly destroyed bridge in the foreground (*ENI*, III, 405), the Jerusalem convent, also in a state of semi-destruction (*ENI*, III, 397) and the Carmen Gate (*ENI*, III, 55). One's first impression is that Galdós the artist is delighting in the portrayal of minute architectural detail such as the straight lines or angles of walls and façades, even of lumps of rubble, upper arches, buttresses, windows, pinnacles and cupolas. In short, the same sort of classical linear composition for which he had shown preference in his early art work, like the watercolour of the city hall in Las Palmas.[12] The illustrations are admirably executed and provide a pleasing effect for the eye, but they remain ornamental decorations rather than vital visual eluci- dations of important scenes or locales. The value of the illustrations is secondary or incidental to the development of the printed word. Naturally not all of the illustrations in the ten volumes can be accused of the same role. Many of the fifty or so illustrations to each *episodio*[13] do contribute effectively to the rapid visual appreciation of the direction of the printed text, especially those full-page drawings depicting crowd-, battle-, or street-scenes. Yet the desire to impress the viewer with artistic virtuosity, as Galdós so clearly did in his own studies, is prevalent, notably in the most gifted of the illustrators, Arturo Mélida. His intricate patterns of lines and arabesques, often

---

[11] With characteristic modesty Galdós refrains from extolling the skills of his collaborators and their submissions to the 1884 Madrid Exhibition lest he appear to his *La Prensa* readers to be advertising the sale of his own illustrated *Episodios* (*CP*, 103-04). A fellow novelist, Armando Palacio Valdés, was equally confident of the ability of Spanish artists, but lamented the low quality of the printers: see the letter of 4 December 1889 he sent to José Yxart, reproduced in David Torres, "Del archivo epistolar de Palacio Valdés", *Revista de Literatura*, 86 (1981), p. 271.

[12] Reproduced in Ruiz de la Serna and Cruz Quintana, *Prehistoria*, p. 187.

[13] *Memorias de un cortesano*, with about forty illustrations, and *La batalla de los Arapiles*, with about sixty, are exceptions to the average.

with classical figures as a base, exercise a strong visual fascination that causes the reader to ponder and then question their relation to the printed text which they accompany. For example, in *La corte de Carlos IV* Mélida draws an absolutely delightful miniature of a cat knocking over some salt; this black picture is framed, so to speak, by the figure of the Devil. The origin of the illustration lies not in any momentous incident of the narration but rather in some verse included as comic relief:

> The egg wants salt
> and the devil of the cat
> knocked over the salt cellar. (*ENI*, I, 325)

One wonders how far Galdós' own fascination with intricate designs and optical effects swayed him into accepting these far from relevant graphics from his close friend.

José Ortega Munilla naïvely imagined that each illustrator sketched out a rough copy of his illustration in the margins of the novels as he read along.[14] The surviving correspondence between Galdós and his collaborators shows that there was wide consultation, but, obviously, he could not and would not dictate which scenes were to be illustrated. He had made that task somewhat easier by inventing scenes and characters that were highly colourful in themselves. Moreover, like all historical novelists, whether of the distant or immediate past, Galdós, in his *Episodios* (and this applies to all five series), could consult the large amount of pictorial records available, be they portraits, paintings, prints, maps or illustrations in history books. In turn, the illustrators themselves could reasonably bypass Galdós' written account or transcription and refer back directly to the pictorial source. This must have been the case particularly in the number of bust illustrations that conveniently dot the *Episodios*: the picture of Wellington in *La batalla de los Arapiles* (*ENI*, V, 251) is an obvious reproduction of a famous Goya portrait. In *La corte de Carlos IV* the scene showing Goya in top hat and frock coat (*ENI*, I, 334) supervising the decoration of the Marquess' palace is clearly based on the many self-portraits the painter was wont to make.

The question of Galdós' own reliance on pictorial sources, especially in the first two series, has been frequently raised by critics.

---

[14] "*Los Episodios nacionales* ilustrados", *La Ilustración Española y Americana*, 2 (1881) p. 378.

Bravo-Villasante has been particularly insistent in identifying parallels.[15] More often, however, the suggestions are qualified; for example, Stephen Gilman writes: ". . . we might compare the sinister reunions in the dark and precarious dwelling of Don Felicísimo Carnicero in the second series to the painter's vision [i.e Goya's] of the Inquisition or the Council of the Indies."[16] Hinterhäuser wonders whether any of the fictional characters in the *Episodios* are modelled on figures to be found in canvases by such painters as Esquivel.[17] Assumptions and hypotheses predominate, simply because Galdós never makes any crude admission of sources. In view of his great familiarity with the Prado collection and other paintings in Madrid churches and religious houses, it is perhaps natural for these critics to expect that he used well-known pictorial sources for some passages of his fiction. However, his purpose in these instances was never slavishly to describe in great detail the subject of the canvas he was recalling, the easiest and most natural of interart relationships. Indeed, there are many occasions when, instead of unashamedly acknowledging the pictorial source, he deliberately tries to throw the reader off the scent by maintaining an odd reticence or by making some important modifications in the verbal transcription. A good example of this process is his account of the resistance of the Madrid population to the French invaders on the 2nd and 3rd of May, 1808. Goya's famous compositions, the "Charge of the Mamelukes" and the "Execution of the Defenders of Madrid", were clearly in Galdós' mind as he chronicled the events in his *El 19 de marzo y el 2 de mayo*. Yet the verbal transcriptions are brief and starkly factual, hardly sufficient to recall the famous canvases. Of the Charge, Galdós writes: ". . . the famous Mamelukes swooped on the people whirling their swords. Those of us who were in the Calle Mayor got the worst of it because the ferocious horsemen attacked us from both sides" (*OC*, I, 437). There is no attempt to reproduce the vivid colours or dynamic motion of the Goya canvas. The only possible nod of acknowledgement to a pictorial source is the narrator's admission of the impotence of the written word to capture the scene fully: "The Calle Mayor and neighbouring streets gave the appearance of a cauldron of rage, impossible to describe in language. Those of you

---

[15] *Galdós*, p. 141.

[16] *Galdós and the Art of the European Novel 1867-1887* (Princeton: Princeton Univ. Press, 1981), p. 61, note 20.

[17] *Los "Episodios nacionales"*, p. 86.

who did not see the uprising can give up any idea of picturing it" (*OC*, I, 435).

In the companion scene of the shootings in Moncloa on the following day, Galdós has his protagonist, the orphan boy Gabriel Araceli, witness events from the distance of the Holy Spirit church. The flash of gunshot illuminates a tangle of bodies in various postures, an adequate reminder of Goya's study. However, in the painting the illumination had been provided by a large lantern positioned in the centre foreground. In Galdós' transcription, this detail is changed to a number of small lanterns with a flickering light.[18] Hinterhäuser maintains the rather simplistic viewpoint that Galdós deliberately chose the most famous paintings of Spanish artists so that the relatively low-brow audience he was aiming to reach could derive some satisfaction from a recognition of this pictorial source.[19] More to the point, surely, are Galdós' determination not to let the obvious pictorial source dominate his verbal account and his desire to distance himself from an obvious visual art model. The *episodios* of the first two series had to stand by themselves as an original contribution to the corpus of iconographical history of the period. They could not appear to imitate slavishly well-known existing models. In the illustrated edition of the *Episodios* that danger was even more real and capable of subverting the whole venture. Yet, in the last analysis, it is the thematic use (not the transcriptional accuracy) to which Galdós applies these allusions, faint or forced, to famous canvases, as well as his visual art similes and metaphors, that is really of prime consideration in the overall aim of the first two series of *Episodios nacionales*.

---

[18] In Arturo Mélida's illustration of the same scene (*ENI*, II, 201), a further modification is introduced by the large fountain in the centre foreground behind which a hidden lantern illuminates the night sky. The figure of an officer positioned at the side of the firing squad is another original addition.

[19] *Los "Episodios nacionales"*, p. 85.

CHAPTER 5

THE VISUAL ARTS AS COMMENTARY OR METAPHOR

The *Episodios nacionales* (1873-1912)

Hinterhäuser's preoccupation with only one of the visual arts – painting – as well as with detecting only well-known pictorial sources inevitably led him to the erroneous conclusion that Galdós' tableaux, or what he thought were verbal reproductions of canvases, had a very indeterminate structural function in the respective *episodios* and were submerged by the flow of the narrative.[1] A much more subtle and coherent interpretation emerges if we widen the concept of visual arts and examine the manner in which Galdós integrates the allusions to the visual arts into the development of one of the major themes of the first two series: the correct appreciation of historical reality.

Trafalgar (1873), the first *episodio* Galdós wrote, offers an example of this skilful thematic manipulation. One of the earliest sights that the eyes of Gabriel Araceli register is that of the Spanish fleet moored in Cadiz harbour. From the distance he absurdly views them as mysterious structures, toys of amusement like the makeshift boats he and his infant friends propel over the roadside puddles. A closer viewing position does not solve the problem of identity; although his eager eyes observe every detail when he later joins the fleet, his vivid imagination likens the ships to the Gothic cathedrals of Castile and Flanders because of the predominance of vertical and horizontal lines, the whimsical play of colours in the sunlight and a

---

[1] *Los "Episodios nacionales"*, pp. 365-66.

certain historical-religious atmosphere.[2] Gabriel's infant imagination has transformed these weapons of war into beautiful visual art objects that exemplify the national spirit. The vision, it need hardly be added, is far removed from reality and could only be possible before the battle of Trafalgar. After the bloody and tragic slaughter Gabriel's original artistic comparisons are no longer valid. As a justification of that floating castle image Gabriel had cited the erroneous impressions given by lithographic reprints and engravings of the Spanish fleet at Trafalgar (*OC*, I, 213). Yet in trying to correct one misinterpretation encouraged by the visual arts, he unwittingly creates another, again through the medium of a visual art simile. By concentrating on the dangerously equivocal impressions given by the visual arts both literally and figuratively Galdós might well be warning his readers against believing the evidence of their eyes.

In the next *episodio*, *La corte de Carlos IV* (1873), the presence of Goya as a minor participant in the fiction encourages the search for interart analogies. For one of his favourite Spanish artists Galdós creates a "walk-on" role as the house decorator for Marquess X. It is very probable that Galdós is recalling here an early phase in Goya's career, the year 1785, when he was commissioned to decorate the walls of a room in the mansion of the Count-Duke and Countess-Duchess of Benavente, as well as to paint their portraits.[3] In Galdós' national episode, Don Francisco is responsible for decorating the hallways and stairs with garlands of artificial flowers, which, under the bright glare of innumerable lamps and candles, also artistically arranged in garlands and wreaths, give a fantastic appearance to the whole house. The illumination also vivifies such art objects in the main drawing-room as coats of armour, Spanish bullfighting scenes and figures, as well as the more sombre conquistador figures in paintings by Pantoja and Sánchez Coello. However, a discordant

---

[2] In his prologue to Salaverría's *Vieja España*, Galdós reverses this comparison, likening the towers of village churches dotted over the Castilian meseta between La Mota and Madrigal to the masts of ships immobilized in a petrified sea: it is an "elementary landscape, a rest for the eyes and a torment for the imagination" (*P*, 86).

[3] See Gaspar Gómez de la Serna, *Goya y su España* (Madrid: Alianza, 1969), p. 53. Nigel Glendinning, *Goya and his Critics* (New Haven: Yale Univ. Press, 1977), p. 183, presents a very limited view of the Goya material in this *episodio*. In a short fantasy tale, "El pórtico de la gloria", which appeared in the Madrid journal *Apuntes*, of 2 March 1896, Galdós gave a fairly detailed description of Goya: "... an unruly, irritable old man, with lively eyes, a mocking mouth, unkempt beard and restless movements ... always with a dark cloak wrapped around his body and a furry hat pulled down to his neck." He is one of the chief protagonists in the rebellion of bored souls in the Elysian Fields. The text is reproduced and analysed in Leo J. Hoar, Jr., "Galdós' counter-attack on his critics: the lost short story, 'El pórtico de la gloria'", *Symposium*, 30 (1976), 277-307.

note in the décor is sounded by the candelabra and flower-stands which are in the neo-classical style recently popularized by the French Revolution. The carved figures of Olympian goddesses in classical poses contrast with the more vivacious natural figures of the paintings and tapestries. Significantly, the aristocratic inhabitants of the house and their guests are indifferent to and ignorant of this strident clash of artistic styles.

They also fail to discern a similar clash of pictorial styles on the stage curtain Goya has painted for the amateur production of an adaption of Shakespeare's *Othello* to be given in the mansion. The figure of Apollo playing the lyre (or it could be a guitar) in the centre of the stage curtain has all the appearance of a Madrid "majo" or "toff", the nine Muses, that of Madrid beauties, while Pegasus looks like a good sorrel from Cordoba. Thus, the whole canvas is a clever pictorial satire (not the first Goya has designed, says Galdós [*OC*, I, 337]) of the classical world now favoured by Madrid aristocracy as domestic decoration. The implications are obvious: this taste for the cold neo-classical style is bogus, artificial and in marked contrast to the more natural and spontaneous liking of vibrant, colourful art forms depicting national scenes. The conflict in these aristocrats between their national identity and their cultivation of artificial, alien personas is thus captured in the gaudy mixture of Goya's pictorial satire. In the same way the third-hand adaptation of *Othello* is a hollow, pompous display of rhetoric that masks the real, live drama of the aristocratic actors, especially of the two females, Lesbia and Amaranta.[4] Beneath the empty words of the bowdlerized version of Shakespeare's masterpiece pulsates a real drama of marital jealousy and intrigue, but without the actors being able to appreciate the correspondence between reality and fiction. Such a mental perception is really beyond their intelligence, especially when they fail to see the pictorial satire Goya paints before their eyes. Again, is not Galdós' deeper purpose in this highly vivid scene to offer a visual lesson to his readers? The visual arts can offer more than surface delights to the eye; for the more perceptive viewer they provide a whole lesson of moral direction to the narrative in which they are encased.

Gabriel eventually comes to see through the artificiality and

---

[4] Gabriel as octogenarian narrator had given the mysterious Duchess X and Countess X these classical names because they resembled figures he had seen depicted in some of Goya's tapestries for the royal factory of St. Barbara. They are also presented as great patronesses of the arts and friends of Goya.

pretence of this aristocratic circle and to appreciate the naturalness and sincerity of Inés and her mother. The latter's death in an attic atop the mansion of the Marquess affords Galdós the opportunity to fashion a scene whose truly artistic resemblance contrasts with the gaudy imitation scene below. Lying on her deathbed, Doña Juana resembles the statue on a tomb; the reddish glow of the candle points heavenward and the prints of the Virgin and the saints on the walls seem to be affected by the sadness of the scene. Here there is no pretence or artificiality; true and sincere emotions are displayed, so art and reality fuse, no longer the discordant incongruities that they were in the aristocratic apartments below.

Perhaps the most ambitious and sustained enlistment of the visual arts in this aim to convey a contrast between reality and appearances is the series of allusions to various visual depictions of Napoleon Bonaparte in the first two series. In *Trafalgar* Gabriel initially visualizes the French Emperor, then an ally of Spain against Britain, as the typical Andalusian smuggler on horseback. This far from flattering image is slightly modified after Gabriel has become familiar with a print of the Emperor hanging in the house of his master, Don Alonso Gutiérrez de Cisniega. The equestrian pose in the gaudy, cheap print by an unknown artist is the same, but the horse is coloured green and the coat of the Emperor vermilion; it is these colours which fix the image of Napoleon in the boy's mind.[5]

Two *episodios* later, in *Bailén* (1873), as the Spanish army joins battle with the invaders around this eponymous town in La Mancha, Napoleon's presence is once more mediated through a succession of art images. Gabriel forms part of a group travelling over the beautifully barren Castilian meseta.[6] This territory is, of course,

[5] Agustí Durán-Sanpere, *Grabados populares españoles* (Barcelona: Gustavo Gili, 1971), p. 75, notes that Napoleon was a frequent subject for the illustrated sheets of verse called "aleluyas" which were very popular in Spain.

[6] Darío de Regoyos y Valdés, *La España negra de Verhaeren* (Madrid: La Lectura, 1924), p. 53, believed that Castile had an "antipictorial" landscape: "The palette is unable to reproduce those vibrations of such brutal and white light." Seven years earlier in his collection *Campos de Castilla*, the Andalusian poet, Antonio Machado (1875-1939), had drawn attention in the composition entitled "The Manchegan Woman" to the ocular appeal of the same landscape as well as to its sparse pictorial features:

Across this La Mancha . . .
Which beneath the level line of the sky levels its paths,
. . .
Across this dry plain of sun and distance,
Where the eye achieves its high noon
(A diminutive band of birds dots
The indigo of the sky above the white village;

recognized as the home of Don Quixote, who had imagined all sorts
of battles raging over its flat, ocean-like expanse. One of Gabriel's
companions is the father of his beloved Inés, the turncoat French
supporter, Santorcaz, who is so bedazzled by the moonlit landscape
that he believes he is reliving the famous battle of Austerlitz (1805).
The illusion is encouraged by the chiaroscuro effects produced by the
moon intermittently visible behind gaps in the clouds. But for
Gabriel the interplay of light and cloud formations generates an
effect of a serious art caricature: ". . . the greyish and rent clouds,
alternately dark and radiant, drew a thousand large-size figures with
that expressiveness which, while close to caricature, had a kind of
solemn, awesome greatness" (*OC*, I, 477). Gabriel's art-based
interpretations of the shifting, moonlit clouds, like the allusions to
Don Quixote, must cast an ironic meaning on Santorcaz's hallucination: the latter's grandiose account of the famous victory is thus
being ridiculed for what it is, a passing vanity that will soon be
devalued by Napoleon's defeat at the hands of the Spanish at Bailén.
The silhouette of the Emperor is the crowning phantasmagoric effect
produced by the dispersing masses of clouds: ". . . a huge hat was
supported by two lamps and beneath it the shaded reflections of the
moon, as it were, sketched a round face sunk between high lapels,
from which a large, black arm stretched forth, pointing determinedly
towards the horizon" (*OC*, I, 477).[7] Again a pertinent comparison
with Don Quixote is made by one of the group, and doubts are also
raised in Gabriel's mind about the validity of this retinal image that
finally resolves itself into the outline of a caricature. Ephemeral art
forms created by Nature now prophesy the outcome of the approaching battle for a man whose power and dynamic personality
have hitherto been eternalized in awesome art images.
    Galdós rigidly maintains this distanced, silhouettish presentation

And way over there stands a copse of small green poplar trees,
Behind miles and miles of yellow fields)
See *Obras: poesía y prosa*, ed. Aurora de Albornoz and Guillermo de Torre, 2nd ed.
(Buenos Aires: Losada, 1973), pp. 209-10.
    [7] Arturo Mélida's illustration of this hallucination (*ENI*, II, 263) is very striking: it
shows battle scenes, skeletons and the silhouette of the Emperor with right hand under
breast lapel in the celebrated pose. Another engraving by the same artist a few pages
earlier had shown Don Quixote sallying forth on Rocinante with the dark silhouette of
Napoleon projected on a wall behind (*ENI*, II, 256). It is significant that most of the
illustrations that include Napoleon capture Galdós' verbal silhouette. In *Napoleón, en
Chamartín*, another illustrator, Lizcano, shows the Emperor as a silhouette charging
over a fence on the battlefield (*ENI*, III, 110). The only non-silhouette illustration,
again by Lizcano, is at the end of the same *episodio* when Napoleon stands atop a
precipice surveying the horizon in his traditional pose (*ENI*, III, 230).

even when the Emperor, visiting his brother Joseph in Madrid in the next *episodio*, *Napoleón, en Chamartín* (1874), presents the narrator with an opportunity for a direct description. This the latter steadfastly avoids, relying on other witnesses for minor details of physical features. Napoleon's persistent monosyllabic exclamations, the mechanical movements of his left hand over his stomach, the sudden arching of eyebrows or a smile directed to his staff, are touches that humanize and individualize the stereotyped image of the Emperor; yet the most salient feature of this close-up of a living icon is the constant flashing of the famous telescope as the French leader scans the horizon. The immediate question raised by the inclusion of this detail concerns the purpose and benefits of all this physical viewing. In the final analysis Napoleon's remarkable eye for battle will be of no avail. Napoleon's vision is directed towards the immediate objective of battle strategy and power, not to the far more important questions of human existence, finality and moral responsibility. These are some of the considerations that Galdós seems to be raising, logically and pertinently, in the mind of the reader as he focuses attention on this ocular mannerism of the living image.

Having stressed the Emperor's close scrutiny of the immediate reality, the narrator shifts his focus, now presenting the historical figure from the viewpoint of other characters. Significantly, Galdós maintains a distanced silhouettish view, but now adds some movement, as if he were conducting a magic lantern show. Bonaparte is dining with his brother Joseph one night in the Pardo palace just outside Madrid and the whole scene is watched by a group of courtiers from a gallery window opposite the State rooms. With the heavier curtains drawn to one side and the lace curtains covering the panes, the outlines of the two brothers are projected onto this screen, as it were, by a lamp placed at the back of the room. Napoleon's silhouette naturally stands out on the screen, and its varied movements and their meaning are the subject of heated debate amongst the spectators who are not able to hear a word. Their interpretation of the siblings' conversation has to rely, therefore, upon their decoding of the accompanying kinesic language of muscular movement by the principal silhouette. Through these perplexed courtiers Galdós is perhaps representing the difficulties which face any analysis of Napoleon if the viewers persist in considering the Emperor solely in terms of the customary pictorial image. Is not Galdós intimating that his compatriots and others have been bedazzled by the iconographical propaganda on the French leader? A more accurate interpretation of the man and his age has to be made independent of these visual art images. In a key reference to Napoleon in *Gerona* (1874), another *episodio* of the first series, Galdós acknowledges that often the historian is deceived by the optical greatness of something that is in reality very small:

> ... and [he] applauds and admires a crime simply because it is perpetrated throughout an entire hemisphere. Overmagnifying objects can be just as much an impediment to correct observations as diminishing them and causing them to disappear in the mist of invisibility. I am saying this because in my opinion Napoleon I with his ephemeral empire, if you exclude his great military genius, differs only in magnitude from the bandits who proliferated in the world when there was no police force. (*OC*, I, 836).

The closing reference to the bandits recalls Gabriel's first impression of the French leader in *Trafalgar*. The subsequent selection of the impersonal, opaque art form of the caricature and the repeated references to the power of visual appreciation have allowed Galdós to question and demythicize the normally imposing iconographical image of the Emperor.

In the second *episodio* of the second series, *Memorias de un cortesano* (1875), masterpieces of world painting, not the shadowy suggestions of silhouettes, are used to make pertinent comments on the historical figure of Napoleon's Spanish accomplice, Ferdinand VII. The national art treasures in the monarch's room in the Madrid Royal Palace receive each day the holocaust of cigar smoke from the King and his coterie of advisers. The smoke forms a screen effectively preventing the royal owner from appreciating his collection, mentioned only by name and never in graphic detail.[8] Once more Galdós emphasizes the gaze of the figures in these art objects, as he had done with the figure of Napoleon. The silent portraits face each other and their lines of vision converge on the centre of the room where the royal *tertulia* is usually seated. The portraits of these royal ancestors smile or frown according to the tenor of the discussion. One canvas (not of royal forbears) that is signalled out for special animation is Velázquez's "The Topers", whose besotted figures are first presented as if they were real people staring down and laughing at the King and his cronies. Only later is their identity revealed and then the illusion of reality is lost. Emphasis is placed on their insistent staring, as if they were some court of madmen sitting in judgement on

---

[8] The illustration by Sala captures the smoke-screen very vividly (*ENI*, VI, 310).

the living characters in the room. The assumption neatly projected by Galdós' selection of this famous canvas is that Ferdinand and his group are even madder than the pictorial figures in their drunken orgy, because they cannot perceive their faults while the latter apparently can. The reader is being asked to compare canvas and historical personage and to draw appropriate conclusions.

Another famous study, Pantoja's portrait of Philip II, offers a similarly serious comment. Again Galdós starts with the illusion that he is describing a living person: "In a corner, next to the window, hidden in the darkness and almost invisible, was a livid, lifeless man" (*OC*, I, 1332). Then we are informed that this man is a figure in a painting and that his stern look reaches across the whole room. The implication is that King Philip, the empire-builder, is aghast at the dismemberment of the empire condoned by one of his descendants. Ferdinand has cut himself off from the noble tradition established by Philip II, just as his cigar smoke blots out the art works from his visual and mental scrutiny. At this juncture Galdós pertinently recalls the visit of Napoleon Bonaparte one day in December 1808 to the royal palace and his long scrutiny of the portrait of the Hapsburg monarch. In view of the year of the events described in the *episodio* – 1815 – this detail is full of significance for our interpretation of the scene as well as corroborating our earlier analysis of the presentation of Napoleon in the first series of *episodios*. What really was Napoleon thinking of as he stared long and hard, as was his custom, at the portrait of Philip? What lessons did he derive from the canvas? Did he ponder the moral provided by the rise and fall of the Spanish empire or was he vaingloriously ranking himself above the famous Spanish monarch? It was probably the latter trend of thought, when he would have been better advised to adopt the former; the events of 1815 would confirm that lesson. As for Ferdinand VII, he does not even display Napoleon's interest in the portrait, nor would he be able to derive any moral message; his legacy to the Spanish nation was correspondingly more baneful than his French master's; not only did he lose an empire, but he also bequeathed over fifty years of intermittent civil war to Spain.

Ironically, the death of this cultural ignoramus, related by Galdós in *Los apostólicos* (1879), is recorded in an impressively extended scene in which Galdós comes closest to the traditional concept of "ut pictura poesis": the re-creation in words of the arrangement of details on a canvas. The whole sequence opens, curiously, however, with a panegyric of one of Galdós' great mentors, Ramón de Mesonero Romanos. Very similar in content to the article he had written for *La Nación* (*AN*, 258-60, 444-46), this authorial insertion into the fictional thread of the *episodio* stresses two important qualities about the painter of Madrid scenes and customs: first and foremost, Mesonero was a great observer of life, but he also had the uncommon knack of probing below the surface appearance of people and things to reach (all so gently!) the underlying reality. His second great virtue was his ability to express in words these pictures of Madrid life that he caught and immobilized in verbal pictures comparable to the masterpieces of Velázquez.[9]

After this authorial aside, Galdós launches into a verbal painting of La Granja palace where Ferdinand VII lies dying. From the outset the physical features of these manicured gardens, a replica of those in Versailles, are associated with the visual arts: the bushes and hedges have been converted by the gardener's shears into all kinds of artistic shapes, while the flower gardens form a thousand mosaics, tapestries and arabesques. Neo-classical statuary in the fountains projects tall spouts of water skywards in fascinating geometrical and architectural shapes, all the more appealing to the attentive eye when there is an interplay of sunlight. Galdós, we recall,

---

[9] Mesonero Romanos was constantly using pictorial analogues in his articles. In "Adiós al lector", the prologue to his third collection, *Tipos y caracteres* (1862), he refers to the difficulty of the writer-painter in capturing the image of contemporary society: "... society escapes his view; the model disintegrates in his hands; it is impossible to surprise it in a moment of rest; and only by making use of the rapid progress of the times, the steam engine, the photograph and the electric spark, can he perhaps fix its voluble features on the canvas, can he establish instant mental communication with it" (reproduced in Ramón de Mesonero Romanos, *Escenas matritenses*, ed. Federico Carlos Sainz de Robles [Madrid: Aguilar, 1956], pp. 893-94). In his famous 1870 manifesto on the contemporary Spanish novel, "Observaciones sobre la novela española moderna" (*E*, 115-32), Galdós refers to both Pereda and Fernán Caballero as contemporary novelists who paint the life of their local regions. Significantly, he had also spoken of Cervantes and Velázquez in the same breath as great painters of human reality, as if their respective arts were complementary.

In "Cuatro mujeres", his own contribution to a collection of articles on contemporary customs, *Las españolas pintadas por los españoles*, ed. Roberto Robert, 2 vols. (Madrid: J. E. Morete, 1871-72), II, 97-105, Galdós reminds the editor of the aptness of illustrated accompaniments for his four female portraits and ends by handing over his article in the form of an imaginary metal mould from whose admirable turquoise the rest of the gallery of sculptures in the collection have emerged. (Unfortunately, Galdós' article was one of the few in the collection not accompanied by an engraving.) The language of pictorial analogues, so apt in illustrated magazines or collections, was, therefore, a tradition in which Galdós participated.

It is interesting to note that in an early article for *La Nación* Galdós used pictorial language to describe another writer who influenced him enormously, Charles Dickens: "He is like a great colourist who produces his effects with indeterminate masses of colour, shade and light without allowing you to define the objects in particular or delineate the features separately ... He only sees in the object that part, that line which influences the whole of the scene, which adds something to the totality of the painting" (*AN*, 453).

had experienced similar delights inside the Toledo hermitage of Christ of the Light.

Turning his attention towards the people in the panoramic view, Galdós signals the bright colours of the clothes (so unlike contemporary fashions); in 1833 the yellow, green and red fabrics of the courtiers walking around the gardens are like small colourful flowers in a meadow, as the artist-narrator gazes at the distant scene. With a heavy use of pictorial references Galdós confesses that he cannot leave out of the foreground of his canvas the vibrant colours of the clothes worn by local peasant women. The background is then filled in with a military band parading in front of the neo-classical façade of the palace. Now that he has completed his canvas, he stands back for a moment to contemplate his work. At this point Galdós chooses to underline its status as a painting: he immobilizes, freezes his components in a pictorial stasis, for, with the unexpected turning off of the fountains, all other movements and activities come to a sudden halt, the courtiers now assuming that the King is dead. The earlier assimilation of this panorama to a Watteau painting is now justified: the brightly attired courtiers stand immobile in the royal enclosure.[10]

But this passage is only a verbal painting of a beautiful exterior scene. To equal his master, Galdós now has to go beyond this façade and enter the palace to capture the real, live drama surrounding the King's last moments. His description of the scene significantly focuses on the art objects in the regal rooms. The tone is decidedly jocose: the neo-classical figures of nymphs gambolling through egg-white clouds in the ceiling frescoes receive impudent and lascivious stares from King Charles IV, Ferdinand's father, in a hunting portrait (probably painted by Goya). Equally comical are the political moves now enacted in the apartments where pressure is applied to the King's brother, Don Carlos, to accept the post of regent. For his response, the prince turns his eyes to a canvas of the Virgin Mary and declares that She will be his guide and advisor. Yet, despite all the buffoonery, the scene is significant for the history of the country, for from it will spring the civil strife that will plague the

---

[10] Two Watteau compositions Galdós may have had in mind are "Perspective" (1714-15) and "Assembly in the Park" (1716-17). The latter, housed in the Louvre, could have been seen by Galdós on any of his trips to the French capital in the late 1860s; see Anita Brookner, *Watteau* (London: Hamlyn, 1967). The illustration in *ENI*, X, 199 does not really do justice to Galdós' verbal picture. According to R. L. Vicuña ("La exposición de bellas artes de 1876", *RE*, 50 [13 May 1876], 134), by 1876 the fashion for Watteau-style paintings in Spain had given way to a taste for Fortuny's impressionism.

country in the years ahead. No painting, Galdós declares, could capture all the hidden nuances and undercurrents of intrigue; yet, on the other hand, it was so plain and simple a scene that art could well let it slip through its fingers. The implication is that Galdós' account will reconcile this paradox. Like his master, Mesonero Romanos, Galdós can paint a beautiful external scene as if it were a wall painting, yet at the same time he can animate it with the realistic currents of human emotions and scheming. A pictorial reproduction of a historical moment can only achieve so much: its glossy beautiful surface must somehow surpass the mimetic and capture all the dramatic tension of human behaviour, as Galdós recognized so insistently in his appreciation in *La Prensa* of the work of Rembrandt, Velázquez and Goya and even of revolutionary geniuses like Michelangelo. In the type of literature that attempted to imitate the visual arts the same recipe was *de rigueur* too.

As a colophon to this extended series of artistic panels on the character and life of the misnamed Ferdinand the Desired One, Galdós engineers a scene in the final *episodio* of the second series, *Un faccioso más y algunos frailes menos* (1870), in which a Goyesque portrait of the monarch is directly responsible for the death of one of his most ardent supporters. In a drunken state Don Felicísimo Carnicero believes that Ferdinand has stepped out of the portrait that hangs in his office[11] and is coming forward to choke him. Carnicero staggers backwards and soon afterwards the rickety house begins to collapse, crushing beneath it Carnicero, whose flat face is now appropriately likened to a Gothic bas-relief. The fictional character's optical distortion of the visual art object, besides conveying the transcendence of the historical moment, is most apposite, for Ferdinand's repugnant image had been regrettably immortalized by the brushes of compliant artists. Galdós, the artist of words, is thus able, symbolically and momentarily, to reverse that pictorial tradition.

In other *episodios* of the first two series, the metaphor of art is also used to dispel illusions about the character of beautiful females. For example, Jenara Baraona, the lover of Salvador Monsalud in the second series, is presented as a figure of ideal beauty, a living artistic statue who bewitches all males. Andrea in *El grande Oriente* (1876), the fourth number in the second series, is another female who is depicted as the personification of classical beauty daily preening

[11] See Arturo Mélida's illustration (*ENI*, X, 370).

herself before the mirror or comparing herself to a Greek goddess. In both cases, the artistic comparisons are justified in physical terms and yet both beauties lack the milk of human kindness: as human beings they are cold, impersonal in their attitudes to others. The artistic parallels can only serve to stress the surface similarities, but in so doing, the implication always is that they lack the corresponding qualities of character. In other words, the art comparisons are used as shorthand devices to signal human character defects.

It would be idle to pretend that all references to the visual arts in the first twenty *episodios* or, for that matter, in the whole of Galdós' work, are given the same rich function that we have noted in the preceding examples. At times, it is obvious that Galdós is just parading his knowledge of visual art terms. For example, in *Bailén* the narrator describes at some length the wall decoration of a small square in Cordoba, although the context would hardly warrant so much detail: Gabriel is merely riding out of the city and notices these features as he passes through the square. There is no attempt to relate the passage thematically to the rest of the *episodio*. Nonetheless, such sections do indicate Galdós' abiding interest in the visual arts.

★   ★   ★

In the last three series, which Galdós wrote from 1898 to 1912, the secondary intention of bringing out an illustrated edition did no longer control, consciously or unconsciously, the composition of the respective tomes. Furthermore, by this time Galdós had largely abandoned his interest in the external observable world in order to concentrate his exclusive attention on the working of that inner, spiritual world which he had always regarded as the ultimate reality. Consequently, it is not surprising to record that references to the visual arts in the last three series are fewer and more isolated. The series of royal and political portraits in the office of the Finance Minister, Mendizábal, in the second number of the third series, *Mendizábal* (1898), or that of family portraits of the Emparán dynasty in *Las tormentas del 48* (1902), the first number of the fourth series, fulfil no other purpose than to provide examples of the poor-quality art work favoured by the ruling classes of the time. The same insipid style is followed in the decoration of the ceiling of the Senate Chamber in *España sin rey* (1907), the first number of the last series. The stilted portraits in the Madrid Royal Palace are the catalyst which determines the abandonment of Spanish society by Santiago Ibero, the protagonist of *La de los tristes destinos* (1907), the last *episodio* of the fourth series.[12] And the view of the cyclical nature of Spanish nineteenth-century history held by another fictional character, the cynic Santiuste, is couched in architectural terms: the 1868 revolution is like a "scaffolding erected to whitewash a building and give it an external coat of paint. It was rather dirty and now it is somewhat clean again, but it will soon get dirty again . . . and then another scaffolding will be erected" (*OC*, III, 780). Art works in these last three series thus represent the hollow values of official society; in their tawdriness and unaesthetic appearance they are an immediately recognizable cipher for the correspondingly repellent spiritual values of Galdós' compatriots. No longer do the art works project a visual puzzle, suggesting one dimension and hiding another: their true qualities are clearly exposed for all to see.

In one area at least, Hinterhäuser contended, the last three series of *episodios* were more pictorial than their twenty predecessors: in the representation of picturesque landscape. This development, he maintained, was the result of greater attention given to landscape painting by contemporary painters, like Casto Plasencia, Aureliano de Beruete and Sorolla, most of whom were personal friends of Galdós. A second factor was the interest in landscape colouring shown by the new crop of writers of the Generation of 1898, many of whom Galdós again knew on intimate terms.[13] Whilst there is undoubtedly some truth in this diagnosis, it does underestimate the nature and quality of the picturesque landscaping that Galdós essayed in the earlier series. For example, the dawn view of Cadiz in *Trafalgar* reveals Galdós' attention, not only to line and space, but also to colour: a light purple hue tinges the water towards the east where the sky is also dotted by a few gold and red clouds. The city slowly fading from the view of the Spanish fleet as it heads to battle is like a gyrating panorama successively presenting different facets of its vast circumference, with the sun sprinkling gold dust over its glass-covered balconies. The nocturnal description of Godoy's palace at Aranjuez in *El 19 de marzo y el 2 de mayo*, Solita's panoramic view of Toledo from Benigno Cordero's *cigarral* (country estate) in *Un faccioso más y un fraile menos*, snow scenes in *Juan Martín el Empecinado* and *Un faccioso más y un fraile menos*, are all

---

[12] For a study of this scene see my "Galdós, the Madrid Royal Palace and the September 1868 Revolution", *RCEH*, 5 (1980), 1-17.

[13] *Los "Episodios nacionales"*, p. 367.

examples of Galdós' interest in the shapes, colours and spatial arrangement of natural landscapes, duly expressed in pictorial terms, well before the Generation of 1898 writers and painters had launched the vogue for landscape studies in literature and art. One particular landscape, the salt mine, also embraces Galdós' fascination with the optical puzzles offered by artistic arrangements of lines and colours. Moreover, a comparison of two examples taken from the respective periods in which he wrote the *Episodios nacionales* contributes to an understanding of how he deepened his landscape descriptions. In *Un voluntario realista* (1878), eighth *episodio* in the second series, the mine at Cardona resembles a diamond dropped from Heaven when the sun's rays produce magical, colourful reflections on the slopes of the salt pile: "Its crests flicker, its sides shine and, in its fanciful grottos, vie the reflections of all the precious stones" (*OC*, II, 30). The whole scene is a visual, artistic intoxication for the eyes of the artist. In *España sin rey* (1907), the first number of the final series, there is a very similar, albeit more extensive, description of the salt mines at Salinas in Northern Spain: the beautiful shapes of the substance give the impression of a snowscape, of a city of porticos of wood and Paros marble. The essential difference between the two passages lies, not in the description of the salt mine itself, but in the pleasure the spectator now derives from the sight: in this instance it is the character Urriés who never "tires of gazing at the beautiful, amusing and funny sight; he kept moving from one position to another in search of different perspectives" (*OC*, III, 863). In the first example, the scene is mediated through the omniscient narrator, but no relationship is established between viewer and scene. In the second example, this relationship does exist, although it has nothing to do with the traditional Romantic concept of pathetic fallacy, the correspondence between the emotional state of the spectator and the appearance of the natural landscape. Urriés' only concern is to obtain as many views as possible of this wonderful sight. It is the spectacle offered by the landscape and the ocular reaction of the viewer that are all important in this second group of *episodios*.

The same development is discernible in a comparison of two descriptions of the plain of La Mancha. In the first period, as we saw in *Bailén*, Galdós had, through the narrator, depicted a boring landscape suitable only for dreamers like Don Quixote or the madman Santorcaz. In an *episodio* of the fourth series, *O'Donnell* (1904), the flat desert becomes a source of incessant visual delight for the fictional character, the erstwhile prostitute, Teresa Villaescusa, as her train travels over the plain: "*Teresa never tired of looking* at the grey lands with no vegetation, only part of which had been ploughed for the imminent sowing. She *enjoyed looking at the land* and making out the different shades of that impoverished land. *She looked* at the villages as grey as the earth, the miserable-looking houses and a petulant tower ... *she did not see anything agreeable, fresh or pleasant pastures, and yet everything interested her because it was part of her*" (my italics; *OC*, III, 187).[14] The train window, it could be said, frames this essentially beautiful picture of an ugly landscape. There are three important aspects about this scene: firstly, as with the previous example, Galdós accentuates the role of the spectator: the scene is a direct challenge to the eyesight of the human viewer. Secondly, the scene is viewed as if it were a landscape picture. Thirdly, for the viewer the scene is beautiful despite its very obvious ugliness. This is not an example of a conscious distortion of reality; what happens is that the viewer is able to see the beauty within the ugliness and to enthuse over that beautified ugliness. It is a paradox, of course, by classical standards, but in Galdós' later aesthetics, as we shall see in some of the contemporary social novels, normal values are inverted: ugliness is beautiful. Yet by concentrating on the action of viewing carried out by the spectator and the enthusiasm derived by the spectator from the picture of the countryside, Galdós is able to remind his readers of that basic flaw in all appreciation of art work, whether human or divine: the tendency of the human eye to be seduced by a glimmering, shiny surface. Furthermore, that weakness is encouraged by the eye of the mind, the imagination; the eye sees what the imagination wants it to see. The point is brilliantly made in one of the last *episodios*, *España trágica* (1909), the second number in the last series, when Segismundo García Fajardo and his friend, Vicente Halconero, comment on the beauty of the working-class areas close to the Manzanares river in Madrid:

> ... Just cast your eyes to both sides and you will cover a magnificent setting, worthy of sublime historical dramas. On the left you will see the hamlet of Las Peñuelas which, *if it is humble in reality, becomes*

---

[14] Another character in the later *episodios* who expresses a similar passion for the landscape of La Mancha is the eccentric Doña Leandra Carrasco, whose nostalgia for her native province is so strong that, unable to tolerate the urban landscape of Madrid to which her husband dragged her, she often escapes into reveries and visions of the flat tableland so dear to her heart.

magnificent in our eyes ... If you look into the distance you will see
the pretty backcloth of the Sierra [Guadarrama] and the bowers that
border the banks of the poor but pleasant Manzanares.
"I do not deny that this landscape has a certain charm," said
Halconero. "*It is not beautiful; it is pretty.* The bits of washing and the
sun give it its piquant colouring ... I love this slope of earth and
prefer it to what is higher up the city where everything is artificial,
imported and a trick." (my italics; *OC*, III, 974-75)

The individual human retina can transform the nature of any object
or landscape into a work of artistic beauty, if that more dangerous
inner eye, the imagination, so directs. This basically Romantic
aesthetic has now totally replaced, it seems, the antithetical classical
concept of beauty to which Galdós had in his early years generally
subscribed. As we saw in the newspaper articles, however, Galdós
had been repeatedly attracted by artistic patterns which appealed to
his imagination, so long as they were controlled by a master idea,
discernible to the viewer's intelligence, or reflected human reality.
But even on these exceptional occasions Galdós was always aware
that the instrument by which man appreciated works of art, the
human eye, was an imperfect tool, even more impaired by its
inextricably close association with the imagination. Visual distortion
is generated when the inner eye of the imagination controls the whole
viewing process, as in this exchange between García Fajardo and
Halconero. The cycle has come full circle: reality is no longer
perceived exactly by the eye or analysed logically by the mind, it is
now created by the mind and set before the eye. This is a development
that will also be evident in the contemporary social novels.

CHAPTER 6

THE THEMATIC COMMENTARY

La Fontana de Oro (1870) and El audaz (1871)

Galdós' first two published novels of any length were two historical novels that can be regarded to some extent as prototypes of the later *episodios*. If *La Fontana de Oro* covers a period, 1820-23, that he will treat again in the second series, the period of the second novel slightly antedates the *terminus a quo* – 1804 – Galdós selected for his first series. Not originally conceived as numbers of an on-going series, these two novels were also longer than the *episodios*, allowing Galdós greater freedom to incorporate visual art motifs and develop them as easily recognizable thematic commentary according to the individual demands of each novel, in the same technique he will adopt in his contemporary social novels.

La Fontana de Oro

The question of Galdós' use of pictorial sources for the novel is implicitly raised in the opening paragraphs when he reminds his readers that St. Jerome Avenue in Madrid, the main locale in the novel, presented a far different appearance in 1820 from what it does in 1870: "But today, when you see the greater part of the street formed by private dwellings you cannot understand what then was a public thoroughfare occupied almost completely by the gloomy walls of three or four convents" (*OC*, IV, 11-12). Galdós must obviously have consulted early prints of the street to make such a statement, but he does not confess his sources. Nonetheless, it is clear that he wishes to fix the physical contours of this street, Main Street, Spain, 1820-23, its edifices and inhabitants, in our mind's eye, as if indeed it were a historical painting or print, but one of a particularly caricaturesque nature. Galdós deliberately distorts the shapes and sizes for comic effect. Standing outside the street limits, the statue of Mari-Blanca in the adjoining Puerta del Sol, with its indecent pedestal, is the "most concrete artistic expression of Madrid culture" of the period (*OC*, IV, 11). The tone is thus set for the rest of the street architecture. Carroll B. Johnson reckons that what is important in this street scene is the alternation of buildings identified with opposing political or ideological tendencies: Liberal beside Conservative, or Republican against Monarchist, and so on.[1] Probably of greater significance for our study is the comic distortion that Galdós applies to the outlines of all structures and inhabitants, whatever their political persuasion. For example, the positioning of the Victoria monastery at the top end of the Avenue, with the large palace of the Dukes of Medinaceli at the bottom, aptly represents the power bases of traditional Spanish society, the Church and the Nobility. But of greater relevance is Galdós' focusing on the outlandish size of these buildings; the large walls of the monastery along with the dirty and decadent garden wall of the old Happy Outcome church cast a darkness across the mouth of the street that present-day readers could not imagine. The ducal palace, on the other hand, had an enormous façade with a large coat of arms, countless windows, a spacious garden and a private chapel. The physical arrangement and effect of these structures are a pointer to their more harmful spiritual effects on Spanish society over the ages: exploitation and obscurantism. Perched on the most precarious point of the street's steep gradient is the Holy Spirit church, later to become the Congress of Deputies. The implications are obvious: Spain's parliamentary liberal democracy in the nineteenth century, buffeted by opposition from the Church and Nobility, will prove to be a tottery edifice.

Criss-crossing the street, Galdós draws attention to the irregular shapes and sizes of various buildings and their owners: the classical portico that gives entrance to an old palace, now converted into a tenement house, is a favourite urinal for passers-by, much to the indignation of stall vendors on the other side of the entrance way. Opposite this imposing architectural specimen stands the narrow

---

[1] "The café in Galdós' *La Fontana de Oro*", *BHS*, 42 (1965), p. 113.

door of the barber's shop where a thousand members of the Liberal party are shaved each week. The reactionary Irishman who owns a dry goods store is fat and succulent, with the shiny round face of a Dutch cheese. On the other hand, Don Anatolio Mas, the proprietor of the dark, cramped stationery store, has the eyes of an owl. The profusion of merchandise in the wool shop of the cyclopean and proletarian Doña Ambrosia is matched by the display of meats in the high-class grocery store of Perico el Mahonés.

The same technique, which Marie-Claire Petit adventurously labelled surrealist,[2] is applied to the dress of the pedestrians in the street: the flaps of the frock coats are sharp-pointed, whilst the top hats have a crown that resembles a pile of sugar. The ham-like shirt sleeves would be the ultimate absurdity but for the hyperbolic toupees that transform human heads into those of macaws. The carriages of the rich that splatter mud on pedestrians are like ships of the line on iron frames or large boxes in whose depths are glimpsed the noble profiles of some notable lord or some notably ugly old lady. The marionettish figures of the lackeys are represented by large coats and three-cornered hats. After these hilarious cartoons Galdós reaches the point of his major interest: the entrance to the café-cum-political club, La Fontana de Oro, which is also presented in terms of opposing sizes: it has a very narrow entrance, yet it must have a great internal capacity,for the crowds that are eagerly making their way to this establishment are all accommodated.[3] At this point Galdós draws some pertinent thematic parallels: these revolutionary orators of 1820 who used the Fontana as a pulpit for the most radical of ideologies were to become in later life (that is, at the time of the novel's composition) the conservative rulers of the country. The antitheses, contradictions in political affiliations, which become the centre of the subsequent fiction, are anticipated, then, by the description of this important street with its human and material furniture in terms of an engraving or cartoon.

Of the interior of the café, Carroll Johnson has accurately remarked: "The first description of the interior of the Fontana de Oro creates a definite mood of ignorance, imitation and inferiority.

---

[2] *Galdós et "La Fontana de Oro": génèse de l'oeuvre d'un romancier et les sources balzaciennes de "Fortunata y Jacinta"* (Paris: Ediciones Hispano-Americanas, 1972), p. 82; she remarks at another point: "You already find in this text the sense of tints, forms, lines in movement, which will give the descriptions of his Naturalist period their unforgettable character."

[3] Antonio Alcalá Galiano, *Recuerdos de un anciano* (Madrid: Austral, 1951), p. 152, recalled that the main room of the Fontana was very long and of some width too.

These are the ideas repeatedly hammered home throughout the expository paragraphs. Nothing is real here. Nothing is as it seems to be."[4] What he could also have observed is that in this picture of the café Galdós again emphasizes the artistic irregularities in a manner that continues the series of cartoons he had established of the street outside. The Fontana is narrow, irregular, low and almost subterranean; the beams supporting the ceiling are asymmetrical. Such a space had to be decorated by the best artists in the capital, the disciples of the painter Maella, but in actual fact they are terrible painters and their achievements in the café disastrous. The capitals pasted onto the columns look like good fat sausages from Extremadura; the frieze around the walls, suitably pasted on as a roll of paper instead of being carved on as a bas-relief, depicts a grotesque anacreontic group: the heads of goats are intertwined with bunches of fruit. If the white, pink and green paint on the columns is supposed to give the impression of jasper, the mirrors are covered with green cloths to keep away the flies; the smoke from the gas lamp, coffee cups and pipes has almost obliterated some of the decoration. In short, this café-cum-political club is a grotesque structure, with correspondingly grotesque decoration.

Our first acquaintance with the leading villain of the novel, the monarchist spy, Don Elías Orejón, who emerges from the penumbra at the back of the café, alerts us to the purpose of the series of cartoons, for again the contrasting lines and forms of the old man's face, that mirror of the soul, are emphasized: his forehead is extremely convex, while his mouth and cheeks are reduced to very insignificant proportions and his ears are large and transparent. The extreme disparity of size between these anatomical features suggest the variance of attitude the spy will show towards his Liberal nephew, Lázaro, the protagonist of the novel. Don Elías' striking physiognomy also prefigures that of his royal master, King Ferdinand VII, whose description is reserved until the later stages of the novel and constitutes the first example of a number to appear in the *Episodios*, as we have already seen. The monarch, Galdós gratuitously reminds us, has been immortalized by a number of artists from Goya to Madrazo: "The infinite abundance of that repulsive face is frightening. Spain is infected with effigies of Ferdinand VII, whether in print or on canvas" (*OC*, IV, 176). If the most prominent feature of Elías' face is the upper part, that of his sovereign's is the lower half,

---

[4] "The café", p. 113.

with the nose standing as the emblem of duplicity. So, the extended series of suggested cartoons which had opened the novel is now balanced by references to precise, historical canvases painted by Goya, Madrazo and others.

Real, not suggested, paintings are also to be found in the vestibule of the house of three impoverished aristocratic spinsters, the Porreño sisters. The ancestral portraits stand out because of their extravagant costumes or hair-styles, made all the more ridiculous by holes or damp patches on the canvas.[5] Inside the rooms the same state of decay is observed in the faded forms of some Chinese drawings or the old-fashioned Watteau pastoral scenes on some folding screens. A mystical study belonging to the Toledo school is the revered family icon because it represents their traditional Catholic beliefs. However, the composition, with miniatures of Dominican friars arranged around a centre-piece of the Virgin and the Order's founder, is rendered even more grotesque than it would otherwise appear by the loss of the saint's head through dampness and old age. Like the statue of St. Librada which hangs in Paulita's room or the old prayer stool, both crudely repaired, the painting makes an effective commentary on the antiquated and distorted spiritual values held by the three sisters. Their first appearance in the novel is, fittingly, cast in an artistic mould: like models posing for a painting, they sit silently in a symmetrical group, either praying or sewing.

The later residence of Lázaro and Elías in the upper rooms of the women's house disturbs this world of static art objects and effigies. As Lázaro makes his way through the portrait gallery, the figures look at him in anger with moth-eaten eyes. For his part, he is so terrified by their gloomy faces that one night he suffers a nightmare in which the images of Elías and the Porreños expand first to an enormous size (Elías' bald head resembling a planet) only to diminish the next moment to infinitesimally small objects. Lázaro is rescued from these distortions, as it were, by the regular features of the image of his beloved Clara, prisoner of the Porreños: her image is not "disfigured, but an exact portrait" (*OC*, IV, 110). In a physically and spiritually abnormal world, she is the only attractive figure for Lázaro's eyes. On her first appearance, Clara had been compared to

---

[5] Chad C. Wright, "Artifacts and effigies: the Porreño household revisited", *AG*, 14 (1979), p. 16, observes that "the hanging pictures thus become grotesque visions of a dead and rotting past, of which only the splendour of gold medallions and velvet survives".

a beautiful sculpture as she arranged her hair: "Her breast muscles stretch forward, the back arches and the angle of the elbow and the gentle curves of the shoulders describe in their expansion graceful lines which give a sculptural expression to her whole figure" (*OC*, IV, 46). But this beauty is incarcerated, first in the prison of her room at Elías' shabby house (only lit by the sun for half an hour each day) and then in the Porreño household.[6] When, eventually breaking loose from the harpies, she flees to her servant's house, she suffers vertigo and spatial disorientation in the Madrid streets. The entire hallucination does, in fact, recall the vivid physical cartoons which had opened the novel, for when she reaches the head of St. Jerome Avenue, Clara believes she is on the summit of a mountain. Then, as she goes down Segovia Street, she imagines that she is lost in a deep ravine and surrounded by the witch-like figures of the three spinsters. The climax of the hallucination is the appearance of the horizon beyond the Manzanares river during a violent storm: the reddish light impresses Clara's eyes and mind so much that she believes there are waves continuously emanating from this distant hot point and that they contain millions of stars and planets in the shape of human beings "oscillating with capricious evolutions" (*OC*, IV, 165). The comic shapes of the opening chapters are indeed recalled, but now they have been transformed into disconcerting, nightmarish lines and colours. The lovers have no choice but to abandon this madhouse of exaggerated forms and seek happiness in a country paradise.

El audaz

Galdós' second extended historical narration also incorporates exaggerated art forms as a recognizable shorthand device to telegraph the deeper meaning of events. The aristocratic heiress, Susana Cerezuelo, is attracted by the plebeian revolutionary leader, Martín Muriel, whom she invites one night to her uncle's mansion in Madrid. To seduce her social inferior, Susana has arranged lamps in such a way that the art decorations on the walls and tables emit strange glows that attract the surprised glances of Martín as he makes his way to an inner room. The large ivory carving of Christ on the Cross seems to move its arms like some marble reptile zigzagging across the wall; the cornucopias are animated, shiny and oscillating

---

[6] See Petit, *Galdós*, p. 86.

bodies. The bulls in the tapestries, like a portrait of Susana's father as a young man, stare intensely at the young plebeian; the Madrid "majas" in another canvas seen to advance to meet him with their castanets. As Matías Montes Huidobro has recently suggested, these animalized, aggrandized art objects that assault Martín's eyes, in what Galdós pertinently labels one of the most significant episodes in the novel, are visual art symbols of the intense sexuality lurking not far beneath the surface of the heiress' social snobbery.[7] On a different plane, one could also argue that Galdós is exposing the basic sexual instincts behind the national preoccupation with religion, bull-fighting and flamenco.

The sexual frustration felt by Susana in this orchestrated seduction attempt is well conveyed in the constant shifting of her posture on the couch. When she does remain still for a moment with one arm supporting the back of her neck, the pose, illuminated by a nearby lamp, is clearly that of the Maja in Goya's famous diptych, "The Naked Maja" and "The Clothed Maja", although Galdós throws the reader off the scent by suggesting a comparison with a Greek statue (*OC*, IV, 328).[8] It is significant that when later Susana, asleep in the dungeon of the madman Don José de la Zarza, dreams of Martín as the perfect leader of society, she should imagine a setting that recalls the art-filled rooms of her uncle's mansion. This dream soon vanishes, of course, like "the images of an optical game when the light behind them is extinguished" (*OC*, IV, 367). The implications of the earlier scene are now made clear: Susana can only accept Martín as an equal in love in an artistic setting. Consequently, the visual arts come to represent the inauthenticity of her feelings, her lack of real love for Martín.

The same function is discharged by the description of picturesque landscapes in the novel. That of the Ocaña convent garden has been hailed by Francisco Ynduráin as an anticipation of the techniques employed by such Generation of 1898 writers as Azorín.[9] What in fact Galdós stresses, in this picture of the sun's last rays falling over the garden, is, however, the pattern of lines traced on the rectangular patch by the oblique shadows of the oak trees, a pattern which is so

---

[7] "*El audaz*: desdoblamiento de un ritual sexo-revolucionario", *Hispania*, 63 (1980), p. 494.

[8] Leonel-Antonio de la Cuesta, *El audaz: análisis integral* (Montevideo: I.E.S., 1973), p. 14, regards Goya as one of the "sources" of the novel. The old gossip, the abbot Paniagua, when dressed in carnival costume, is immortalized by the pen of Goya in a caricature.

[9] *Galdós entre la novela y el folletín* (Madrid: Taurus, 1970), pp. 51-53.

pleasing to the eye. Another picturesque panorama, and again in an ecclesiastical context, follows a short while later: the skyline of the old cathedral city of Alcalá de Henares with its dreaming spires and towers, which is enjoyed by Susana's father from the upstairs room of his mansion located just outside the city. Similarly beautiful scenes at Aranjuez delight the blue-stocking Pepita Sanahuja and her wealthy family: the sun's rays leave "dazzling traces of light and shimmering outlines of a thousand colours" (*OC*, IV, 379) on tree-tops, roofs and the waters of the river Jarama. The realistic counterpoint to all these idealized, picturesque skylines and land-scapes is the tumbledown house of Don Rotondo in Madrid, where the demented veteran of the French Revolution, La Zarza, and his modern ideological follower, Martín, share lodgings for a while.

The terrain on which the traditional and revolutionary forces in Spanish society finally clash is imperial Toledo, which, as we saw in Part I, had been the subject of Galdós' article "Las generaciones artísticas", published the previous year in the *Revista de España*. Galdós' description of the city's streets, buildings and surrounding landscape has been faulted by some critics,[10] but the manner in which he is able to relate it to the significance of the plot's dénouement also validates the other examples we have discussed. First and foremost, the Inquisition is able to represent Martín's street attack on their ramshackle, lugubrious building as a sacrilegious affront to the adjoining Cathedral, which, as it is the symbol of the city and the achievements of its inhabitants through the ages, now becomes the focus of opposition to the insurgents. In other words, rebel Martín, who had successfully resisted the artistic seductions of Susana, is now presented as a barbaric iconoclast.

The conflagration that his band of supporters initiates illumi-nates the night sky and roof-tops with vivid hues and tints (light purple, vivid scarlet); the buildings, towers and minarets cast huge shadows on the ground as if they were gigantic monsters. The chiaroscuro patterns do suggest a Goya canvas,[11] but they also serve to arouse Susana's awareness of the true nature of her relationship with Martín, whom she has followed to Toledo. "In one of those

---

[10] Cuesta, *El audaz*, p. 88, accepts the relevance of the description of the Alcántara bridge, but not that of the streets at night. A. H. Clarke, "Paisaje interior y paisaje exterior: aspectos de la técnica descriptiva de Galdós", *Actas del primer congreso internacional de estudios galdosianos* (Las Palmas: Excmo Cabildo Insular, 1977), p. 247, objects to the intrusion of the narrator's voice into the landscape description presented from within the disturbed mind of Susana.

[11] "Village on Fire" (c. 1808-12); see Gassier and Wilson, *Goya*, p. 265.

intense glances of the spirit which instantly illuminate the conscience" (*OC*, IV, 406), she realizes that her dreams of Martín as a noble, equal in social rank, are an illusion: "The large castle she had constructed in her imagination ... was like one of those multi-coloured spheres made with soap suds" (*OC*, IV, 406). This castle analogy immediately refers the reader to the Alcázar or castle of Toledo, aglow with the reflections of the fires burning around the city, and these are the destructive "art works" of the iconoclast Martín. So, the metaphor of an ephemeral art work is balanced by the reality of an attempted destruction of a city that is not only a collection of separate art works, but whose daily life through the ages is symbolized by a work of supreme architectural beauty.

It is the sight of another architectural treasure, the imposing Roman structure of the Alcántara bridge, that provides Susana with the solution to her emotional and social problems: she will commit suicide by jumping off the bridge into the swirling, blood-red waters of the Tagus. Galdós often referred to the colour of the river in his newspaper articles (see *OI*, I, 52; *OC*, VI, 1583), but here he presents the reality behind the literary metaphor: one individual human being will indeed add her blood to the foaming torrent, an individual, furthermore, who likes to surround herself with beautiful art objects and whose own figure suggests visual art comparisons. The river, so often depicted in art work, now offers her a release from the unbearable reality of Martín's social status. Susana's social snobbery, "that great passion and that great pride" (*OC*, IV, 408), triumphs over natural impulses. Hence the appropriateness of using this arresting specimen of architecture as the means by which to achieve her tragic end. Galdós' description of the bridge highlights features that anticipate and encourage Susana's final act. In the moonlight the reflection of the great semicircular arch in the water resembles a large hole opened up in the great mass of shadows formed by the rocky edges of the river.[12] This brutal and violent image suggests the eventual hole that Susana's body will bore in the surface of the water. But the actual fall from the dizzy heights of the bridge is presented as if it were the result of Susana's gazing at art works: firstly, she looks at the Toledo skyline, which, with the turrets on the bridge, the crenellations of the castle of San Servando and the Alcázar, recalls

---

[12] Galdós could well have had in mind the picture of the bridge, similarly moonlit, given in a woodcut illustration by Castelló in Amador de los Ríos' *Toledo pintoresca*, p. 200. The circular reflection of the bridge's main arch is also a prominent feature of the drawing.

the earlier Alcalá landscape of spires and turrets. She is so overwhelmed by this panorama that she moves forward to the edge of the bridge. Secondly, when she is about to jump, she is made to appear as if she is bending over to inspect something on the inside of the bridge's arch, as if it were some exhibit in a museum. Her eyes, red with the glow of the fire's reflections in the sky, are like two large dots, miniatures of the bridge's two arches. In her final act Susana achieves an artistic stasis that conforms her with the surroundings: she has merged with architectural and artistic landscape in a pretty picture. Living with the reality of Martín's social status would have been unaesthetic, unbearable. In *El audaz*, as in *La Fontana de Oro*, Galdós is able to integrate his visual art examples coherently and consistently into the thematic fabric of his narrations, allowing them to become automatic and immediate ciphers of commentary for the reader. Galdós will use this technique to even greater effect in his contemporary social novels.

PART III

THE VISUAL ARTS AND
THE CONTEMPORARY SOCIAL NOVELS

CHAPTER 7

INTRODUCTION

The proposition that the relationship of a contemporary social novel with the visual arts hardly differs from that of a historical novel might be difficult to accept at first sight. Yet there is no logical reason why the former, like the latter, cannot have graphic illustrations interspersed amongst its pages, cannot rely on the visual arts for specific source material, even weave them into the fabric of the novel for thematic effect, or cannot apply the metaphor of art with frequency. In fact, the social novel may promote some interart topics (like the discussion of aesthetics or the description of the practice of art through a fictional protagonist) which in the historical novel may be difficult to develop. In other words, it is possible that the social novel is a more suitable vehicle for the marrying of literature and the visual arts.

Though Galdós never published illustrated editions of his contemporary social novels during his own lifetime, some have appeared since his death[1] and there is evidence to suggest that in his later years he had thought seriously of such editions. In a letter to Galdós of 6 April 1898, Pereda refers to the rumours that his friend has contracted Pellicer, one of the illustrators for his 1881-85 edition of the *Episodios nacionales*, to illustrate *Doña Perfecta*. Pereda also takes advantage of the opportunity to recommend to Galdós another artist, Pedrero, who could do superb illustrations for *Marianela*.[2] Whilst these suggestions and rumours did not materialize into anything concrete and may have more to do with Galdós' acutely

---

[1] See Manuel Hernández Suárez, *Lengua y literatura*, Vol. I of *Bibliografía de Galdós* (Las Palmas: Excmo Cabildo Insular, 1972).

[2] The letter is reproduced in Ortega, *Cartas*, p. 190.

desperate financial situation after the ruinous lawsuit in 1897 against his former publisher, Cámara, it is interesting to note that in an earlier period another artist friend, Apeles Mestres, had also broached the question of doing an illustrated edition, again for *Marianela*.[3] Galdós must have been tempted to try his luck and fortune with illustrated social novels.

After all, his good friend, Pereda, had had illustrations engraved for his *El sabor de la tierruca* of 1882, for which Galdós had written the prologue (although without commenting on the graphics), whilst another close friend, Leopoldo Alas, was very partial to having illustrated editions of his novels published.[4] But apprehensions about costs and delays of time must have inhibited Galdós' enthusiasm for any ventures of this kind. Moreover, his experience on the de luxe edition of the *Episodios* had been salutary in that, though he saw the opportunity and need for such an edition of those particular historical novels, he clearly recognized that not all types of fiction benefited from an illustrated accompaniment, nor would they, with such an ornate form, necessarily reach the wide Spanish and international audience for which he was always craving. Galdós knew that he had to appeal to his readers first and this had to be done through the printed word. The graphic arts could be profitably enlisted for a subsequent edition, but for that a writer needed time and money, neither of which was in bountiful supply in Galdós' schedule.

Furthermore, like Tolstoy[5] and Bécquer,[6] to name only two other writers, Galdós had already done his own illustrations for the social novels, as it were. As he composed his manuscripts, it was his practice to sketch in the margins the busts of profiles of his characters, as he had done in the books of other writers in his possession. Years later Galdós made this astounding claim to some journalists who interviewed him: "Before creating literally the characters of my works, I sketch them with my pencil so as to have them in front of me when I talk about them. It is very strange . . . I have drawn all the characters I have created."[7] It is impossible, of

---

[3] In a letter of 17 April 1883, quoted by Bravo-Villasante, *Galdós*, pp. 137-39.

[4] See Josette Blanquat and Jean-François Botrel, *Clarín y sus editores: 65 cartas inéditas de Leopoldo Alas a Fernando Fe y Manuel Fernández Lasanata 1884-1893* (Rennes: Université de Haute-Bretagne, 1981), pp. 58-59, 71-72.

[5] See Edward Crankshaw, *Tolstoy: the Making of a Novelist* (New York: Viking, 1974).

[6] See King, *Gustavo Adolfo Bécquer*, p. 36.

[7] Quoted by José María Carretero [El Caballero Audaz], "La figura de la semana", *Nuevo Mundo*, 9 Jan. 1920.

course, to verify this claim, for not all the manuscripts of his fiction are extant, nor is it certain that Galdós always sketched his figures in their margins – he could easily have used mere scraps of paper. But what has to be stressed is that for Galdós himself (and there is no reason to doubt his claim) at an important point in the creative process it was necessary to enlist the aid of the visual arts. If at a later stage he forgoes this direct reliance, the presence of the visual arts in the fiction, through verbal transcriptions of art objects or the metaphors and vocabulary of art, is still very prominent and bespeaks the important role Galdós accorded them in the development of his themes and of his major concern: the correct ocular and spiritual appreciation of reality.

The techniques Galdós used to incorporate this visual art material were obviously varied, but, because they were also repeated, the novels can be assembled into certain categories. This classification is not meant to be exclusively rigid, for some novels contain features which receive great emphasis in other groupings. In rejecting a chronological discussion of the novels I am not intending to preclude any examination of the development and perfection of these techniques. As we shall see, there is a discernible progression in the presentation of certain visual art material, but my main purpose has been to codify the different approaches Galdós adopts for the greater elucidation of each novel's particular theme.

Our division is as follows:

Group I: novels in which the visual arts are used as a mirror of reality for the wealthy noble: *La familia de León Roch*, *Lo prohibido*, the *Torquemada* tetralogy.

Group II: novels which open with significant descriptions of visual art forms: *La desheredada*, *El amigo Manso*, *Tormento*, *Fortunata y Jacinta*.

Group III: novels in which the initial descriptions of picturesque landscapes play an important role: *Doña Perfecta*, *Gloria*.

Group IV: novels which combine features of some of the previous groups (initial art forms, picturesque landscapes) with a prominent discussion about the advantages or disadvantages of the ocular perception of reality: *Marianela*, *El doctor Centeno*, *La de Bringas*.

Group V: novels in which visual art references, again presented at the beginning, now prove to be enigmatic signs: *Miau, La incógnita, Nazarín, Halma, Misericordia.*

Group VI: novels which represent the summit of Galdós' use of the visual arts, which now serve as the principal determinant of the novelistic action: *La sombra, Angel Guerra, Tristana.*

CHAPTER 8

MIRRORS OF REALITY FOR THE WEALTHY NOBLE

La familia de León Roch (1878), *Lo prohibido* (1884-85), the *Torquemada* Tetralogy (1889-95)

La familia de León Roch

At the centre of *El audaz*'s reconstruction of a past age lies what, as we saw in the last chapter of Part II, is essentially a class struggle between a proletarian "have-not" and an aristocratic heiress. In *La familia de León Roch* the struggle between the protagonist, León Roch, and his wife, María Egipcíaca, is not based on social origins, for all belong to the same class, the moneyed bourgeoisie or aristocracy. Nonetheless, visual art material is again used to highlight artificial attitudes in human relationships.

As an early proof that our classification of novels is capable of overlap, the opening sequence of *La familia de León Roch* could justify its inclusion in either of our groups II, III or IV, since it seems to concentrate attention on the difficulty of gauging correct dimensions of people and human character. León is first seen reading a letter from his wife, María Egipcíaca, which is full of misrepresentations about Pepa Fúcar, who, as the daughter of the Marquess of Fúcar, will eventually be her rival for León's love. María Egipcíaca reckons that Pepa, whom she has seen at the health resort from which she is writing, is too tall to be beautiful, too thin to be elegant and that you would need a microscope to see her tiny eyes. The reference to the microscope is a neat auto-referential device that suggests the difficulty of correctly appraising visual reality. María Egipcíaca's picture is somewhat removed from the truth, for she admits that she only caught sight of Pepa from the distance, either on the beach or the balcony of the spa where she was staying. Now that Pepa has moved along the Cantabrian coast to where León is staying, María Egipcíaca wishes she could climb to a tower to spy on her and, presumably, misread what her eyes might see: getting the right ocular focus on Pepa's figure is for María Egipcíaca as difficult as judging her rival's character. The exaggerations of the dimensions of the physical world are recalled by the context in which León is reading this portrait of Pepa: he is walking through an avenue of tall trees, at one end of which is the health spa, a low building with a portico of Greco-Roman pretensions, and at the other, the cramped residence where the holiday-makers are lodged. Tall trees suggest a thrusting vertical axis, like Pepa's tall body (in María Egipcíaca's eyes) while the low buildings at the distant extremities draw a contrasting horizontal perspective, suggestive of the distance from which María Egipcíaca had viewed the other woman.

León's first view of Pepa in the novel is hardly less distorted, this time, however, because of the artistic appearance of her image. He catches sight of her late at night at the window of her room in the spa residence: "A white shape ... showed its bust ... it would have appeared to be a marble statue, had it not been for the dark hair and the movement of the hand playing with the branches of a nearby plant ... Pepita Fúcar stood out in the black square of the window like the blurred and pale figure of some old canvas" (*OC*, IV, 791-92). The effect of this pictorial pose is to make Pepita appear more beautiful to the eyes of León, so the narrator says, than she really is.

León's fascination with female beauty is, of course, the reason he is attracted to the sublimely beautiful María Egipcíaca. As she combs her hair before the bedroom mirror she is the perfect image of a Greek statue, a living piece of Paros marble, just like Clara in *La Fontana de Oro* in a similar boudoir scene. Galdós makes the significant observation that María Egipcíaca is one of those "mortal statues that do not need a soul in order to possess life and beauty" (*OC*, IV, 821). León's wife is indeed a sculpturesque beauty with no soul; her treatment of her husband, insensitive and calculated to hurt, is the outcome of her religious mania, which, in a strikingly beautiful girl, Galdós finds absurd. He transposes this idea into a plastic image: María's resemblance to Minerva, the Greek goddess, is diminished aesthetically by the presence of a prayer book in her hand.

The only occasion María Egipcíaca deliberately exploits her physical appearance, and then at the prompting of her wounded pride, is when she tries to seduce her husband back from Pepa, after being told by a friend of the liaison of the two. The emphasis now to be placed on the artistic appearance of María Egipcíaca is heralded by the title of the chapter (XIII): "A figure who seems to be painted by Zurbarán but is really by Goya" (*OC*, IV, 890). María is trying to impress the world with her religiosity by suppressing her natural instincts and beauty as if she were a figure from Zurbarán's brush. These impulses are now allowed to come to the surface, as if she had become a figure in a Goya painting. Yet again Galdós emphasizes the narcissism of María Egipcíaca: the sudden refurbishing of her beautiful exterior is really an exercise in egotism, with numerous allusions to the visual arts underlining this attitude of mind encouraged by what the eye sees. Her careful toilette is a protracted session of auto-erotic delight: the veil that had previously shrouded the mirror is now removed and "so to speak, the bewitching image of María Sudre was born on the brightly-lit, clean glass. It was like a pretty example of the creation of the world . . . Her green eyes shone with a passionate radiance, and gazed in charmed absorption at their reflection, as if saying: 'How beautiful God made us!' Then María positioned her head in two different half-profile poses, twisting her eyes round so that she could see herself. What a beautiful sight!" (*OC*, IV, 898). The re-emergence of María's beauty to her own eyes is thus presented as an artistic creation on a mirror that appeals totally to the eyes of the beholder. Further contemplation of the rest of her sculpturesque body takes place when she washes in the bath: the water from the taps pours over the marble and porcelain of the tub and then onto "the ivory parts of a human statue [i.e. María's body] . . . like in the mythological fountains where tritons, nymphs and alabaster jets . . . and inlaid work *form a most beautiful whole for the eyes to see*" (my italics; *OC*, IV, 901). This voyeurism, possibly unequalled in the rest of Galdós' work, is practised, not by the prurient narrator, as one initially suspects, but by another art object, a humanized decorated clock. Its chimes add another layer of ironic comment when María restores the portrait of León to its former prominent position in the room, smothering it with kisses: the scene captures perfectly the artificiality of María Egipcíaca in her relationship with her husband; like Susana in *El audaz*, she can only approximate to any intimacy with León through an assimilation to visual art objects which beautify and at the same time distance the reality of the person. The crowning artistic touch to María's display of beauty is the stunning hat she dons before setting out to reconquer her husband: "It was the great brush-stroke, the supreme touch missing hitherto in the sublime picture ... A great victory for beauty! María Egipcíaca was most elegant, and bewitching; she was elegance itself, the living model. In her person she incarnated the infinite ideal of sartorial elegance which, with natural beauty, produces the marvellous statues of flesh and fabric before which sometimes the prudence and dignity of men, other times their health and wealth, succumb" (*OC*, IV, 899). Galdós has now introduced a further consideration into his art picture: not only is she dazzled by her own beauty, but that beauty is a moral and social trap for men. The auspices for the future of León, now to be visually assaulted by this beautiful art object, are not promising.

María Egipcíaca's subsequent reception at León's apartment is appropriately framed by artistic comparisons. Firstly, she is met by Pepa's daughter, Moñina, carying a doll; not unnaturally, to the young girl this Greek goddess appears like a doll too, propelled by an inner mechanical device. Secondly, León's entry into the room is plasticized: the sight of his wife immobilizes him in the frame of the door "like a statuette in its niche" (*OC*, IV, 904). Inevitably, the hoped-for reconciliation fails to materialize as both partners soon quarrel. María's tearful recriminations end in a tight embrace of her husband followed by a fainting fit. With her head slumped over her breast and hair hanging down, María is likened to Velázquez's famous picture of Christ on the Cross. Alfieri's comments on the comparison do not really do justice to its apt incongruity.[1] By choosing a well-known canvas that captures the exact position of María's drooping head, Galdós is able to bring more attention to the incongruity of the reality and the art comparison: María Egipcíaca is not stretched semi-naked on a cross dying for all humanity; she has just witnessed the dismal failure of her attempts at seduction. The final ironic touch is that María Egipcíaca has temporarily put aside her religious fanaticism to attempt this conquest.

During the deep sleep that follows this faint María has a nightmare vision of Hell that is built upon fragments of images retained from visits to German and Spanish factories with León. Trains, machines, tunnels, furnaces consequently abound in this "whirlwind of visions, which, because it possessed all colours and all

---

[1] "Few characters in Galdós' novels share with María Egipcíaca the distinction of being likened to a specific painting of Christ" ("Images", p. 31).

shapes, practically did not have any shape or colour at all" (*OC*, IV, 911). Some scenes of infernal torment, like the pouring of molten liquid into a victim's skull, seem reminiscent of scenes painted by Hieronymus Bosch in "The Seven Deadly Sins", which Galdós would have seen in the Prado. Yet there is no explicit reference. The sight of her husband as one of the souls in Hell causes María to awake in panic. The nightmare presents a pictorial study that is the reverse of the art world suggested by María's radiantly beautiful appearance. The murky inner mind contrasts with the delightful pleasing exterior: and yet both faces are extreme pictorial forms that suggest an exaggeration of mind, of purpose and interpretation. Towards the end of this visit María strikes the artistic pose: when Pepa intrudes on the couple in a room, María grasps León's head by the hair "in the same way that they paint the executioner taking hold of the victim's head to show it to the crowd" (*OC*, IV, 935). The art parallels traced for the reader by the perceptive narrator aptly capture the artificiality in her behaviour with her husband.

The rest of her family are also presented in terms of art objects, but of a very different ilk. María's sickly twin brother, the mystical Luis Gonzaga, is compared to a piece of brightly coloured furniture or a Japanese figure.[2] The heavily-rouged face of their mother, the Marchioness of Tellería, is as deceptive as the pastoral scenes painted on the stage curtain of a theatre. The paterfamilias, whose elegant dress coats adorn his body like the de-luxe binding of a book devoid of ideas, has a face which is "the transfiguration of a beautiful face, or rather the caricature of a whole race" (*OC*, IV, 808). So the Tellería family is a disturbing contrast of classical beauty and grotesque decadence, the one offsetting the other.[3] The art decorations

---

[2] A statue of his patron saint is found in the chapel of the Fúcar family where at the novel's end it stands guard over the corpse of María Egipcíaca, its eyes staring menacingly at all who enter.

[3] John W. Kronik, "Galdós and the grotesque", *AG*, anejo (1978), p. 42, sees one of the uses of the grotesque in this novel as a technique for the plastic rendition of decadence. Paul Ilie, "Bécquer and the romantic grotesque", *Publications of the Modern Language Association of America*, 83 (1968), p. 319, points out that the grotesque as a genre is incoherent and "devoid of any apparent law from which it might derive congruence", in other words, the antithesis of classical order. Hence Galdós' reference to the Marquess of Tellería as the antithesis of the beauty of his daughter. V. A. Smith and J. E. Varey, " 'Esperpento': some early usages in the novels of Galdós", in *Galdós Studies*, ed. J. E. Varey (London: Tamesis, 1970), pp. 195-204, note the description of the Marquess of Tellería as an "esperpento" or scarecrow image. Ramón del Valle-Inclán's later, more comprehensive treatment of the literary device was based on an appreciation of Goya's painting of grotesque shapes; in fact, he says that Goya invented the genre of the "esperpento", in *Opera Omnia* (Madrid: Rivadeneyra, 1924), XIX, 224. In an article of 19 January 1884 for *La Prensa*, Galdós refers to Goya's "brave, original and slightly extravagant" genius (*CP*, 53).

which this parasitic family is able to purchase with the money sponged off their son-in-law is a collection of imported French works. However, it is an insignificant display when placed alongside the veritable museum of valuable works on which the Marquess of Fúcar lavishes his money, but because he has no aesthetic sense, the collection is a hodgepodge of styles. In one of the many rooms with their own special designation, like the Arabian or Japanese Rooms, historical portraits, Poussinesque pastoral scenes on tapestries, a statue of Christ in the arms of the Dolorous Mother, hundreds of bullfighters, "majas", erotic watercolours, Rubenesque nymphs, equestrian studies, porcelain cats on the tops of glasses and flower-stands supported by mythological animals, all stand side by side in a nauseating and dizzy arrangement that defies analysis. Galdós captures this incongrous mess linguistically with the oxymoronic juxtaposition of two familiar phrases: "the podgy nymphs of Rubens and the skinny steeds of the turf" (*OC*, IV, 855). The dining-room is so cluttered with still life studies that a better title would be the Palace of Indigestion.

The chapel of the Fúcar family on the estate of Suertebella outside Madrid also falls into the same depressing category of unaesthetic jumble. With an impressive command of technical vocabulary, reminiscent of his review of the Happy Outcome church for *La Nación* a decade earlier, Galdós masterfully debunks the Greco-Chino-Roman architecture that he had first mistakenly described as a "beautiful monument"! The interior is covered with plaster imitations of marble and jasper, gold leaf and gold powder; it dazzles like a profusion of gold braid and polished buttons. Likewise, the angels (formerly nymphs) and theological virtues (formerly sprightly muses) painted on the ceiling give off the kind of glitter one normally associates with bedroom walls! The satirical interpretation of the allegorical figures by an unnamed wag adds a further layer of ridicule: the blindfolded lady with a chalice in her hands is bankrupt Spain, the skiff sinking on the Sea of Tiberias is the Ship of State and the four doctors of the Church writing on scrolls are the Press! As well as being immensely comic, the description offers in miniature a very important lesson on the subjectivity of all visual art inter-pretation. What presumably is appreciated by the Marquess as a work of great art is clearly the antithesis in the eyes of the narrator. But a third party provides completely original and unsuspected associations, more profound than those of the other two. Art appreciation is a very subjective experience which, perforce, is governed by the ethical values of the beholder.

The chapter in which this description of the Fúcar mansion is given (Part II, Chapter IV) opens with an important painting of the Madrid bullring during an afternoon fight. Galdós' intention to paint a picture in words is certainly evident both from the use of pictorial terms and from the way he gradually moves from one item to another across his canvas to complete the picture, in much the same way that he executes the landscape study of the La Granja Palace in *Los apostólicos* (1879), the *episodio* which he was to write a few months after the completion of *La familia de León Roch*.

Galdós begins by noting the condition of the sky, then he moves slowly earthwards noting the architectural frame of the ring, then the various sections of the stands and finally the scene at ground level in the arena, although the coverage here is scanty. The style of the descriptions suggests that Galdós is deliberately avoiding a picture which one might have expected to be colourful and impressionistic in the style of Mariano Fortuny's famous canvas "The Bullfight", which he might well have had in mind as he wrote. From the beginning, however, the tone is unremittingly unpicturesque: the sky is a mixture of blue patches and overcast clouds, which eventually resolves itself into a downpour to interrupt the fiesta. The morbid, lead colours of the metal structure of the stands ill accord with the traditionally gay image of the event. Worse still, the clothes worn by the spectators are uniformly drab, except for a few bright blobs of colour in the section where the prostitutes are stationed, with white mantillas, heavily-rouged faces and attached flowers. Far from emphasizing the picturesqueness of the traditionally colourful scene, Galdós focuses attention on other senses: the pungent smells and the animal-like noises of this gathering. The bullfight is an orgy of strong impressions for the workers and idlers, a relief from the routine drabness of their daily lives. Some of the plebeian types appear to be, both in dress and behaviour, caricatures of the bullfighters. Galdós' original "demythicization" of the national sport is more than an indulgence of a pet hate; the whole sequence is pertinently related to the subsequent description of the Fúcar mansion where *objets d'art* and canvases glorifying tauromachy are to be found in profusion.

The collector and promoter of this mishmash of art work, the Marquess of Fúcar, is duly incorporated into the surface of the chapel in a rather clever way by Galdós, who again creates a highly comic effect as well as underlining the responsibility of the Marquess for the whole disgusting show. The latter watches the public mass for

María from a window that opens onto an interior space adjoining the chapel. This space is called the Gallery of Laughter because of the countless political cartoons cut out of the world's newspapers and spread over the walls. Thus, by standing in this gallery and looking into the chapel, the Marquess is able to join both areas and insert his own image into the mural arrangement, ensuring that the hilarity of the cartoons is transferred to the decoration of the chapel and to his own image. The Marquess' status as an icon in this scene is consolidated by the appearance of his bust in the window-frame of the chapel by the side of an image of St. Luke, patron saint of artists. If for the art collector and living icon, the Marquess, the chapel is "a most beautiful basilica", for the anonymous wag, for Galdós and for the perceptive reader it is "une catédrale pour rire", an architectural symbol or mirror of the social and mental attitudes of this type of parvenu aristocrat for whom glossy, gaudy externals mean everything.

The Tellería and Fúcar families are oblivious to these codes or signs transmitted by the art works with which they surround themselves, but is León Roch? We have already seen his artistic appreciation of the outline of Pepa at the beginning of the novel and his pleasure at the sight of his wife's beautiful body. The detailed description of the art treasures in the Fúcar rooms is also mediated through his observant and, at this moment, undisturbed eyes. But there are other occasions when León's retina, under great emotional strain, produces some alarming images of visual art objects. The first example occurs after he has watched his wife and her twin brother talking in the garden one evening about his lack of religious conviction. León moves towards his study through a series of rooms where mirrors bounce back reflections of his figure. Arriving in the semi-dark study, he imagines that he is confronted by an art object, "a Japanese figure, dark, rigid, uneven, standing out against the background of illuminated colours. The wretchedly small body remained stiffly upright in its seat . . . and the gelatinous, cadaverous, face . . . lifted its emerald eyes to the ceiling, or with stupid indifference rolled them over the walls covered with watercolours, maps and prints" (*OC*, IV, 841). The imaginary figure (duly set against a background of various visual art objects) which León in his anger proceeds to throttle and reduce to a bundle of sinews, is, of course, Luis Gonzaga. León's antipathy towards his brother-in-law is thus translated into an imagined assault on a humanized art object.

In Part III, León finds himself in another emotional, though not so hallucinatory, state, when he becomes the target for the unjust upbraiding of his pompous father-in-law. The scene takes place in the Japanese Room of the Fúcar palace, one of those interconnecting rooms with special names that are like the pages of a picture book. On the walls of the rooms all sorts of objects, animals and figures are suspended, with gold and silver butterflies reproducing the hiero-glyphic smile of the Marquess of Tellería. A far more disturbed vision befalls León a short while later after a discussion with Pepa in the so-called Incredible Room of the palace. Careening around before his troubled eyes like fixtures on a merry-go-round, the painted figures, china objects and statues take on an absurd appearance: clothes and bodies merge, people become like birds, "men and women ran in a rapid cyclone, a motley comic mob" (*OC*, IV, 960). Clearly, these aristocratic types, in particular the Tellería family, are made to appear dehumanized and ridiculous by association with these art collections, yet the corresponding assumption has to be that León is at times and in special circumstances an unusually perceptive interpreter of visual art forms; indeed, if his picture of the Marquess of Tellería is a cartoon, then he is an unconscious cartoonist.

In reality, León does try his hand at the visual arts: he may not be much good at conventional painting, which he soon abandons, but he is interested in the colouring of geological diagrams. However, these are downplayed in Chapter VIII, Part II, first by the naïve comments of the servant, Facunda, and then by the sacrilegious actions of Pepa's daughter, Moñina, and some friends. Insisting on making their own additions to León's composition, they daub paint across the diagrams, or superimpose their own drawings. Galdós chuckles to his readers: "Undoubtedly, they have greater esteem for the ideal of artistic perfection: for them there was no work of art which did not need one brush-stroke more ... she had a box of paints and knew how to do paintings, almost as good as those by Velázquez" (*OC*, IV, 871). The obvious inference to be drawn from the whole scene is that León's art work is not much better than the children's primitive strokes, and that he is really dispersing his talents in an unstructured attempt to fathom out the meaning of life. After all, his interest in geology is only one of a number of amateur pursuits he eventually forsakes. A correct appreciation of life in the historical context of nineteenth-century Spanish society is only possible for León, then, through the special experience of an art-based halluci-nation.

Doubts about the reliability of normal optical vision for such a purpose are raised in a comic manner in the same chapter when the children send León's telescope crashing to the floor.[4] The instrument and also the oversized model of the human eye in León's study reveal his absorption with the question of physical sight and its application to astronomy. Ironically, it is the personified art object, or walking dummy, the Marquess of Tellería, who, departing from his usual custom of uttering inanities, is given the task of making the perceptive gloss on this amateur interest of León: "Tell me, and can you see the soul with this [the telescope]? ... Of course! If you cannot see it, you maintain that it does not exist" (*OC*, IV, 807). Galdós seems to be ridiculing this scientific pursuit of León as a means to approach the reality of life: León may be able to scan the universe and measure sidereal distances, but can he penetrate the human soul, both his own and those of the people he lives with in society?

Some space is devoted to León's interest in astronomy and it is important to note that Galdós employs art terms to render the night landscape that is the subject of León's ocular scrutiny. The star-studded heavens are an indescribable monument: "The blue dome is so high ... that the mind and gaze of man are, as it were, out of breath when they look up to it. You cannot stare at this peerless firmament fixed over the great steppe of Castile without holding your breath" (*OC*, IV, 833). In fact the beautiful night sky is Madrid's own special picturesque landscape, the equivalent of a Constable-like meadow panorama enjoyed from other cities. This nocturnal landscape is also for León a source of relief from his inner torments: "The saddened spirit throws itself at the immensity of that shoreless sea as if back to its natural home" (*OC*, IV, 840). A very similar consolation is derived from the same landscape by the moribund Luis Gonzaga: for him, the sky is a confirmation of God's kindness in freeing him from earthly torments and calling him to Heaven. For the two antagonists the night sky has a spiritual meaning that is prompted and encouraged by its beautiful appearance. The ecstasy of both men is the result of an upward view of the sky's curved dome which completely ignores the flat prosaic base of the earth, the Castilian meseta where no prominence, mountain or forest disturbs the straight surface. Galdós explains the purpose of his night

---

[4] The language of the chapter title is pertinently pictorial: "In which the Invasion of the Barbarians is painted in bright colours. Alaric, Attila and Omar live again." Galdós is referring to the invasion of Rome by the Barbarians in 410 A.D. He was later to comment in one of his *La Prensa* articles on a painting on this topic by Checa (*CP*, 247).

landscape when he refers to the Castilian meseta as "the reclining image of Humanity, sleeping or dead, which dreams in the darkness of its mind of the infinite splendours of above" (*OC*, IV, 834). The sky-gazers like León and Luis Gonzaga are, thus, to be regarded as dreamers who escape from the boring flat reality of the earth into the architectural majesty of the Heavens.[5]

Galdós is no such escapist; he resolutely includes a vivid counterpoint to the nocturnal skyline. His daylight description of the Madrid landscape is rendered, significantly, in art terms which underscore the contrastive function of the piece: León's house is situated directly on the line of the city limits which urban planners have traced on the map. Beyond this boundary there are only a few scattered structures at which the swallows and beavers would laugh. The rest of the horizon comprises the sad, barren expanses of La Mancha, lightly tinged with an unflattering green which in summer becomes yellowish and ashen. Resisting the plough's attempts to trace furrows, the earth propels dust clouds that shroud the horizon and obstruct the eye of the viewer. As we saw in our discussion of the *Episodios* in Part II, La Mancha's sea-like terrain often formed an ideal springboard for the imagination of dreamers like Don Quixote. The novel development of this motif offered by *La familia de León Roch* is that the night sky over Castile is an equally potent agent of escapism. But, like all the other art objects in the book, both landscapes (terrestrial and celestial) raise pertinent questions, first about the accuracy of the human eye's capturing of physical reality, and, secondly, about its ability to see the art object unclouded by considerations of the mind. In other words, how far can the human eye perceive the totality of the world around it? For the spiritually blind like the Tellería and Fúcar families, such lessons are beyond their capabilities. But even the inquisitive prober, León Roch, amateur artist and astronomer that he is, is unable to perceive the inner truth completely. Only in privileged moments of hallucinatory vision does the absurdity of the aristocratic world he inhabits emerge with total clarity through the medium of distorted visual art shapes. This is, unfortunately, not accompanied by a vision of his own shortcomings.

[5] Clarke, "Paisaje interior", p. 249, makes the same point.

Lo prohibido

Not all of Galdós' moneyed aristocrats or high bourgeois are accorded this negative presentation through the medium of the visual arts. But as, more often than not, they are the only social groups in nineteenth-century Spain able either to buy art objects or to dress in beautiful clothes, they become immediate candidates for Galdós' refractive lens. *Lo prohibido*, written six years after *La familia de León Roch*, resembles it in that the world of the novel, an autobiography of the seductions or attempted seductions of his three cousins by the member of parliament, then stockbroker, José María Bueno de Guzmán, is essentially that of the moneyed classes who lavish expenditure on such items as art works. Eloísa is perhaps the member of the Guzmán family most guilty of this vice.[6] In her mansion compositions by contemporary Spanish painters like Palmaroli, Villegas, Román Ribera and Martín Rico are all represented. Like other art objects (figurines and candelabra) the painting becomes the pre-eminent status symbol. Yet for Eloísa it becomes something much more serious, a mania which must be regularly satisfied, and is satisfied so long as José María's fortune lasts. When it is not, then she experiences sleepless nights. A feature of this mania is that Eloísa believes that any art object she sees has a high value; for instance, any old painting is surely a Velázquez; if the object is a tapestry, then it can only come from the collection in the Royal Palace in Madrid. Eloísa candidly admits the falsification: "This way I deceive myself, I drug my vice . . . yes, my vice. Why give it any other name?" (*OC*, IV, 1719). To this extent she and José María are more conscious of the self-deceit induced by this artistic collection than were the Tellerías and Fúcars in *La familia de León Roch*. They are not only more conscious of the deceit, they openly crave for it. Another artistic pose of self-deception is adopted when the two lovers spend a secret tryst in Paris and imagine themselves to be Latin Quarter types, "the student and the 'grisette', the painter and his model living from day to day with only two francs and a huge ration of carefree love" (*OC*, IV, 1729). The reality is far different: they spend an immense sum of money on the purchase of expensive art objects to take back to Spain. Were he richer, José María would have bought

---

[6] Eloísa, according to one love-smitten newspaper columnist, is a beautiful, living piece of Parian marble over whose creation the Creator and Phidias would have fought (*OC*, IV, 1737). Her sister, María Juana, when angry, resembles one of Michelangelo's sibylline figures in the Sistine Chapel in the Vatican.

the most expensive items on the market (a Rembrandt, a Murillo or a Veronese) so that Eloísa could "play with them and lick her lips with pleasure looking at them" (*OC*, IV, 1732). As Arthur Terry perceptively noted a decade ago, the language of love and that of finance are intimately linked in this novel.[7] Indeed, in this instance José María's words describing what he hopes will be the reaction of his mistress to these presents is strongly suggestive of a sexual response: art becomes a necessary stimulant to their affair.

The climactic scene in the novel which conveys the full extent to which these two characters have wittingly confused art and life occurs at one of Eloísa's lavish Thursday house-parties or soirées. On display on this occasion are two full-length portraits, one by Domingo and the other by Sala, a friend of Galdós and one of the illustrators of the 1881-85 edition of the *Episodios nacionales*. The portraits are so realistic that the narrator initially believes that the two figures are ordinary guests at the party. This illusion is due to a number of factors: firstly, the positioning of the two canvases on either side of a doorway in a manner reminiscent of the placement of the two Goya studies, "The Naked Maja", and "The Clothed Maja", in the Prado; secondly, the arrangement of lights illuminating the canvases; and finally, the supreme skill of the two artists in creating such living figures: ". . . the brush, converted into a physiological power, had created the flesh, the epidermis, the muscle, . . . and finally the gleam and meaning of the glance . . . 'This is not painting,' said Eloísa, *exaggerating things*, 'it is performing miracles . . .' It was not a fiction, it was life itself. Undoubtedly, it was going to speak to us . . . we knew her from previous contact. *To think that a colour-covered surface should breathe and be alive like that!* Eloísa kept remarking, obviously enjoying our surprise: 'What a soul she has!'" (my italics; *OC*, IV, 1738). For the two lovers the aim of this exhibition is to create a great surprise amongst the party-goers, just as the previous week the star attraction had been two Brueghel tapestries.

José María is perceptive enough to note the insistent stare of the two figures: the old man in Domingo's picture squints at the viewer, as if the bright lights of the display lamp hurt his eyes. On the other hand, the girl in Sala's portrait stares suggestively at the audience, as if enticing them forward with her smile. These are only personal

---

[7] "*Lo prohibido*: unreliable narrator and untruthful narrative", in *Galdós Studies*, ed. J. E. Varey (London: Tamesis, 1970), pp. 62-89.

hypotheses José María advances to explain the meaning of the glances of the two figures. As to their respective identities, he is even more dubious: the old man may be a beggar or perhaps an unemployed civil servant; the girl may be from the working class, or even an aristocrat dressed up as one. Other important considerations, however, seem beyond José María's ken. He never pauses to meditate on the transformation of these vulgar types into attractive polished surfaces through the medium of paint. Nor does it seem to occur to him that the two portraits might well be prefigurations of Eloísa and himself at a later date when they have been reduced to a sorry plight through the extravagant and ruinous purchases of art works such as these two. Though he is aware of the figures' insistent stare, José María does not for one moment consider whether the portraits speak to his intelligence and moral sight, as well as to his retina.[8]

Confusion of life and art is also generated, deliberately, by the author; Galdós introduces as an actor in the fiction one of his closest friends, the artist Arturo Mélida, the leading illustrator of his *Episodios nacionales*. Eloísa hires the celebrated and multitalented artist to decorate the patio of her new house so that it will rival the renowned enclosure of the Duke and Duchess of Fernán-Núñez.[9] More precisely, Mélida is to design and decorate the scotia of this space in an original pattern of Hellenic figures that represent the ideals both of the ancient and modern worlds; thus the figure of Philosophy alongside the telephone of Edison, for example. Eloísa is so excited at the thought of the project that she would have wished to see it all completed in one day! Galdós' humour is, of course, directed towards this female character, but he is also playing games with his regular readers, as well as sharing a joke with his friend Mélida. By the time the second part of *Lo prohibido* had appeared on the

---

[8] Balart, *Impresiones*, p. 236, wrote as much ten years later: "Painting speaks to the eyes, true; but as if they were the intermediaries of the soul." Juan de Dios, an important secondary character in the first series of *Episodios nacionales*, who is the perfect image of one of the court jesters painted by Velázquez, notes in *La batalla de los Arapiles*, the last *episodio* in the series: "The soul's eyes are the ones that are never deceived, because they always have a ray of eternal light. Body sight is an organ the Devil uses at whim with which to torment us. What we see with it is often illusory and fantastic" (*OC*, I, 1064).

[9] Galdós possessed in his library a copy of a sixty-three page publication by Emilio Bravo y Moltó and Vicente Sancho del Castillo, *Recuerdo de un baile de trajes. Reseña del verificado la noche del 25 de febrero de 1884 en el palacio de los excelentísimos señores Duques de Fernán-Núñez* (Madrid: El Liberal, 1884). The account of the splendid ball is preceded by a tour of the palace; the covered patio or loggia and its art contents are described on p. 7.

bookstalls, the final volume of the illustrated edition of the *Episodios* was ready for sale. Galdós' regular readers would have been amused to see his principal illustrator subject to the crazy whims of a fictional character like Eloísa. There is one final touch of irony that would be deliciously enjoyed by *cognoscenti*: Arturo Mélida had designed one of the cover illustrations for the 1884 booklet by Bravo and Sancho on the Fernán-Núñez palace which Galdós had consulted for this novel. Now Mélida is being asked by Eloísa to make a counter-design for her patio that will outshine the Fernán-Núñez enclosure! Eloísa wants to cocoon herself in a world of art.

As in *La familia de León Roch* there is one perceptive, sensitive actor in the cast who is a painter of sorts: the eccentric Raimundo, Eloísa's brother.[10] His forte is the pencil caricature, but he is too much of a butterfly to develop this skill; he lacks what Galdós, in a rather serious-sounding authorial comment, calls, "a proper depth ... an intimate force ... that moral propulsion which is as indispensable for acts of artistic creation as for works of charity" (*OC*, IV, 1702). However, his moral map of Spain with its various shades and colours indicating intensity of particular vices across the country is a bold visual piece of moral art that José María praises for its insight. Even so, despite these warm words of praise and his financial help in publishing a de luxe edition of the map, José María fails to perceive the relevance of the map for his own life and that of his social acquaintances.[11] That is to say, until his accident on the staircase of his house which precipitates a spiritual awakening before his death. Raimundo's coloured map of Spain is perhaps an anticipation, then, of this development, as well as a visual art contrast to those beautiful objects on which Eloísa and José María squander so much money, passion and, ultimately, moral vision.[12]

---

[10] The third and most unconventional sister of the Guzmán family, Camila, has primitive and unacademic art forms (often in a damaged condition) in her house: photographs, bullfighting posters and cheap prints.

[11] See Vernon A. Chamberlin, "Galdós' chromatic symbolism key in *Lo prohibido*", *HR*, 32 (1964), 109-17, for an analysis of this coloured map. Alfieri, "Images", p. 32, notes that the comparison of Raimundo to an old statue of Christ is "another way of indicating the poor state of religious painting in Galdós' own times besides of pointing out the apathy and indolence of the character". In view of Raimundo's skill with the moral map of Spain, however, the comparison with Christ becomes more apposite.

[12] In contrast, the visual moral painted in every watercolour landscape by José María's relation, the Anglo-Spanish Pastor y Morris, is plainly vulgar. The young woman's other artistic accomplishments include decorating porcelain plaques or pieces of rice paper. José María acts as her dutiful guide around the Prado during her visit to Madrid.

The *Torquemada* Tetralogy

Francisco Torquemada, eponymous hero of this series, starts his fictional existence as a successful money-lender amongst Madrid's lower-middle-class circles before rising to become the Marquess of St. Eloy, financial wizard and adviser to the Spanish government. This development is charted over four novels, the first of which, *Torquemada en la hoguera* (1889), is separated from the others, not only by date of composition, but also by a different treatment of art material, due to the change in social status of the protagonist. The tone of the novelette, preponderantly comic, is reflected in the incorporation of the visual art material. For example, the miser's spiritual adviser during the troubling time of his son's illness is the renegade ex-priest, Bailón, who is the exact image, first of one of Michelangelo's Sybil figures on the ceiling of the Sistine Chapel in Rome, and then of the well-known profile of the great Italian poet, Dante Alighieri. The disparity between the impressive anatomy of the man and the theological nonsense he expounds to console Torquemada is clear for all to note: Bailón's only resemblance to these famous figures of world art is superficial, limited to the external artistic outline. Another comic art form is the tableau the money-lender erects around his son's talented mathematical drawings after his death. The revered icon is then placed on a kind of private altar to the boy's memory in Torquemada's room.

Not all of Torquemada's behaviour during this emotional crisis is comic; he does try, albeit briefly and hesitantly, to develop a sense of true Christian charity towards others.[13] These half-hearted attempts are surrounded by strong suggestions of visual art scenes. In the first, Torquemada is stopped in the street by an old beggar who needs clothing to cover his exposed body on a cold night. Instead of giving the man the fine cloak he is wearing, Torquemada rushes home to fetch his second best. The venerable appearance of the man's face, it is reported, can be matched only by pictures to be found in the religious publication, *The Christian Year*; there is indeed a strong resemblance to the traditional image of St. Peter. The exchange of the cloak also brings to mind another pictorial scene, the famous study of El Greco, "St. Martin and the Beggar", especially when the painter Torquemada will help next is also called Martín. This second act of charity begins with a street encounter between the money-

---

[13] See my "Sallies and encounters in *Torquemada en la hoguera*: patterns of significance", *AG*, 13 (1978), 23-31.

lender and a young woman, Isidora Rufete, the protagonist of the earlier novel *La desheredada*, who has been forced into prostitution. She tugs at Torquemada's coat sleeve as he passes in the street in what obviously is an overt allusion to a scene in the New Testament when Jesus was similarly stopped by Mary Magdalen. Galdós makes the inverted parallel obvious by referring to Isidora, with her beautiful hair barely covered by a red-and-blue-chequered handkerchief, and her sad countenance, as the image of Mary Magdalen.[14] Having been rebuffed by the intended recipient of his charity, Torquemada is eventually able to distribute his interest-free loan to the penniless painter Martín, laid low by tuberculosis in his attic studio. Martín's reaction to the present is one of elation and he promises that when he is feeling better he will paint a portrait of Valentín, Torquemada's son, who, he is sure, will soon recover from his illness. Given the state of Martín's own health, this promise seems as unrealistic as the idyllic landscape scenes that stand in all sorts of strange positions in the attic. The frequent recipient of canvases from defaulting clients, Torquemada has developed a sharp sense of the marketability of art work and the sad truth in this case is that Martín's landscapes will not sell. The comparisons of people and scenes to art figures, noted earlier, besides underlining the semi-artificiality of Torquemada's attempts to practise Christian charity, become even more appropriate in the light of this occasional art dealership.

Further (retrospective) irony derives from the fact that in the subsequent three novels of the tetralogy Torquemada becomes, through his marriage into the aristocratic Aguila family, a prisoner of this artificial art world. Cruz, the leader of the family, constantly urges him to live up to his new social rank by buying the outward symbols of that position: a title, carriage, palace and art collection. To overcome her brother-in-law's resistance to the last item, Cruz reminds him that if the need arises, he can always sell his Rembrandts, Sartos and Van Dycks to the National Gallery in London, or any other famous gallery, for a handsome profit. The collection is fully described in the last novel, *Torquemada y San Pedro* (1895), which opens with the dawn sun filtering onto the armoury of the Torquemada palace and spreading Nature's colours like a painter over what are, after all, man-made art objects. Torquemada's only

---

[14] Alfieri, "Images", p. 27, comments, rather excessively: "It is as if Galdós himself were subsidizing art and also re-telling a portion of the Mary Magdalen story."

interest in these and the paintings lies in their commercial value, as appraised annually by the experts. Otherwise, he shows complete indifference or scorn towards what he considers preposterous shapes. Masaccio's "The Baptism of the Master Redeemer", before which the art experts stand in awe with open mouths, has, for Torquemada, all the appearances of the inside of a bottle of ink, against which the torso and leg of a human body barely stand out and which, in Torquemada's own words, would not even be recognized by the mother who bore it.

As in *Lo prohibido* Galdós selects one particular historical canvas to project a special shaft of significance on his protagonist's development. Rubens' "Prometheus" is for Torquemada nothing more than a revolting, ugly figure whose punishment (a bird feeding on his entrails) is well deserved. Partly because of his preoccupation with the illness of his wife Fidela, Francisco fails to appreciate the relevance of the study for his own predicament; as Ricardo Gullón and Gilbert Smith have pointed out, in his relationships with the Aguilas, Torquemada has become another Prometheus.[15]

For the funeral of his wife, the family's art treasures are assembled in an awesome display: a Van Eyck triptych and a Morales "Ecce Homo" as well as Murillos and Zurbaráns cover the walls of the main rooms. Torquemada is overwhelmed by such a profusion of art works and escapes from the palace in search of his old haunts in the less aristocratic areas of Madrid. In the beautiful spring sunshine, the working-class areas he sees and the people he meets rekindle in him a contentment with life; yet it is emphasized how this joy springs from an appreciation of the artistic appearance of the scene as appraised by Torquemada's eyes: "... as he made his way to the suburbs, *everything he saw*, ground and houses, trees and people, *presented themselves to his eyes as if Nature had been given a coat of happiness or repainted*" (my italics; *OC*, V, 1165). Because the people look happy they must feel happy, is his simplistic conclusion. Torquemada has been unable to avoid the effects of living in an art museum; he now comes to judge people and life by the artistic appearance of external features. The point is reinforced later the same day when during a bout of drunkenness at the tavern of his old

[15] In *Psicologías del autor y lógicas del personaje* (Madrid: Taurus, 1979), pp. 81-85, and "La elaboración del mito de Prometeo en las novelas de Torquemada", in *Actas del segundo congreso internacional de estudios galdosianos* (Las Palmas: Excmo Cabildo Insular, 1977), II, 361-68, respectively.

friend, Vallejo, Torquemada believes that the innkeeper has summoned him to discuss the sale of his art collection. Torquemada cannot escape the influence of his new social surroundings, even when not in full control of his faculties.

The exhibition of art masterpieces at Fidela's funeral was appropriate for a woman who adored portraits and is herself compared by the narrator to one of the Hapsburg princesses painted by Velázquez and other artists, and to the type of woman painted by one of the artists represented in the family collection, Quentin Massys. Fidela's brother, the blind and nostalgic Rafael who detests the parvenu philistine Torquemada, is also likened to a visual art object, this time a religious statue:

> Image, I said, and I will not change the word, for he certainly had some relationship of line and colour with the carved saints, young martyrs or handsome Christ figures at prayer. With that absolute tranquillity of posture, inertia of members, that curly little chestnut beard which stood out darker against the very white skin of shiny wax, that over-effeminate, grief-stricken, death-like beauty of his features, his inability to see, that lack of a visible soul, or in other words, the human look, the similarity with an image was complete. (*OC*, V, 948)

The most important detail of this portrait is, of course, Rafael's blindness; once more Galdós concentrates the reader's attention on the eyes of the art object (here a human being), emphasizing the visual appeal of the artistically shaped body to the eyes of others and, more importantly, to Rafael himself, whose blindness is only a recent illness. Rafael might well be in love with his own physical image, as he remembers it; but he is even more narcissistic spiritually. When, free of the intervention of the medium of the eye, he could have developed a deep insight into other people's characters, especially that of his brother-in-law, he prefers to cling to images of the family's past glories which exclude Torquemada. In *La familia de León Roch* comparisons to beautiful art works had suggested María Egipcíaca's physical narcissism; in the *Torquemada* series, the same technique is slightly adapted to suggest an even greater spiritual narcissism.

The visual arts are used to underline this shortcoming in another way. A favourite pastime of Rafael is to relive his pre-blindness visits to the Prado museum in the company of a friend, the art student Melchorcito, who in his ambition to become another Fortuny or Rosales has already made some good sales on copies of Velázquez or Murillo works. Two aspects of this frequent exercise in escapism command attention. Firstly, Rafael sees again the famous canvases of the Prado through his own and his friend's verbal descriptions; the images are re-created in his mind by the power of the spoken word. Secondly, like his sister, Rafael has a preference for portraits, in particular for those of historical figures: both men enthuse over the historical portraits of Velázquez, Raphael, Goya and Van Dyck, in much the same way that Galdós himself had done in his articles for *La Prensa*. This is a good example of how Galdós adapts what may be his own private opinions on art to the demands of his fiction, where they take on a completely different complexion altogether. In this example Rafael's praise of the historical portraits may be eminently sensible and accurate in itself, but, when compared to the contempt in which he holds his brother-in-law, it becomes a sign of his dangerous removal from contemporary reality.

This absorption in art is also directly responsible for an important development in the fiction: Rafael's escape from the family home for a brief period. While Melchorcito goes home to fetch a review he has written on the latest art exhibition (Galdós might well be laughing at his own art reviews for *La Prensa* a decade earlier), Rafael slips out of the house bought with Torquemada's money and makes his way through the streets of the capital back to the family's ancestral home, which he remembers for its beautiful collections of tapestries and ceramics. Although he is recaptured and returned to the new house, he is never able to accept the presence of Torquemada and finally commits suicide. In the climactic conversation between the two men that precedes this final act, there is an important cluster of references to the visual arts which repays attention. Torquemada happily admits that he will always remain an ordinary piece of earthenware, no matter how much artist Cruz tries to shape him into some kind of Chinese vase; the torment he has to endure under her domestic tyranny is comparable to that depicted in prints of Hell or the Inquisition. The arts are not mentioned here by Rafael but rather suggested by the various postures of his body. He concludes his conversation with Francisco by placing his arms behind his head in the same pose adopted by Goya's famous naked and clothed "majas", a comparison Galdós had first used, as we have seen, over a quarter of a century before in his description of the seductive pose of Susana Cerezuelo before Martín Muriel in *El audaz*. The incongruity of this image at this point in *Torquemada en el purgatorio* is obvious: Rafael is certainly not trying to seduce Torquemada to his way of thinking. Moreover, Galdós chooses this point to recall the similarity of Rafael's appearance to that of Christ, more precisely of Christ in the tomb. This image is the last of a triptych Galdós has painted for his blind nobleman in the tetralogy. In *Torquemada en la cruz* (1893), as was noted above, Rafael had been compared to Christ at prayer. Later in the same novel, when tearfully embracing his sister Fidela, before her marriage to the former money-lender, his sad face, slumped forward with dishevelled hair hanging over his forehead, recalls the picture of Christ on the Cross known as the "Ecce Homo" (*OC*, V, 985). Finally, before his egotistical suicide he is compared to the figure of Christ in the tomb. The progression in the triptych towards Christ's last earthly posture reflects Rafael's trajectory towards his death. But, of course, the parallels between Christ and Rafael are inverted: there can be no comparison of spirituality, for Rafael is an egotist who puts an end to his own life to escape the burden of Torquemada's company, while Christ was crucified for all humanity. The body postures may be similar for both corpses (or soon-to-be corpses), but that is the only point of comparison. Moreover, the pose is entirely appropriate for a man who adores historical paintings and clings to pictorial images of the family's past glory. Lest the reader may be tempted by the Christ parallels to feel sympathy for this hard, self-centred bachelor, Galdós inserts that final incongruous, sensual reference to Goya's reclining "maja". The technique may be an inversion of that used in *La familia de León Roch* when María Egipcíaca had been compared on one occasion to Velázquez's painting of Christ on the Cross, but the results are the same: the incongruity of mixing a religious image or appearance with those of great sensual beauty inevitably provokes doubt about the validity of the religious component of the analogy.

For Rafael, like the other aristocrats and bourgeois in the novels of this first group, interest in the visual arts signals a concern for the external appearance of their social standing. These beautiful art works cost money and therefore exteriorize the social merit of their owners as assessed in financial terms. But this pleasure at the surface gloss of the brightly coloured and decorative objects is at the expense of any awareness of the meaning or, indeed, relevance of these art works for their own lives. Only León Roch in his hallucinations, José María as he nears death and Torquemada in his stubborn philistinism, capture, and then only partially and unconsciously, the hollowness of this social preoccupation with the visual arts. The majority of these aristocratic characters cocoon themselves in the pleasant world of glossy, attractive art works as an escape from the more rigorous demands of mental and spiritual insight. For the reader the narrator's constant deployment of ironic, incongruous metaphors offers an alternative guide, a more correct moral vision of the beguiling world of art.

CHAPTER 9

INITIAL ART FORMS

La desheredada (1881), *El amigo Manso* (1882), *Tormento* (1884), *Fortunata y Jacinta* (1886-87)

Our second category comprises those novels which can be grouped together because they all contain significant descriptions of visual art forms at the beginning, forms that Galdós appears to be holding up to the fictional character as well as the reader for his or her special mental viewing. Because Galdós positions this art form or object at such a strategic position the reader is forced to evaluate its significance for the interpretation of the rest of the novel, where other references to the visual arts repeat the opening motif. This is not to say that these Group II novels do not exhibit other aspects of the visual arts that we consider separately in subsequent groupings, but rather that this initial deployment of an arresting art form is one of their most distinguishing aspects. At the same time Galdós remains vitally concerned with the relationship of the visual arts to the human eye's perception of physical and spiritual reality.

La desheredada

Galdós' first novel in what he was later to call "the contemporary series" was introduced to an old friend, the Krausist founder of Madrid's Free Institution of Teaching, Francisco Giner de los Ríos, in terms of the traditional metaphor of the writer as a painter: "In fact, in this work I wanted to travel on a new road or to start my second or third 'manner', as they say about painters.''[1] In actual fact, Galdós opens his novel with a detailed verbal picture of the Madrid mental asylum of Leganés where Tomás Rufete, the father of the protagonist, Isidora, is incarcerated. The whole architectural mass of buildings is presented as a visual puzzle that defies visual art reproduction: "Oh, Leganés! If they tried to represent you as a theoretical city, like those that in days gone by were drawn by philosophers, saints and engravers to express a moral or religious plan, no, there would not be any architects or physiologists who would dare to mark down with a sure hand where your hospitable walls begin or end" (*OC*, IV, 987). In *La familia de León Roch* the urban planners had experienced no such difficulty in demarcating the city limits and placing León's house within its confines. Leganés, on the other hand, defies such a rigid demarcation because its dimensions appear on the moral map of Spain, like that to be painted by Raimundo in *Lo prohibido*, where boundaries are not so clear-cut, for madmen can be also found outside the walls of Leganés.

The second visual art form suggested in Galdós' statement is that of the illustration or print to be found in old religious or moral treatises, where its function is traditionally to reinforce the meaning of the printed word, as we noted in Part II of our study. Despite Galdós' overt denial that Leganés corresponds to this traditional book illustration, the idea of a parallel has been raised, the seed planted in the mind: the reader has been made to entertain, if not accept, the possibility that the description of the building of Leganés is intended as a pictorial illustration, like a frontispiece that opens Galdós' treatise on the social madness of Isidora Rufete and her circle, in short, as if *La desheredada* were in the tradition of the medieval treatises. Having launched this notion, Galdós may indeed officially deny its plausibility but he has at least mooted the idea. The perceptive reader might be willing to assess the idea's validity especially when he notes other artistic aspects woven into this initial picture of Leganés.

The inmates are able to look out of the asylum's windows at the surrounding countryside; but through bars which, acting as a frame, cause this landscape to take on the appearance of a beautiful picture, of a paradise beyond their reach: "... the happiness of the intense verdure reached their eyes diminished and almost lost" (*OC*, IV,

---

[1] Reproduced in Manuel B. Cossío [M.B.C.], "Galdós y Giner: una carta de Galdós", *LL*, 20 (1920), 254-58.

988). Yet at dawn, "that pleasant opening of the day's eyes", the sun, "father of all beauty ... spreads the same wonders of form and colour" in the asylum as in the Retiro Park, that lovers' haven, in the centre of Madrid (*OC*, IV, 989). At one moment, the beauty of Nature is shut out of Leganés; at another, it overwhelms its precincts. Leganés is, thus, an architectural enigma: it seems to transcend the physical limitations of the walls and reach into Madrid and the rest of Spain. The asylum appears to be an illustration to a religious treatise, yet the narrator seems to quash this notion. A third visual art reference climaxes this process of enigmatic identity: the walls of the asylum resemble the ramparts of the Egyptian pyramids because areas where the plaster has fallen off and become discoloured in the rain give the appearance of a thousand Pharaonic figures on the flat surface (*OC*, IV, 988). Galdós' selection of the ancient pictorial language of hieroglyphics is brilliantly apt, for it suggests the difficulty, not so much in perceiving exterior forms, as in deciphering the meaning of this visual art form that is Leganés, and also relates that enigma to an ancient style in the history of world architecture.

These comparisons to art forms, encouraged by the exterior dimension and appearance of the asylum, give way to a concrete visual art form on the inside of the edifice, which is again exploited by Galdós as a lesson for his principal character. Isidora, waiting to see the director of the asylum in the main administrative office, spends her time looking at objects in the room. An impressive wall map of Spain captures her attention. This is no precisely coloured moral map of the country like Raimundo's in *Lo prohibido*. Indeed, it is quite the opposite: it seems to be a statistical map of the country's industrial production, for tables of statistics below the outline are accompanied by flags and circles denoting urban centres. Furthermore, dominating the map is a vignette with pictures of all the machines of modern industrial production and transport: trains, ships, factory chimneys, balloons and lighthouses. At the centre stand the figures of a lion and a lady (somewhat indecently attired), presumably representing Spain and Prosperity respectively. At this stage in the novel there is no indication that the illustrated map will play any prominent role in the subsequent fiction, although the alert reader may be puzzled by the length of its description and its presence in an insane asylum office. In retrospect, however, the map's illustrations do seem to prefigure in an ironic fashion the main outline of Isidora's story. The real driving force behind her obsessive claim that she belongs to the aristocratic Aransis family is her thirst for the visible and tangible material trappings of that class. The means by which she achieves this goal when her moral and legal claims fail will not be hard work or industry, as suggested by those dynamic instruments of modern power on the map (later she will even show indifference to the operation of the Relimpios' Singer sewing-machine), but by sexual liaisons with powerful and wealthy men. Anticipation of this alternative course, for the attentive reader, might be detected in the features of the semi-naked lady and the lion on the frieze of the map, which Isidora finds so pretty, especially if we consider the lion as the symbol of Spain, for the string of Isidora's lovers can also be viewed as representatives of the successive stages in Spanish political history at this time, as I have shown elsewhere.[2] In this sense, then, the illustrated map does continue the enigmatic warning contained in the initial description of Leganés: artistic appearances can be deceiving, their true meaning may be buried beneath some layers of ideas which the inquisitive mind of the onlooker (fictional character or reader) has to explore.

Isidora is fascinated by the pretty colours and designs of the map and whilst it would be unjust to expect any great foresight of her at this point, she does not try to decode the message of the visual art form: her appreciation is confined to surface shapes. The point is emphasized by her appreciation of another art object in the room, the plaster bust standing atop a bookcase. Again she expresses delight with the pretty appearance of the bust as well as of the books, revealing a sharp eye for the erotic appearance of the bust: the shoulders have the contours of a female figure in a low-cut dress. She also notices that the figure has no pupils in its eyes. The observation is brief, but suggests that Isidora's eye is still attracted by the outlines of objects. However, in the following chapter we are informed that she does possess a very vivid imagination which anticipates events before they happen, seeing them as frozen images with all the proportions, perspective, colours, and arrangement of paintings. Her imagination can also distort the size of things and people she has seen: small things become miniscule, ugly things horrible and pretty things divine.[3] An example of this ability is provided immediately in the following paragraph when she pays a visit to the leech-store

---

[2] See my *Galdós's Novel of the Historical Imagination: a Study of the Contemporary Novels* (Liverpool: Francis Cairns, 1983), Part I, Chapter 1.

[3] Isidora also proves to be an accomplished verbal portraitist: her succinct sketch of the external appearance of her protector, José de Relimpio, is praised for its accuracy by the narrator (*OC*, IV, 1034).

owned by her aunt, Encarnación Guillén, which is appropriately announced by the hieroglyphic picture of small snake-like creatures on the store sign (again we recall the hieroglyphics on the walls of Leganés). Isidora, perturbed by the sight of this and other twisted store signs, sloping lamp-posts and dilapidated house fronts, believes she is not in the real world of Madrid at all, but "in the caricature of a city made of rotten cardboard" (*OC*, IV, 998).

Two chapters later, on a Sunday afternoon excursion around Madrid with an old childhood friend from La Mancha, Augusto Miquis, Isidora's dangerous propensity to distort reality is again highlighted and also in a visual art context, a visit to the Prado museum. On the way there Isidora stops from time to time to gaze at objects for sale in shop windows; but at the same time she wants to see the reflection of her fine figure in the glass window. In most women this is a natural action, but in Isidora's case its repetition through the novel[4] suggests an excessive preoccupation with her own beautiful figure, as if the mirror reflection were an art object separated from her real self. Thus, in this small scene Galdós captures the narcissism of Isidora and also her need to buy objects to adorn that beautiful external image she cultivates. The scene also serves as a timely introduction to Isidora's visit to the Prado, alerting the reader to her fascination with beautiful images. This is indeed her response to the museum's masterpieces: intuitively, she recognizes that their beauty is superior to anything she has seen before. However, this aesthetic response also has its social-class component: she is upset when told that the lower classes are also allowed into the

----

[4] See Part I, Chapter II and Part II, Chapter X. In the latter example she whirls around ecstatically before a mirror in a boutique after trying on some new dresses. Finally in the last chapter of the novel, before she plunges into a life of prostitution, she takes one further look at her figure in a mirror. Now, however, it is only a small mirror and Isidora has to contort her partly-clad body, adopting a series of grotesque postures, in order to view the whole figure in stages. Still proud of her fine shape, she fails to note that the grotesque physical postures might well represent the degree to which her moral principles have sunk. On other occasions, such as when she stares intensely at the Singer sewing-machine Relimpio is trying to explain to her and her thoughts are miles away, her eyes are unutilized, non-absorbent reflectors of the images of external reality. Miquis offers a shrewd description of these optical organs: ". . . they were a deep and luminous sea in whose crystalline bosom floated like nereids dreamy imagination, indolence, ignorance of positive arithmetic and the nescience of reality" (*OC*, IV, 1072).
Relimpio himself is another mirror-gazer, always fussing over his appearance. His portrait, in oils, hanging in the family living-room, is another booster of his self-confidence. Whenever his jealous wife, Doña Laura, lambastes him for his amorous proclivities with other females, she takes inspiration from a print on the opposite side of the room, showing Sardanapalus, the sybaritic Assyrian king, immolating himself and his concubines!

gallery to see the great works of art; for Isidora great artistic beauty must be synonymous with aristocratic standing, art is a natural accompaniment for nobility, a belief that was dominant amongst the aristocratic and bourgeois characters in our first group of novels. The visit to the Prado *is* an important event for Isidora: she is genuinely bedazzled by the display of artistic beauty which only serves to strengthen her attachment to the world of art forms. In his account of the visit Galdós concentrates exclusively on the reactions of delight from Isidora: when he enjoyed a golden opportunity to impress the reader with his knowledge and love of the Prado's collection, he scrupulously avoids any mention of details about technique, identity, authorship or subject. He forgoes all digressions and focuses exclusively on this fascination of Isidora with surface beauty. At the same time, the visit might well be construed as a sly, humorous dig at the seriousness of such art gallery visits, actively encouraged by Galdós' friend, Giner de los Ríos, and other Krausist teachers.[5] On this particular occasion a confrontation with some of the world's art masterpieces does not open new vistas of spiritual understanding of reality, life or world history, but rather increases the viewer's dangerous absorption with externally beautiful forms.

Miquis' clowning antics during and after the same visit provide a necessary foil to Isidora's spasms of aesthetic rapture: for a dose of plebeian reality he drags her to a crude eating establishment, with its vulgar wall etchings, sketched by impatient customers. For Isidora the Retiro Park close to the Prado is a picturesque delight, an "ingenious adaptation of Nature to culture" (*OC*, IV, 1007). With its spring vegetation, sunlight filtering through the branches of the trees, white clouds dotting the blue sky, it looks the picture that the narrator had briefly anticipated in his description of dawn at Leganés. Miquis, however, punctures his friend's pastoral romanticizing by conducting her through some very inhospitable and far from picturesque pieces of terrain (gullies, earth tips and embankments with hardly any vegetation) between the Aragon Road and Pajarillos. Adding insult to injury, Miquis launches into an ironic panegyric of the landscape whose first feature instantly reminds the

---

[5] Francisco Giner de los Ríos, *Educación y enseñanza*, Vol. XII of *Obras completas*, 2nd ed. (Madrid: Espasa Calpe, 1933), p. 60, was hoping that guided tours of the art galleries could also be extended to the general public. Curiously enough, in the last piece of fiction Galdós wrote, the *episodio* of the fifth series, *Cánovas* (1912), which chronicles the same period in Spanish history covered by Part II of *La desheredada*, the protagonist, Tito, takes his female companion, Casianilla, to the Prado to give her lessons in art history.

reader of the initial depiction of Leganés: "There are the pyramids of Egypt which we call tile factories; here the ruined amphitheatre of these mud-brick walls ... What vegetation! Look at these age-old thistles ... Look at those buildings: Saint Mark's of Venice, Saint Sophia, the Escorial ... Oh, Isidora, I love you, I adore you. How beautiful the world is, how attractive the afternoon! How the sun gleams! How pretty you are and how happy I am!" (*OC*, IV, 1012).

Miquis' amorous banter deflects the force of his preceding parody, whose effect is soon completely nullified by the appearance in the Castellana Avenue of a procession of carriages transporting wealthy, titled ladies. As Miquis instructs his friend, this is no ordinary evening "paseo"; it is a political demonstration by these female aristocrats (all wearing white mantillas in support of the pretender to the throne, Alfonso XII of Bourbon) against the Italian prince, Amadeo of Savoy, who had been offered the Spanish crown in 1870 by the Revolutionary Government of Prim.[6] The colourful scene, which confirms for Isidora the existence of a refined aristocratic world in which beauty, grace and wealth exist and to which she feels entitled, is seen by the young girl from La Mancha through the filter of the artistic figures and scenes that had overwhelmed her senses earlier in the day at the Prado museum:

> So reality became a fantasy before her dazed eyes, taking on the dimensions and shapes proper to fever and art. The beauty of the horses and their grave trot, their elegant tossings of the head, became, in her eyes, as in those of the artist, the implausible figure of the hippogriff. The busts of the ladies, appearing between the procession of stiff coachmen and so many horses' heads, the various colours of the parasols, the liveries, the furs, produced before Isidora's eyes an effect similar to that which the sight of a magnificent fresco of apotheosis with nymphs, pegasuses, clouds, triumphal chariots and floating drapes would produce in any of us. (*OC*, IV, 1014)

Isidora, the impressionist artist, has succeeded masterfully in freezing the kaleidoscopic movements of animals and people into an artistic tableau; but in so doing Isidora is distorting the historical reality and ignoring uglier elements like the counter-demonstration by some prostitutes.

Her next session of picture-viewing takes place in the less grandiose setting of the Aransis palace whose brick and plaster

---

[6] For a discussion of the political implications of this scene, see my *Galdós's Novel*, pp. 4-7.

eighteenth-century façade seems to reflect the mediocrity of the art collection inside. For Isidora the focus of her devoted attention is the portrait of her putative mother, the daughter of the dowager Marchioness of Aransis, in the room where she had been confined until her death for giving birth to an illegitimate child. Prior to Isidora's visit in the company of Miquis and José de Relimpio, this portrait is discussed with the reader. First the narrator gives his interpretation: he is particularly struck by the contrast in the picture between the melancholy of the woman's eyes and the burlesque smile on her lips. The interpretation of the dowager Marchioness, as reported by the narrator, is somewhat different: she prefers to highlight the hair style, the enchanting complexion of the face, the graceful movement of her daughter's hand sweeping back the black mantilla, touches that one normally associates with a Madrazo portrait and correspond to the nostalgic mood of the mother as she recalls the sad story of her daughter's life and death. This elegiac mood is underscored by the simultaneous playing of a Beethoven piece on a nearby piano by the dead woman's young son. Galdós' purpose in contrasting these two interpretations of the portrait is surely to underline the greater subjectivity of the mother's viewpoint. Completely objective interpretations of any art work are, of course, impossible, but there are also great differences in subjective responses, depending to a great extent on the emotional and cognitive perspectives of the viewer. This scene is, then, another important lesson by Galdós on the essential perspectivism at work in art appreciation, or, in starker terms, on the ability of the visual arts, through the appeal to the optical senses, when controlled by the imagination, to mislead the viewer.

In the context of Isidora's visit to the Aransis palace, this difference of opinion between the narrator and the Marchioness serves as a prologue to Isidora's climactic confrontation with the portrait of her putative mother. Her viewpoint, of course, is far different from that of the narrator or even of the woman's mother: Isidora is overcome with reverence and love for this image of the person she believes is her natural mother, with the result that she is sure that the divinely drawn eyes on the canvas are speaking to her. The exaggeration in this response can be readily appreciated after the preceding lesson in subjective perspectivism, but now Galdós goes further and sets out to ridicule his protagonist's interpretation. The presence of Augusto Miquis provides the perfect means: his irreverent clowning before the paintings and then on the piano is as much a burlesque parody of the traditional, serious art gallery visit or concert as a timely deflation of Isidora's exaggerated and spurious filial devotion which is "foreign to the emotions of art" (*OC*, IV, 1049), as the narrator pointedly remarks: "Miquis, *who was a master at playing the role of artist*, began to show that dumb wonderment of the enthusiastic tourist and to shout out and twist his neck in order to look at the ceiling, with his mouth open for a good while . . .: 'I could spend my whole life looking at those shepherdesses jumping around and those children riding a swan' " (my italics; *OC*, IV, 1048).

In the disastrous interview with the Marchioness at the end of Part I there is no reference to the palace's art treasures that surround the couple. Instead, particular interest is now focused on the resemblance of Isidora to the image of her putative mother. The girl from La Mancha insists: "I am the living portrait of my mother" (*OC*, IV, 1075). The old woman is forced for a moment to agree that there is some resemblance, but suggests that it is purely accidental: Isidora's trump (and final) card, as it were, that reliance on the beautiful physical appearance (eternalized in the Madrazo-style portrait) to clinch her argument, proves ineffective and she has to withdraw from the Aransis palace, her claim rudely rejected.

In Part II, Isidora, like Don Quixote, makes a third sally to the palace of her illusions, and this time there is another pertinent mention of the art collection. By now, however, Isidora is in a desperate situation: her lawsuit against the Aransis family is bogged down in the courts and she has to depend on male admirers for financial support. Her current lover is the Catalan anarchist and lithographer, Juan Bou, who takes her to visit his sick sister, the wife of the caretaker of the Aransis palace. Bou's sarcastic interpretations of the aristocrats' art decoration are coloured by his political prejudices, of course, but they also owe something to his artist's eye; his interpretations are far more grotesque than the comic distortions of Miquis: " 'Well now, there; who can this animal be?' said the lithographer, stopping in front of the portraits. 'What stiffness! Sorry, sir, I thought you were a stick. And he is looking so angrily at us . . . It is alright, sir; we are not going to eat people . . . Look, here's a nun, also. And she is beautiful. I bet you are a lively bit, sister!'" (*OC*, IV, 1124). Isidora, too annoyed and ashamed at this savage distortion of her putative forebears, remains silent. It is not a question of her interest in art waning, for a few moments earlier in the caretaker's apartment she had keenly studied the cheap prints of the Virgin and saints and etchings on events from Spanish history (pertinently, the failed revolt of "Los Comuneros" or urban rebels in the sixteenth century), oblivious to the conversation of the man's sick wife. On the contrary, in the Aransis apartment her appreciation of the family paintings is entirely subject to her preconceived notions of the importance of her position.

Still naïvely believing that, despite the legal setbacks, her cause will eventually triumph, she promises Joaquín Pez that one of her first actions as a legally recognized Aransis will be to become a patroness of the arts, buying masterpieces, both ancient and modern, like those she has seen on her repeated visits (now totalling three or four) to the Prado. The figures with which she identifies in these Prado paintings are either dressed in fine clothes or, like Greek goddesses, such as the allegorical figure on the wall map in the Leganés office, semi-nude. This identification confirms Isidora's obsession with body appearances, whether bare or clothed; she feels the identification so intensely that she claims that this painted world in the canvases is the proper world to which she belongs and that it is rightfully hers (*OC*, IV, 1143).[7]

Less noble art forms like the cheap prints in the Relimpio household, where she first lodges on her arrival in Madrid, are not to her aesthetic taste; she would dearly love to remove the prints, which treat of the sentimental scene of Princess Poniatowski learning of the death of her husband, an allegorical figure of Hunger and two emaciated, almost grotesque lovers, swearing eternal love beside a stream. Isidora's antipathy is determined by more immediate considerations than aesthetic taste; she will shortly be visited by the son of her protector in Madrid, Don Manuel Pez. The widowed Marquess of Saldeoro, as Joaquinito Pez is first known, would not appreciate these cheap art forms. The irony in this snobbish rejection of the prints is that, in retrospect, they will appear to offer an amazing visual anticipation of Isidora's relationship with Joaquinito: their declaration of eternal love in dire financial straits will appear as unromantic and squalid as that of the lovers in the prints; hunger will be the constant companion of their affair; and eventually Isidora will have to lament, like the Polish princess, the loss of Joaquinito, her first and true love. To foresee this outcome is, of course, an impossibility at such an early stage, but, nevertheless, there is still an appreciable contrast between the vulgarity of these prints and the

---

[7] Disguised in typical Madrid costume to attend the annual San Isidro fair, Isidora looks like a Flamenco Venus (*OC*, IV, 1113).

romantic, beautiful ambience with which Isidora would like to surround herself for the visit of the young widower.

No such visual vulgarity offends Isidora's eyes when she makes a subsequent visit to the Pez house for some financial support. The walls of the family study are decorated with prints of beautiful, semi-naked classical females, which, as we know already, are an immediate source of visual enchantment for Isidora. She is somewhat puzzled to note that there is a reproduction of Velázquez's "Christ" on another wall. Before she can resolve her confusion, the dashing young Joaquinito enters. The implications of the opposition between the subjects of the two sets of pictures are important. We have already seen in *La familia de León Roch* and the *Torquemada* tetralogy the use of the same technique (and in the case of the former, the use of the same famous painting) in order to contrast the carnal narcissism and spiritual poverty of the fictional character. In this example in *La desheredada*, there is a slight variation of the technique: the contrast is not now between person and painting, but between two paintings. Yet the lesson is still the same: a preponderant interest in corporal charms involves a neglect of spiritual values. The entry of the handsome Joaquinito at this moment of bewilderment in Isidora's mind augurs ill for the arousal of any religious conscience in the young girl; by the end of Part I sexual instincts have triumphed, as Isidora, now rejected by the Aransis family, is ready to follow Joaquín for her financial salvation. The Pez art collection is not without significance either for this middle-class, bureaucrat family: the incongruity of subject-matter surely sums up the hypocrisy of the family: on the one hand, we see their social propriety and religious conformity; on the other, their more natural instincts and desires.[8] In short, Isidora's experience of art viewing may delight her eyes, but the moral consequences of this visual fascination seem to be disastrous. Cautioned by the initial art lesson of the Leganés asylum presented by the narrator, the reader, while noting the delight of Isidora, realizes that there might perhaps be a deeper significance to this motif of which the fictional character is still ignorant. The world of art only encourages her dangerous propensity to mistake visual, artistic forms for reality, to bask in the visual, epidermic pleasures of the canvas at the expense of the more important messages that their

---

[8] In the *pied-à-terre* the two lovers will occupy in Hortaleza Street, there is another clash of art styles; Isidora is forever gazing ecstatically at the magnificent photograph of her beautiful aristocratic figure on the mantelpiece. Joaquinito, on the other hand, enjoys the comic figures of gluttonous, drunken friars and other popular types.

subjects might convey. Paintings are selected for their power to boost her illusions of a world that includes only things beautiful, noble and wealthy. Anything that upsets that illusion, like the prints in the Relimpio household or the vision of the setting sun over the Guadarrama, which, immediately after her expulsion from the Aransis palace, is regarded as a visual confirmation of her devastating blow, is condemned as unaesthetic because it does not correspond to her rosy, colourful vision of art and life.

Miquis is only the first of a number of secondary characters who, with their consciously or unconsciously parodic view of art, are marshalled alongside the protagonist to expose this basic self-deceit. In this respect, it could be said that the first appearance of Mariano, her epileptic brother, at work in a rope factory is a deliberate negation of the picturesque setting or landscape in fiction. The only light that reaches the work area comes from a narrow inner patio of the building. Mariano works at the winding machine in total darkness. The imbalance of light and darkness, the difficulties in appraising space and distance, the combination of the horizontal lines of the hemp strands being wound around the moving circular wheel, the wooden disc of the machine (which resembles "the strange optical aberrations of the retina when we close our eyes dazzled by a very bright light" [*OC*, IV, 1002]), all present a challenge to the eye's ability to perceive shapes, distances and angles in the almost complete absence of light. The inability of the stranger (here appropriately Isidora and her aunt Encarnación) to make out any kind of shape, human or inanimate, is the main point of this description. The whole scene forms a striking contrast to Isidora's subsequent Prado visit, where the luminosity of the varied colours dazzles her eyes and filters into her whole nervous system as if by osmosis. In the rope factory Isidora, "who was used to seeing in objective shapes and movements the actions and tremblings of her own person" (*OC*, IV, 1001), suffers the reverse identification: she is bodily disturbed by the infernal noise of the machine. So, beside the aristocratic art world of the Prado is juxtaposed the cavernous industrial world of the rope factory, one the antithesis of the other. Yet there is a common link that seems to corroborate the inverted parallelism we are claiming: the hemp that is being stretched and wound in Mariano's grotto is the same raw material from which the more aristocratic and artistic fabrication of the picture is made to arise: the canvas board.

Carmen Bravo-Villasante has stated that the character of

Mariano owes its origins to the popular illustrated texts of the "aleluyas" or broadsheets traditionally distributed in segments to the congregation at Easter Sunday masses.[9] The claim is rather excessive; more probable is her other suggestion that the gang-fight in Part I, in which Mariano kills a rival, is based on a very popular nineteenth-century "aleluya" called "La pedrea" or "The Rockfight". Certainly, Mariano's connections with the visual arts increase dramatically when he is sent as an apprentice to the lithographer Juan Bou. He is pushed into this job by his sister, who believes that it is a noble and dignified profession, far preferable to that of a rope-winder precisely because it is connected with painting. Mariano cannot be allowed to sully the beautiful impression Isidora wants her family to present to the world, however slight his artistic aptitude or slender the financial rewards of the job; her own considerations of social snobbery must take priority: "It was agreed, then, that Mariano would learn a trade; but even on that exceptional occasion Isidora's aristocratic urges predominated over her anger, because she would not allow her brother to become a cobbler, mason, locksmith, tailor, or even a hairdresser, and thinking about which industry he should enter, she decided he would become an engraver, that is to say, a manufacturer of those pretty prints which adorn illustrated publications, and of those magnificent reproductions of the Museums ... *For industry to be able to appear as noble, it needs to pretend a relationship with art*" (my italics; *OC*, IV, 1097-98).

With time Mariano does come to like lithography and the printing of "aleluyas", even displaying some skill in operating the printing machine. Furthermore, Bou's business is experiencing some prosperity as there is a current boom in decorated merchandise. The giant with the delicate fingers for drawing (and also a face like a Greek mask when paying court to Isidora) is considered an innovator in his field, for he patents the process of printing kitchen-shelf paper with the figures of popular types like bullfighters and "majas". The premises of his lithography business, the detailed description of which (Part II, Chapter IV) shows Galdós' intimate knowledge of this aspect of the visual arts, resemble those of the rope factory, with their dark, labyrinthine structure, whilst the creaky,

---

[9] "El naturalismo de Galdós y el mundo de *La desheredada*", *CHA*, 77 (1969), 479-86. On the "aleluya" see Alison Sinclair, *Valle-Inclán's 'Ruedo ibérico': a Popular View of Revolution* (London: Tamesis, 1977), pp. 25-26. Julio Caro Baroja, *Ensayos sobre la literatura de cordel* (Madrid: Revista de Occidente, 1969), p. 426, maintains that Galdós' work did not manage to exert any influence on the genre, which reached its peak just at the time he was making his mark as a novelist.

dye-stained printing press gives the appearance of a tavern rather than that of a temple of the illustrated word. In all these aspects of Mariano's apprenticeship in the lithography business it seems as if Galdós is once more holding up a more prosaic reality to counter the fantasy vision of Isidora. Mariano is no apprentice artist, he is just a manual labourer, the "estampador" or printer. The work area is no artist's studio but a dark dungeon, and the art work on which Bou and his workers thrive is at the bottom of the artistic scale: not the reproductions of etchings by Doré or of famous works of art, but kitchen decoration or broadsheets for beggars and blind men to sell at street corners; not really the fine world of art so beloved by Isidora; somehow the reality of Mariano's job does not match up to Isidora's dream world.[10]

But Mariano's apprenticeship with this minor branch of the visual arts does have important consequences in another sphere of human activity that Isidora does not foresee. Her brother imbibes all the anarchist rhetoric spouted by Bou during his labours; the boy comes to hate the upper classes with equal intensity and to yearn for a revolution that will allow the poor to take over the position of the wealthy and powerful in society. This increasingly dangerous obsession reaches its climax when Mariano, watching one day a procession of royal coaches on their way to the Basilica of Atocha, curses this extravagant display of wealth and power. Sitting down by one of the fountains in the nearby Plaza Mayor (Main Square), he re-creates in his mind's eye, as he is wont, the picture of the procession he has just seen, a facility that contrasts with his sister's ability to foresee events. This mental re-creation takes place against the backdrop of the geometric shapes and figures fashioned by the jets of water from the fountains and the interplay of the sun's rays. Galdós' liking for these patterns had been seen two years earlier in his description of the fountains in La Granja in the *episodio Los apostólicos*: but in *La desheredada* the aquatic picture is more

---

[10] Another character connected with the minor art world of lithography is Melchor, son of José de Relimpio. His art work, at first in collaboration with Bou, centres on a project for a national lottery or raffle. The walls of his studio are covered with examples of his work (coloured signs) which to Isidora's impressionable eyes or "mad fantasy" appear like tropical birds on branches in a South American jungle. Significantly, there are also maps of Madrid and Spain in his studio, recalling that important map in the Leganés asylum office. Galdós remarks that the maps played the same role as a railway- or mine-plan in a prospector's office. Melchor has designed a prospectus for the national venture and the undistinguished illustrations again call to mind the Leganés asylum: Sisters of Charity are leading beggars to an asylum, the façade of which is composed of Greek columns, with a sun and the triangular insignia of Jehovah superimposed.

integrated into the development of events. First, the shapes and lines of water act as a kind of shifting convex lens, against which the normal shapes of people and things behind them are distorted, a prototype, as it were, of Valle-Inclán's later deforming street mirror which produced his "esperpentos": ". . . the water, gushing out of imitation rocks, forms an elastic sphere, whose walls expand and contract according to the strong or weak puffs of air which hit them. On this mobile liquid crust the sun creates fanciful rainbows, and convex images of the gardens and pedestrians are sketched" (*OC*, IV, 1166).

But if the aquatic backcloth acts as a transparency that distorts the scene behind, it must also distort Mariano's re-creation of the procession. The effects of this superimposition of a distorting lens are still evident when the royal coaches return from the suburban basilica to the city centre. Mariano's vision is now also affected by one of his epileptic seizures, so that his picture of historical reality becomes distorted by the elastic shapes of a water fountain picture: "Crowd, troops, horses, uniforms, plumes, colours, tinsels, noise, made him so giddy that he could see only a pale, moving mass of objects, like the iridescences and contorsions of the ball of water that he had been looking at moments before" (*OC*, IV, 1167). In many ways this view of the royal procession corresponds to Isidora's impressionistic view of the mantillas demonstration at the beginning of the novel. Both visions of reality are strongly influenced by previous viewings of artistic forms of one kind or another, so that reality is perceived in terms of isolated components of a canvas. The only difference is that Mariano's picture of King Alfonso's procession is the grotesque inversion of his sister's beautiful frieze of Amadeo's controversial "paseo". Furthermore, whilst Mariano's intense loathing of the pageantry is again the reverse reaction to that of his sister on the earlier occasion, he acts to change the immobilized picture (Isidora had desperately wanted to form part of hers) by rushing forward to fire his pistol at the king: this dynamic movement will, he believes, change the order of Spanish society forever. However, the attempt fails and Mariano is put to death by garrotting. This is the final blow to Isidora's social pride, determining her subsequent descent into street prostitution. Thus, her attempt to turn Mariano into a kind of artist worthy of her own social status has rebounded with a savage vengeance: the main lesson her brother has learnt at Bou's lithography studio is not one of the beauty of art, but of the need for political violence, an apprenticeship which now terminates in this tragic humiliation for her. Fascination with the beautiful world of the Prado canvases has not only fuelled her own aristocratic pretensions, but has also dictated the upbringing of her brother. One person's infatuation with the beautiful world of art has, paradoxically, resulted in a grotesque moral and physical action by another. This strange pattern of cause and effect accords well with the initial enigmatic description of the asylum at Leganés: immersing oneself in the sumptuous world of beautiful art does not automatically confer nobility and virtue on the art-lover or those closest to him or her. On the contrary, an absorption with the surface appeal of canvases to the eye, to the total exclusion of any spiritual insight or moral reflection, will inevitably lead to the kind of distortions of reality that Isidora practises upon herself and her brother. In truth, the boundaries of Leganés cannot be represented by a visual art introduction to Galdós' text, for the greater madmen are to be found outside its walls in the city of Madrid. There can be no frontispiece or colour illustration to Galdós' moral tale, because, paradoxically, his main fictional character overindulges her liking for the visual arts.

El amigo Manso

Galdós' second novel in "the contemporary series" opens with the baffling statement from the narrator that he does not exist, that he is a spiritual entity, an artistic condensation, a diabolical creation of the human mind, another example of those falsifications of man sold from time immemorial by artists, poets and others. In other words, narrator-protagonist Máximo Manso, who is able to speak to the reader because of his literary creation, is an art object, an image of man in words comparable to those in paintings. For a man conscious of pre-existence as a spirit and who in his earthly form teaches the abstract subject of philosophy to university students, the most startling aspect of the account of his early years given in the opening chapters is his frequent use of metaphors and references to the visual arts, especially to sculpture. It is almost as if he needs the language of solid sculpture to counteract the etherealness of his origins, fictional status and profession. For example, he modestly claims that in his role as a teacher he is only "an assistant of those noble craftsmen who have from age to age been fashioning the beautiful figure of the divine man from the block of the human animal" (*OC*, IV, 1186). He also hopes that his learning from books and life's experiences will be a firm structure for the reality of his own life, with powerful foundations in his conscience, rather than shaky constructions of wind and smoke. Later in the novel he will lecture his brother, a newly-elected deputy to the Spanish parliament, on the need for a new type of national politics and again the language of architecture is pertinently used: "It is necessary to knock down the empty catafalque of painted canvas and open up new foundations in the firm bowels of the true country so that on them might be established the construction of a new and solid State" (*OC*, IV, 1208). In all of these examples, both at the beginning and throughout the novel, the use of the language of petrification and sculpture seems to surpass a traditionally rhetorical use and to be an unconsciously-felt need on Máximo's part.

The reality of the material counterpoint to this figure of speech is presented in another section at the beginning of the novel: the account of Máximo's terrestrial birth in Cangas de Onís. It so happens that this town is situated in the Asturian mountains, close to Covadonga, the traditional birthplace of Spanish resistance to the invasion of the Moors in the eighth century. Máximo believes that he has absorbed some of the melancholic pleasantness of the region's valleys and the greatness of the mountains' granite masses. As a boy, he and his brother were often taken by their father on hunting expeditions in this area, so that he became accustomed to the strange feeling of appearing to walk on clouds up the mountainside. It is a paradoxical sensation: stationed on some of the most solid rock formations on earth, Máximo feels the closeness of the sky and clouds. The relevance of this location for Máximo is that it is the point where the contrasting physical worlds of sky and earth appear to be contiguous; it is also an expression of the dual constituents, matter and spirit, of Máximo's and Everyman's being. The mountain-top location also serves to represent visually Máximo's special status and origins as an artistic creation. Having compared himself to a figure in a painting, he now objectifies his origins in a beautiful landscape vision.

The climax of all these early allusions to rock forms and mountains, whether literal or metaphoric, is reached in the strange episode Máximo recalls of his frequent childhood visits to a ruined local monastery, St. Peter of Villanueva. At the top of the decaying Byzantine column of the portico appear carvings of some grotesque figures over which Máximo and his young friends daub paint or of which they mutilate isolated features. Ironically, the most destructive boy is now the chairman of the provincial committee on monuments, a wise and respected individual! One particular set of figures, a king leaving his palace and queen and then being devoured in a forest by a bear, so impresses Máximo's young mind that he has nightmares after each visit.[11] The carved figures still affect him as an adult, for whenever he sees a bear, he believes that he is a king ready to be devoured, or alternatively, when he sees a king, he feels like a bear ready to gobble him up! This art work, like the mountains, is an intimate part of Máximo's being: "I have with them the relationship of configuration, not substance, that the cast has with its mould ... I feel as if the capitals which reproduced that terrible story are printed or traced in my encephalic mass" (*OC*, IV, 1188). The irony, of course, is that this visual art example is no work of beauty; in shape and appearance it is grotesque, its subject-matter is chilling, tragic. The ultimate relevance of this art object, so heavily embedded into the text at the early point of Chapter II, is that it foreshadows Máximo's own experience as an art object (fictional protagonist): he will be devoured, not by his mission to spread the benefits of philosophy and to educate modern youth, as he initially and idealistically believes, but by an all-consuming romantic passion for Irene, the girl-friend of his pupil, Manuel Peña (a significant name in the context of our argument: it means Mr. Rock, the star pupil whom Máximo intends to shape into a rational human being).

Máximo is given this task, the main development of the novelistic action, as the result of an interview with Peña's mother, the flamboyant Doña Javiera, in Chapter III. This interview also succeeds in confirming Máximo's visual art status. Doña Javiera has such a high regard for Máximo's intellectual ability that she has cut out and framed a portrait which had been recently reproduced in an illustrated review; it now replaces her engraving of St. Anthony. Moreover, she claims that Máximo is equal to the four great figures of world culture represented by plaster busts in the study where this interview takes place. For Doña Javiera, Máximo is the fifth "father of learning" beside Demosthenes, Quevedo, Marcus Aurelius and Julián Romea. R. M. Price has explained the aptness of these plaster figures: all four represent elements that are given some prominence in Máximo's relationship with Manuel and Irene: oratory, literary and

---

[11] Galdós probably culled the details of this legend from a copy of the *Semanario Pintoresco Español* in his library.

other satire, active stoic philosophy and drama.[12] I prefer to interpret the plaster busts as an ironic comment on Manso's unsuccessful attempts to instruct and fashion the personality of Peña. He is a failure as a moral and spiritual teacher; he does not achieve the status of those bust figures. Doña Javiera's fanciful comparison fails to take into account – through ignorance – the provenance of these art objects: Máximo's mother had purchased them at random in a plasterer's store; there had been no logical criterion, apart from size, in their selection. Javiera's plastification of Máximo, besides being very amusing, is also highly inappropriate, for he has only the outer appearance of a figure of universal wisdom. Furthermore, aesthetic musings on the beauty of Javiera a short while earlier have to be taken into account. When she had entered his study, he had been in the middle of writing a prologue and notes for a friend's (note, not his own) translation of Hegel's *System of Fine Arts*. At this particular moment his mind is filled with a whole jumble of ideas on aesthetics, but Javiera's unexpected entry immediately dispels the chaos and brings clarity to his mind; Javiera, Manso loudly proclaims, is "aesthetic authority" in person. That day she looked particularly attractive with her jewels and black mantilla setting off her pallid complexion. Yet, like those three famous female figures in the Louvre portraits Galdós had analysed in his *La Nación* article fifteen years previously, as we noted in Part I, Peña's mother has one imperfection when judged by normal standards of aesthetics: she is fat! However, Máximo is moved by the incongruity to ponder the prospects of adding another chapter to the Hegel translation, on irony in the fine arts! So, in this third chapter that launches the momentous relationship of Manso with Manuel, and eventually Irene, ironic comparisons to visual art forms infuse the whole interview: Máximo is famous (in Javiera's eyes) for his newspaper photo and status as a hypothetical bust figure; Javiera seems to Máximo's eyes an ironic distortion of the model of female beauty as established by such philosophers of aesthetics as Hegel. The main

---

[12] "The five 'padrotes' in Pérez Galdós' *El amigo Manso*", *Philological Quarterly*, 48 (1969), 234-46. Doña Cándida, an old friend of the Manso family, strongly resembles the bust of Marcus Aurelius in Máximo's study. Because of her increasing debt, she is forced to sell off some paintings by Ribera and Paul de Vos. Later in her new apartment, paid for by Máximo's brother, José María, she immediately decorates the walls with engravings of two famous canvases: Turner's "Sinking of the Intrepid Before the Cliffs at St. Malo" and the "Sinking of the Medusa" by Gericault. Both paintings seem to be pertinent pictorial commentaries on her regular propensity to incur financial insolvency!

point of this double ironic comparison is surely to bring out Máximo's blinkered vision when directed to his own character (he is, after all, congenitally myopic and needs to wear gold-rimmed glasses). He may be very perceptive about Javiera's disproportionate body, the miniature art work (cardboard-box palaces or wire-frame models of El Escorial) executed by her current lover, Ponce, or later the gaudy colours and decoration of her new house. But he is, amazingly, silent on Javiera's hyperbolic comparison: is it that he is flattered by such a comparison? Its high comedy, so apparent to any reader, is completely ignored by this supposedly introspective narrator-protagonist. If he is blinded by the calculated flattery of his neighbour, then his acceptance of her commission to educate her son, with all its consequences, must stem from that fascination with Javiera's imperfectly aesthetic appearance and her elevation of him to an icon status.

Máximo's tutoring of Javiera's only son begins optimistically and again with the metaphor of art: "The pleasure I experienced [with my pupil] was like that of the sculptor who is the recipient of a perfect block of the finest marble from which to carve a statue" (*OC*, IV, 1193). An integral part of the curriculum is the frequent visit to the Prado museum to view and appreciate directly the great works of art. This Krausist practice, which Galdós had also incorporated in *La desheredada* with disastrous results for Isidora, is successful in *El amigo Manso*, with Peña admitting that although he had been to the Prado before he had never "viewed" the paintings in the way Máximo now teaches him. Unfortunately, this promising beginning to the course of tuition soon gives way to loss of interest on Manuel's part and finally to a complete separation from his master, since Manuel gains quick success with his good looks and eloquent speech in those spheres of Spanish society (politics and social gatherings) that put great store by appearances rather than spiritual depth.

Máximo discontinues his character sculpturing as he, too, is sucked into the ebb and flow of social reality away from his ivory tower of philosophical meditation. He even comes to reject his belief in an objective definition of aesthetics, maintaining that each individual's personal preferences dictate artistic appreciation. This realization now greatly affects his view of Irene. No longer for him the incarnation of beauty and reason or the graphic representation of the allegorical figures of Theology and Astronomy, Irene has some important blemishes: her nose is scandalously incorrect, her eyebrows are too thin to allow a proper projection of her melancholic eyes and her mouth is bigger than it should be (*OC*, IV, 1218). Máximo then discovers to his horror that this individual image of beauty has human passions and weaknesses like anybody else. This nasty realization, hastening his return to the world of pure spirit, Limbo, and bringing the novel to a close, first prompts an important outburst of disillusionment from Máximo to Doña Javiera: "What you see, Doña Javiera, is the least important part of existence. Everything that is great, all laws, all causes, all active elements are invisible. Our eyes, are they anything more than microscopes?" (*OC*, IV, 1308). In his love for Irene, Manso has been deceived by the visual appearance of her artistic beauty: the philosopher of ideas has fallen victim to his traditional enemy, corporal beauty, with its deceitful image of stasis and permanence. The implications both of that early incongruous use of the language of sculpture and of the nightmares of the monastery carvings have now been realized. Fortunately, Manso, like José María in *Lo prohibido*, is able to escape the tyranny of his eyes by dying. For less privileged characters, there is no such escape. As Galdós had shown in his earlier description of the cloisters of the abbey of Santillana del Mar in his "Cuarenta leguas por Cantabria", death brings its own realization of the eye's vain obsession with artistic forms.

Tormento

Like its predecessors in our second group, Galdós' fourth novel in the "contemporary series" contains an important visual art form inserted in its opening chapters, the purpose of which is to guide the reader in his or her interpretation of the rest of the novel.

After an initial dramatized dialogue between the hack writer, José Ido del Sagrario, and the young serving boy, Felipe Centeno, the scene moves to the new house of the Bringas family, where husband and wife are busily engaged in arranging their furniture. These two characters are pointedly given physical appearances that are related to the visual arts: Rosalía Bringas with her prominent bosom is likened to one of Peter Paul Rubens' classical figures. The affiliation of her husband, the civil servant, Francisco, is more contemporary: he can be recognized by all readers familiar with the photographs or etchings of the great nineteenth-century French statesman, Adolphe Thiers. The resemblance is purely exterior: Rosalía has none of the allegorical representativeness of Rubens'

Greek goddesses, nor even the spirituality of some of the heroines of the great seventeenth-century playwright, Calderón de la Barca, whose name she bears and to whom she believes she is related. For his part, Francisco lacks all the intellectual insight of the great French politician. The art comparisons of both are further downgraded by the unpoetic or unartistic circumstances in which they are first seen: clouds of dust and piles of furniture momentarily conceal their celebrated figures.

However, when all the moving is completed, they both stand back and appreciate the artistic arrangement of furniture, amongst which the family's collection of paintings receives special attention. There had been some dispute as to where certain canvases should be hung: while Francisco opines that a picture of Christ should go in the place of honour in the main room, Rosalía is adamant that this position should be occupied by the canvas of the Queen (Isabel II). At first the regal picture appears lopsided and has to be straightened, a small detail that would have been without significance had not there been an exchange of opinion about the two leading monarchist politicians of the period, O'Donnell and Narváez. It now becomes clear that through this incidental talk on the paintings Galdós is able to suggest the totteriness of the Isabelline regime: both political leaders were to die soon after this scene (November 1867), leaving the Queen virtually undefended against the revolutionary coalition which was to overthrow her in September of the following year.

Moreover, with the mention of the sovereign's portrait Galdós is also able to suggest the similarity between the physical features of Rosalía and her royal mistress, a parallelism that is enlarged throughout *Tormento* and its sequel, *La de Bringas*, to include moral resemblances too. Likewise Francisco's concern for the picture of Christ is a subtle suggestion of a link between him and the Royal Consort, Francisco de Asís, a parallel that is also consolidated in the remaining pages of the two novels. Justification for this dual parallelism is provided by a final detail in this opening scene of *Tormento*: as the couple admire their new drawing-room, with the art objects all neatly arranged, Francisco exclaims that the room is the perfect image of the famous room in the Madrid Royal Palace called the Gasparini Room. The paintings, furniture and other art objects consequently take on the status of royal art treasures. A key element in this romantic distortion of the Bringas' room is the lighting: the coloured candles create a magical effect worthy of any illustrated editon of *A Thousand and One Nights*. Yet this single room of elegant radiance has to be viewed alongside the remaining rooms in the house, which are cramped, small and poorly lit. Galdós is in fact deliberately contrasting the artistic, unreal appearance of the one against the dark, unpleasant reality of the remainder. Unlike the aristocratic art-owners in *La familia de León Roch* and *Lo prohibido*, the bourgeois Bringas strive to appear wealthy art collectors when they are not; that pretence is all the more fragile and temporary when it is surrounded by a contrasting reality of poverty and ugliness. This contrasting pattern of extreme radiance and darkness established by the discussion of the Bringas' rooms in this early chapter reverberates throughout the novel as an indictment of the superficial values and attitudes of this particular social class.

As befits two characters strongly associated with a number of art forms, Rosalía and Francisco are made to appear within this chiaroscuro pattern from time to time. Normally Francisco is trying to economize on the use of light to balance the precarious family budget. On one occasion when in conversation with his rich cousin, Agustín Caballero, recently returned from years of business spent on the Texan border, Francisco tries to enlist his financial support for his daughter's piano and French lessons. Galdós chooses this moment to draw a picture of his character carrying a lamp aloft from one room to another. The effect of the illumination is to reinforce the physical resemblance to Thiers: "... my Don Francisco seemed the Beacon of History shedding light on events" (*OC*, IV, 1488). The irony, of course, is that he is unconsciously shedding light, not on recent political events (well beyond his ken), but on the real reasons for his friendliness towards his cousin: he needs Agustín's money to maintain a social appearance beyond his current economic means. For her part, Rosalía loves basking in the bright lights of the theatre performances and the Royal Palace ball, but in the semi-darkness of her sewing room, coldly and unashamedly, she calculates the material advantages for the family of an absurdly impossible marriage between Agustín and her own daughter. In both examples, then, darkness is used to express the real attitudes and thoughts of the Bringas couple, while excessive illumination is used to underscore the physical and social appearances they would always like to display.

However, it is not the Bringas couple, but the main characters of the love triangle – Agustín Caballero, Amparo Sánchez Emperador (a distant cousin of Rosalía and the object of Agustín's wooing) and the dissolute priest, Pedro Polo, former lover of Amparo – who are consistently presented in scenes marked by this contrast between light and darkness and very often in a visual art context. For instance, the first opportunity that Agustín has to talk to Amparo alone in the Bringas house occurs one evening when Amparo is baby-sitting the Bringas children. When Agustín arrives, Amparo is browsing through one of the only two books in the Bringas house, the edition of the Bible published by Gaspar y Roig. Significantly, Amparo is not glancing at the text, but rather at the illustrations whose colours dazzle under the lamplight in the room. The plate she is looking at when Agustín enters is of an angel standing between two columns of light; another illustration she shows to Agustín is the portrait of a bronzed man. A few moments later Agustín himself draws attention to a third picture: "What about that plate? ... It says 'Who is this man who arrives from Edom?' ... Well, sir ..." (*OC*, IV, 1492). Galdós' selection of illustrations and his presentation of them are full of significance: the biblical figures are clearly attractive to the eye and only to the eye; no mention is made of their identity or of the text they are supposed to illustrate. In Agustín's case, the print proves to be a convenient diversion that enables him to avoid an embarrassing silence as he struggles to remember the speech he had prepared on his way to the Bringas house. Inevitably, the significance of the caption of the print for his own life-story and moral predicament goes unnoticed. As for Amparo, at this moment she can only appreciate the Bible as a picture-book. Furthermore, the plates Galdós has selected suitably suggest the handsome, tanned figure of a male remarkably similar to Agustín. The added impli-cation is, of course, that Amparo's attraction to Agustín is primarily based on an exaggerated visual appreciation of his masculine beauty. This suggestion is underscored when later, on a guided tour of Agustín's mansion with the Bringas couple and others, Amparo is overpowered by the dazzlingly handsome appearance of her husband-to-be as he carries a lamp aloft. Significantly, when Amparo tries to commit suicide later in the novel, her unconscious body is discovered by Agustín in a darkened bedroom of the same house: the immobility of the scene and Agustín's frozen posture at the door emphasize the exaggerated pictorial effect for which Galdós is aiming.

But if we return to the initial private meeting of the two lovers, we note that Galdós exposes Amparo's tendency to pay more attention to the glossy external pictures of the Bible than to the printed verses of the text, taken from the Book of Isaiah: "I am sunk in deep mud where there is no footing; I have fallen into abysses of water and the current has drowned me" (*OC*, IV, 1495). Amparo's eyes just glide over the text without absorbing its meaning, which is full of relevance for her own moral predicament at this point. Her inability to reveal her past affair with Polo will bedevil her whole relationship with Agustín and constitute the dramatic core of the novel. So, if illuminated biblical illustrations are the dream world into which Amparo would love to plunge, the black characters of the printed text represent the moral reality which she needs to perceive clearly and to ponder. It is all so easy to allow the eye to rest on the pictures instead of deciphering the meaning of the text. As at this time Galdós was also still very much engaged in editing the illustrated edition of the first two series of the *Episodios nacionales* – volumes VI, VII and VIII (i.e. six *episodios*) appeared in 1884 –, he was obviously very much aware of the possible tensions between printed text and graphic material in any illustrated book.

Before looking at more scenes which continue this pattern of chiaroscuro, it is important to realize that both Agustín and Amparo are presented with features that are related to visual art forms. Amparo has a classical beauty, far superior, according to Nicanora, the wife of Ido del Sagrario, who has seen her undressed in the changing rooms of the St. Jerome baths, to that of any museum statue; she is a special artistic creation of the Almighty. For the besotted Polo she resembles "one of those beautiful religious images which, dressed in velvet, with varnished face and handkerchief in the hand, represented with their eternal weeping salvation through repentance" (*OC*, IV, 1508). Moments later he is comparing her to a Goya figure on the famous dome of the Madrid church of St. Anthony. Refugio, her younger sister, has certain imperfections in her figure: a flat nose, a diminutive face and an oversized bosom, not to forget her missing tooth! Nonetheless, with this Venus Calipije figure, she is a popular model with artists. Her first appearance in the novel is, significantly, in a state of semi-nudity (she is getting ready to visit her artist employers-cum-lovers) and holding aloft a lamp to show her sister the way upstairs to the open door of their apartment. In many ways Refugio is a companion figure for her sister, not only putting into relief Amparo's more classical beauty, but also her more tragic moral dilemma.

As for Agustín, a black beard with white flecks and a tanned complexion give him the appearance of one of the Aztec figurines he has collected during his years close to the Mexican border. This similarity is reinforced by the vividness and verisimilitude of the art figures themselves. Agustín is a man who does appeal to Amparo (and Rosalía) through a physically handsome appearance and he clearly sets much store by the surface appearance of objects and people: the display of modern luxuries and comforts in his new mansion is deliberately intended to impress his bride-to-be. He also makes the equation between external and inner beauty: because Amparo is so beautiful and kind in manner, he automatically assumes that she is virtue personified. He may be shrewd and able to see through the ploys of his cousins, the Bringas couple, but he does not have enough insight, or mental eyesight, to penetrate that pretty picture of his beloved Amparo, as Galdós acutely observes: ". . . he could never read Amparo's heart, because for that kind of reading, the only eyes that see clearly are those of God" (*OC*, IV, 1565). This shortcoming emerges very plainly in a climactic encounter of the two lovers, once more in the Bringas house. Amparo is still unable and unwilling to mention her dark past to Agustín, and pointedly chooses the darkened rooms of the house for her conversation. Even when the maid lights the lamp in the hallway, Amparo takes her suitor to a more distant room in order to ensure her continued effacement in the dark. If she shows her moral cowardice in this successful protection of potentially damaging facial signals, Agustín demonstrates his naïvety by declaring, with a great flourish, that, as a man in love, he has second eyesight and can perceive Amparo's virtuous character. When all danger of an embarrassing confession has passed, the lovers can once more bask in the limelight of their mutual adoration: after they leave the Bringas house later the same evening, they stop to mutter sweet nothings beneath a street lamp which illuminates the scene "with a soft and poetic light" (*OC*, IV, 1527). This insipidly sentimental romance, as Galdós calls it, needs its comforting illumination as much as the art work in the Bringas apartment so that appearances can dazzle and conceal reality.

If Agustín's modern mansion, with its array of furniture and modern gadgets, prominent among which are the electric lights, is the illuminated palace of Amparo's dreams, then Polo's shabby, dark, dusty abode at the top of a flight of stairs that seems like an inverted cistern is the hut of her past reality. In response to Polo's plea for help, Amparo pays a visit and immediately brings light and order into the recluse's cave. By cleaning and polishing the priest's rooms, she is hoping to put an end to his claims on her affections. This does not happen and Amparo is forced to make a second, more desperate visit a while later. On this occasion Galdós chooses to emphasize the resemblance of his characters to art figures and to bathe those likenesses in strong light so as to suggest their artificial pose. Amparo has been forced to hide in Polo's closet by the sudden arrival of his sister, the religious fanatic Marcelina, who is certain that her brother is still seeing his former lover. Marcelina, who on other occasions has been described as a carved church-pew figure and a graceless bas-relief, is now referred to as a Goya figure. Father Nones, who also arrives to see his old colleague, appears to have stepped out of an El Greco canvas. It is his suggestion that Amparo take his arm and leave the house in his company so that she will not be attacked or verbally abused by Marcelina on guard in the street outside. As the couple sallies forth, with Polo shining a light down the staircase, Nones humorously remarks that the two of them make a great picture, as if they were going to a dance in the centre of Madrid. Nones' banter, however, is very much to the point: the two do form a picture, a canvas, especially under Polo's lamp; but it is a picture that deceives none of the figures in the tableau: it is only a stratagem to enable Amparo to avoid the public hostility of Marcelina. For Amparo, the picture comparison is very apt: she prefers the pretty appearance to facing up to the dark reality of her past. Accompanied by Nones she knows that she cannot be attacked publicly by Marcelina. The charade keeps up the appearance of respectability and this is the pose that Amparo maintains until her final departure with Agustín for a life of cohabitation in Bordeaux. When Francisco Bringas arrives at the station to say goodbye to his cousin, he is shocked to see that Amparo is accompanying him; Agustín shows his cousin his companion as if she were a static figure in a picture, seated as she is at the back of the train compartment. This intensely memorable picture does seem to discharge the role of a book illustration, for at this point Galdós chooses to remark that a train's departure is like the end of a book. One is immediately reminded of the illustrations in the Bible the two lovers had glanced at during their first intimate conversation. To some extent and despite some personal suffering, Amparo does achieve her dream of material prosperity with a handsome, angelic man. She has escaped torture like the heroine of *A Thousand and One Nights*, whose scenes had been suggested by the appearance of art works in the Bringas drawing-room right at the beginning of the novel. Art can become reality, but at the clear cost of a moral conscience.

Fortunata y Jacinta

Galdós' masterpiece can be included in our second group of novels because it contains in Chapter II of Part I a reference to a visual art form which will have considerable importance for our subsequent reading of the novel. In the dense history of the Madrid dry-goods trade that occupies this chapter mention is made of the upbringing of Barbarita Santa Cruz in the confined doll-house quarters of her parents' store-cum-home. Her first visual impressions of life had been supplied by the colourful Chinese fabrics worn by the mannequins in the family store, and by the severe-looking, life-sized portrait of Ayún, the Chinese artist-creator of the famous Spanish Manila shawl. These dummies and portrait are the companions of Barbarita's childhood with whom she speaks and exchanges ideas; they are revered as if they were the Host at Mass. The narrator extols the Manila shawl as a work of primitive art: "To wrap yourself in it is like dressing up in a painting . . . the shawl would be a vulgar piece of clothing if it had been scientifically designed. It is not, *because it preserves the character of primitive and popular arts*; it is like a legend, children's tales, innocent and rich in colour" (my italics; *OC*, V, 20-21); it is "that delight for the eyes, that prodigy of colour, that imitation of a smiling nature, illuminated by the midday sun" (*OC*, V, 29). The danger of these passages is that they may lull the reader into believing that Galdós' only considerations in mentioning this garment were aesthetic.[13] The point to emerge most strongly from his long account of its popularity and decline in nineteenth-century Spain is that it has been a great commercial success for the family of Barbarita Santa Cruz (née Arnáiz). As a token of appreciation for the dividends he himself received, the Chinese artist-inventor-creator, Ayún, sent the Spanish firm portraits of his fourteen wives, portraits that emphasize the almost dehumanized nature of these women, "stiff and pallid ladies like you see painted on cups, with incredibly small feet and incredibly long nails" (*OC*, V, 21). In their exaggerated, almost grotesque features, the portraits offer a reverse art form to the supremely poetic beauty of the Manila shawl; furthermore, they are a token of thanks for the commercial success of the latter, not a celebration of its artistic merit. One art specimen commemorates another, but for extra-art reasons. The most persistent wearers of these shawls, subsequently enlarged and adapted by another Chinese

---

[13] Curiously, Palencia, "Galdós, dibujante", pp. 142-43, considers this passage as one of Galdós' best pieces of art criticism.

artist, Senqua, have been the women of the lower classes, who have maintained this colourful, traditional garment while their social superiors have adopted the drabber designs of North European fashions. Commercial exploitation of an art work for the benefit of the mercantile class is the theme sounded by this initial presentation of the "painting" that is the Manila shawl, and when transposed to the human level and the Santa Cruz exploitation of Fortunata, it becomes a theme that dominates the novel. There is one final ironic twist to this prominent sequence on dummies, the shawl and the Chinese portraits: in a novel subtitled "Two histories of married women" the gift of the portraits of Ayún's fourteen wives to Juanito's grandfather is not without significance. Juanito cannot, naturally, emulate this figure, but his extramarital affairs may be more numerous than those publicly narrated (with Fortunata and Aurora). Furthermore, it is precisely the financial success of the Manila shawl and other clothes for the family firm that enables Juanito to carry on his affairs. Thanks to the profitability of the Manila shawl money is no impediment in setting up the mistresses in their own furnished apartments. So, in *Fortunata y Jacinta* we have another variation on the pattern of art tableaux opening the novels of our second group: after the enigmatic frontispiece of the Leganés asylum in *La desheredada*, the language and masses of petrification in *El amigo Manso* and the regal canvases in *Tormento*, Galdós now erects a piece of fabric as the art motif to guide the reader in approaching the novel's meaning.

An early example of bourgeois exploitation of art work is seen in the market scenes in Toledo St., which is travelled by Jacinta, barren wife of Juanito, on her visit to the boy Pitusín, rumoured to be her husband's illegitimate son by Fortunata. Jacinta's mind is so preoccupied with the question of adopting this spurious son that, as she makes her way through the crowded stalls, she retains only a blurred image of the street scene, as if in a reversal of reality it were a theatre curtain moving before her eyes. The bright primary colours of the clothes on display are an instant visual attraction, but equally noticeable is the unique, bizarre sense of art demonstrated by the store owners in the display of wares: clothes are stretched over walls and doorways, and tailor's dummies swing mesmerizingly from the stores' doorposts. Moreover, the scene is mediated through Jacinta's bourgeois eyes which at this point, flickering with emotional excitement at the thought of seeing her husband's child for the first time, exaggerate these artistic cloth arrangements and confuse the dummies with real people. The emphasis on Jacinta's blurred perception of the artistic scene prepares the reader for her imminent and instant fascination with the doll-like Pitusín and his Murillesque eyes. She is typically bourgeois in her preference for the fanciful artistic appearances of objects, which for the impartial spectator or reader seem dangerously exaggerated.

The same point is made on Jacinta's second trip through the Toledo St. market. It is now towards Christmas and Jacinta has been happily preparing for her surprise presentation of the illegitimate heir to the Santa Cruz family. Although her viewing of the scene is no longer emotionally disturbed, the same pictorial impression of imposing artistic shapes is presented. Galdós adds some illumination to the scene in the form of enormous glass lamps, drawing attention, not to clothes as in the first sequence, but, more appropriately, to the mountains of produce on sale for the Christmas season. In the glare of the lamps, the arrangements of the items take on gigantic proportions: barrels of olives are stacked in pyramid formation, marzipan boxes form altars, and dates and raisins are arranged in triumphal arches with the names poetically inscribed on Spanish flags. The pertinent use of architectural forms (altar, pyramid or triumphal arch) conveys very vividly the stallholders' innate sense of art: "... they possess an exuberant imagination and to detain the passer-by and to summon buyers they resort to theatrical and fantastic means" (*OC*, V, 134). But it is imaginative art at the service of business: art has to be used to entice buyers and clearly the buyers of such delicacies for Christmas can only be aristocratic or bourgeois families like the Santa Cruzs and Arnáizs. The main point, however, is that these displays of produce are no ordinary feats of art, but the ingenious products of an imagination that is forced to go to extremes to attract upper-class customers, at times adopting methods bordering on the zany and bizarre, as when two sales-boys from a tailor's store shout out their bargains attired in morning dress and with blackened faces. Nature in the raw is indigestible for the bourgeoisie; it has to be dressed up and given an exaggerated artistic presentation and patina, just as Pitusín will have to be scrubbed and cleaned and his Murillesque locks combed before he is taken to the Santa Cruzs' for all to admire his visual resemblance to Juanito, or so Jacinta hopes.

In terms of individual appearances the Santa Cruzs and their friends are closely associated with the visual arts: Juanito's paternal grandfather had had his portrait painted by the great Romantic artist, Vicente López. Estupiñá, Juanito's tutor and guardian during his youth, has the face that all readers and viewers will recognize from the countless lithographic and photographic reproductions of the composer Rossini, though another similarity to a parrot and to Punch, the puppet, detracts from the original artistic comparison.

However, it is Juanito himself who in this circle is the most heavily identified with the world of visual arts, as befits a man who in all of his personal relationships strives to create an artistic effect and who believes especially in the inviolability of the fine appearance. It is significant that the first page of the novel, in recalling his student days, presents a shot of him sketching caricatures at the back of the lecture theatre. His sense of the picturesque and knowledge of art, put to use in the selection of paintings for the rooms in the family mansion, come very much to the fore during his honeymoon when he takes Jacinta on a trip around some of the most romantic and picturesque old cities in the country. Suzanne Raphaël has shown clearly how this is a far from idyllic honeymoon, with the question of his affair with Fortunata dominating most of the couple's thoughts and conversations.[14] What also needs to be stressed about this unusual trip is the way in which Galdós marshalls picturesque scenery, architecture, painting, and art metaphors to provide an incongruously glossy frame within which the more sombre reality of the couple's preoccupation with Fortunata is sketched. The two cousins' courtship had blossomed in the picturesque surroundings of the countryside around Plencia in Northern Spain: the hills, fields and ocean had provided a most suitable backdrop. Their honeymoon, however, starts on a far from romantic note: at three o'clock in the morning on a bumpy ride from the railway station into the city of Burgos. The next day the two take a guided tour around the magnificent cathedral, Juanito taking advantage of any free moment before altars and statues to kiss and hug his bride; they enthuse over the art treasures, yet they also giggle at this enthusiasm. The idyll assumes a more serious note when Jacinta starts to probe into Juan's sexual past. This happens at the moment they are walking down a straight avenue of chestnut trees. The narrator glosses the symbolism of this space with its straight unending lines: it is like the path of a nightmare, and indeed Juanito has to suffer the torment of his bride's inquisition. Later the next day, as they travel across Castile, it is ex-caricaturist Juanito himself who, under Jacinta's further questioning, notes the symbolism of other components of the landscape: if the

---

[14] "Un extraño viaje de novios", *AG*, 3 (1968), 35-49.

countryside now becomes his conscience, the train track with its dark tunnels represents Jacinta's scrutinizing mind. Juanito shows, then, a sensitive awareness of spatial arrangements and an ability to ascribe symbolic meaning to them. In Saragossa, as earlier in Burgos, he exploits the artistic ambience of the picturesque buildings to distract his wife's attention from the story of Fortunata: in the narrow, empty streets around the cathedral he smothers his wife with kisses.

The subsequent visit to Barcelona's textile factories, inserted into a smoky landscape picture seen from the heights of the Tibidabo, also interrupts Jacinta's line of questioning for a while, because once again her eyes are focused on art objects of a kind: in this pilgrimage to the manufacturers of materials similar to those on which the fortunes of their own families had been built, Galdós superbly stresses that it is the *artistic fabrication* of the textiles which appeals to Jacinta's bourgeois mind and imagination. Although at first she marvels at the manufacture of the dyes from natural plants and substances, she is absolutely fascinated in the Jacquard mills by the incomprehensible interplay of the perforated cartoons. It is this artistic environment which leads her to express sympathy for the lot of the female workers, just as later her bedazzlement with the artistic arrangement of goods and wares in the Toledo St. market will affect her attitude towards her husband's supposed offspring, as we noted earlier. When she tries to resume the interrogation of her husband on the train journey to Valencia, he has no difficulty in deflecting the most awkward questions by pointing out the great artistic beauty of the manicured and well-outlined fruit and vegetable fields unfolding before their eyes, as if indeed they were a moving painting framed by the carriage window:

> The sea-shore villages, situated between the blue sea and a magnificent vegetation, filed past on the left of the tracks. At intervals the landscape took on a blue tinge with the silvery leaves of the olive trees. Further back the vineyards added a happy note with the green finery of the vine shoot. The triangular sails of boats, the low white chalets, the absence of sharp-pointed roof-tops and the predominance of the horizontal line in buildings brought back to Santa Cruz's mind ideas on Greek art and nature. (*OC*, V, 54-55)[15]

Juanito's artistic senses are so aroused that he invents a striking

---

[15] Diana Festa-McCormick, "Proustian canvases in itinerant frames", *Symposium*, 36 (1982), 14-29, notes another example of this technique in *A la recherche du temps perdu*.

artistic image for the bird-populated telegraph wires that run alongside the train track: "They are like the stave of a musical score. Look how it goes up and down. The five lines look as if they are engraved with black ink on the blue sky, and the sky seems to be what is moving, like a half-unrolled stage curtain" (*OC*, V, 55). This ingenious art comparison soon receives its prosaic counterpoint: at the next train-stop the newly-weds lunch on a delicious dish of cooked magpies, the erstwhile notes on the musical score!

The honeymoon had been originally scheduled to end after the visit to Valencia, but the art lover in Juanito prompts him to add an Andalusian segment. Ironically, however, it is in the picture-postcard city of Seville (far more interesting than the flat, boring Castilian meseta, according to Juanito, who seems unable to accept straight, linear formations of any kind) and after a lively visit to a tavern in the working-class district of Triana, whose inhabitants "are very original people, innate artists, poets who seem to paint what they speak" (*OC*, V, 58), that Juanito, in a drunken stupor, blurts out to his startled wife the full truth about his affair with Fortunata. No longer are the ambience and examples of art able to sustain Juanito's attempts to conceal his past from Jacinta. The naked truth emerges at a moment when his artistic imagination is unable to function.

As has often been emphasized by critics, Juanito's acceptance of Fortunata is itself predicated on the need to adorn her beautiful frame with man-made artistic apparel. This attitude is first given philosophical expression by Juanito's friend, Jacinto Villalonga, and, pertinently, with the help of a visual art image that emphasizes the bourgeois male's own role as an artist: "The common people are like a quarry of marble. From it comes great ideas and great beauties. Then come intelligence, art, handiwork: they take out the block of marble and give it artistic form" (*OC*, V, 152). This philosophy, repeated in almost the same words on two other occasions by two other characters,[16] sums up Juanito's basic inability to accept Fortunata unless she is adorned with something, be it dress, customs or language, that gives her an artificial beauty.

Juanito Santa Cruz is not the only male of his class to hold this attitude to Fortunata, or indeed to use the same language of art. The retired colonel Feijoo regrets he did not make Fortunata's acquaintance earlier, for he could have given some artistic shape to this raw diamond. Of far greater importance is the earlier episode when Maxi

---

[16] Juanito to Fortunata (*OC*, V, 278) and Guillermina to Fortunata (*OC*, V, 407).

Rubín, Fortunata's impotent pharmacist husband, endeavours to shape his wife's character before their wedding by sending her to the religious convent of Las Micaelas. He sees these architectural confines, maintained, it should be noted, by the Santa Cruzs and other bourgeois families, as the crucible for the purification of a woman whose external physical beauty he can only compare to that of biblical figures he has seen in pictures or prints. The artistic re-creation of Fortunata by the Rubíns, then, is another bourgeois exploitation of the primitive artistic beauty of the working class. The careful attention to the architectural appearance of the convent and to Maxi's view of it shows, however, that this artistic process of shaping Fortunata's moral character, in its concentration on external appearances, is really a work of artistic destruction, the antithesis of what it pretends to be. Gaudiness of the architectural detail of Las Micaelas prefigures a gaudy spiritual creation. The convent is indeed typical of the new types of religious houses that have grown up on the outskirts of the capital after the loss of Church property in the centre due to the Disentailment policies carried out by Liberal Governments in the 1830s and the 1850s. Galdós shows righteous indignation against the poor architectural style of these religious structures, funded by donations from the faithful. Speed and cheapness of construction have produced brick edifices with touches of Gothic or Mudéjar style on the outside, and flashy, decorated plaster, imitating the style of the Lourdes basilica, on the inside. The establishments are kept clean and tidy, but architecturally they are a deplorable mess. This neat and clean appearance, however, is one advantage they possess over the old plaster-covered churches of the city centre which Galdós had criticized over twenty years earlier in his *La Nación* articles. The "sanitization" or cleaning of art object Fortunata is carried out, therefore, in an institution that believes in the "sanctity of the broom, water and soap" (*OC*, V, 227), but which is, architecturally speaking, a calamity: the temporary chapel has plaster walls like those to be found in the bedroom of most private houses in Madrid (after all, the building was formerly a private residence); the altar is painted a glossy white and gold, the colours usually associated with shop dummies; the paintings on the walls of the convent's reception-room are the work of the same artist responsible for the far from distinguished portrait of Doña Lupe's husband in the house that later in the novel will serve as another prison for Fortunata. In detailing this gaudy, transitional, makeshift architecture, Galdós is suggesting that the hopes of the Rubín family for Fortunata's permanent moral reshaping in this ambience might be overly optimistic.

The transitional status of the building is repeatedly brought to the reader's attention by the accounts of the construction taking place in its precincts. In particular, on one side of the convent, a new wall is being added: a spiritual creation is paralleled, therefore, by an architectural creation.[17] But in actual fact the construction of this wall also happens to be an act of artistic destruction. In the first instance each new line of bricks gradually obliterates the sight of the beautiful landscape to be seen from the city limits, especially in the setting sun: "It seemed as if the builders, as they laid each row of bricks, were not constructing, but blotting out something. The panorama was disappearing upwards, like a world that was sinking ... Finally the roof of the church swallowed up everything and the only thing you could see was the brightness of dusk, the day's tail dragged along the sky" (*OC*, V, 241). Even more disconcerting is the separation of the inmates from the world outside: the wall cuts them off from the rest of society and normal life. This separation is keenly felt by Fortunata and other inmates, but also by her husband-to-be, whose reaction to his wife's spiritual reconstruction is transmitted, in part, by an aesthetic response to the landscape and the architectural construction taking place at the convent. As the wall rises more each day Maxi is forced to retreat further into the distance to catch some glimpse of Fortunata in the yard of the convent. This area of wastelands straddling the city limits, with the occasional tile factory, cemetery and mounds of manure as well as the hut of the excisemen, offers a gloomy contrast to the more poetic and pictorial view of the distant landscape of the beautiful Sierra de Guadarrama with "its strokes of intense blue and dabs of white snow" (*OC*, V, 232). From the distance of the squalid wastelands, the convent of Las Micaelas forms part of this majestic skyline which enchants Maxi. Another source of fascination for his eyes is the convent's water pump which rises over the garden walls. Apart from the obvious sexual connotations of this instrument,[18] there is also an important art simile: it

---

[17] Ortiz Armengol, "El convento", p. 7, notes that the architecture of Las Micaelas is more modest than that of some other religious houses. In an article for *La Prensa* of January 1884, well over a year before he started writing *Fortunata y Jacinta*, Galdós had also remarked that the imposing walls of the new Modelo prison in Madrid when viewed from the heights of Vallehermosa "were an image of public punishment, represented in the synthetic plasticity of the architectural mass" (*CP*, 47). Galdós was very quick – like Juanito! – to read moral symbolism into artistic forms.

[18] See Vernon A. Chamberlin, "Poor man's windmill: aquatic symbolism in *Fortunata y Jacinta*", *HR*, 50 (1982), 427-37.

resembles "a Japanese parasol whose convexity has been removed . . . it was so pretty to look at with its plume-like breastplate of white and red rods" (*OC*, V, 231). Here, then, is another oriental design to complement the Manila shawl that Fortunata and her peers wear, or another art object to appeal to bourgeois eyes. Maxi interprets this art object in two distinct ways: when it is moving, he believes it is signalling the message that Fortunata will soon be leaving the convent; when it is stopped, that she might stay inside forever. His illusions or fears are orchestrated, as it were, by the sound of stonemasons chiselling at blocks of stone in a yard adjoining the garden walls of Las Micaelas: "You would think that they were engraving in immortal tablets the legend that the heart of an inconsolable poet was dictating to them letter by letter" (*OC*, V, 232). The inclusion of this arresting metaphor is important for a number of reasons: surely it is no accident that this form of artistic creation should be situated right beside Las Micaelas; furthermore, another adjacent area is occupied by a factory that makes printing ink. Galdós could well be underlining the artistic act of creation that is being undertaken in the convent and that he is transcribing through the medium of the printed word of his novel. Moreover, the appropriateness of the mason's profession is obvious in the light of the metaphor Juanito and his social circle use to refer to the primitive beauty of Fortunata and her class and, in her moments of anger at the duplicity of Juanito, Fortunata often wishes she had fallen in love with a stonemason rather than a middle-class heir to a family fortune. But the point of Galdós' inclusion of these realistic details is surely to relate the masons' work to the mental mood of Maxi: it is his distress, not that of Fortunata, that he believes is the subject of the masons' chiselling. The panoramic view of the convent, the observation of the Japanese parasol of a water pump and now the distant audition of the masons' creation are all subject to the personal interpretation of Maxi: the artistic dimension of those visions and interpretations conveys, not only the artificial nature of the spiritual re-creation of Fortunata in Las Micaelas, but also the personal, inauthentic distortion of that process by the bourgeois character who believes he stands to benefit most from it.

So far, we have insisted on the exploitation of the common people's innate beauty or wealth of ideas by the ruling middle class. But the inevitable corollary of this argument is that the working-class members themselves are a party to this exploitation, coming to adopt the attitudes of the bourgeoisie and, in so doing, becoming their unconscious parodists. This is a function discharged by José Ido del Sagrario, sometime concocter of sentimental historical novels and now a minor practitioner of the visual arts as a decorator of mass cards. Like his social superiors, Maxi and the Santa Cruz honeymooners, Ido is a sensitive viewer of the landscapes he sees, in this novel that of the Sierra de Guadarrama. But his appreciation is entirely dependent on his moods: if he is feeling happy then everything is wonderfully beautiful; if he is morose, as is more often the case, everything is terribly ugly, for his impressionable retina, under these influences of the mind, always exaggerates the perceived images. In our example, early in Part I, Ido is feeling very elated after receiving a commission from Doña Guillermina Pacheco to transport some bricks for the orphanage she is building. Accordingly, he launches into an enthusiastic encomium of the structures to be seen at the city limits and of the distant mountains: "Over there, the Toledo Gate, what a magnificent piece of architecture! Over here, the gas factory ... Oh, marvels of modern industry! ... Then, the splendid sky and those distant views of Carabanchel, lost in the blue immensity, looking and sounding like an ocean ... sublimities of Nature!" (*OC*, V, 107). The circumstances in which this landscape is painted detract from its validity, and, inevitably, through comparisons with those landscapes that appeal so strongly to Maxi (in the same area) and to the honeymooning Santa Cruzs (in the Spanish countryside), project a parodic light on the reactions of those bourgeois characters.

Ido's namesake, José Izquierdo, like his niece Fortunata, is the proud possessor of a handsomely attractive body which is eventually responsible for his becoming the most famous and prosperous of artist's models.[19] For a man whose account of his prominent role in recent political events is a fabrication of untruths and who has unsuccessfully tried to sell Pitusín to Jacinta and the Santa Cruz family as Juanito's son, there is great irony in his subsequent celebrity as the perfect model for such famous figures of world or biblical history as the Duke of Alba or the Penitent Thief.[20] The pleasure Izquierdo enjoys in this occupation is, in large measure, due

---

[19] In an article for *La Prensa* as he was writing *Fortunata y Jacinta*, Galdós complained of the poor quality of models currently employed by Spanish painters (*CP*, 247).

[20] There is also irony in the fact that the vogue for ancient historical subjects in contemporary Spanish painting was being rigorously denounced by Galdós in his art reviews for *La Prensa* before and after the composition of this passage in *Fortunata y Jacinta*, as we saw in Part I of this study.

to the financial reward he receives for posing. He is exploiting the "treasures of lines" (*OC*, V, 125) in his body, as Guillermina terms his great asset. Art is the means by which he satisfies his craving for fame and wealth. But this exploitation is the suggestion of the aristocratic Guillermina, who backs up this idea with some practical help: it is the waving of Guillermina's calling card that secures Izquierdo an entrée into the world of Madrid art studios. Even more to the point is the reason for this gesture on Guillermina's part: it is her opportune solution to the hoax Izquierdo has practised on Jacinta; by making this obviously productive move, Guillermina is hopeful that Izquierdo will give up his claim. Izquierdo's career as a model is, then, like the primitive painting of the Manila shawl, an exploitation on the part of the Santa Cruz circle for their own benefit: to extricate themselves, and particularly Jacinta, from a vexing and potentially embarrassing situation. This arousal of Izquierdo's artistic vocation, therefore, plays an important part in the change of the plot's direction in Part I.

Equally important is the role discharged by Izquierdo's activities as an artist's model in determining the novel's dénouement in Part IV. Now, ironically, he will be the unwitting agent who sets in motion the process by which an authentic heir is finally introduced into the Santa Cruz family. As Fortunata is in an advanced stage of pregnancy and somewhat immobile in her apartment at the top of the tall building, No. 11, Cava de San Miguel, her uncle helps by running errands for her each day; but this is only possible during the free time (very little) permitted by his duties as a model. On one of these occasions Izquierdo is seen carrying home some dates, amongst other purchases, by Maxi who immediately recognizes this fruit as one of his estranged wife's favourite desserts. This particular fruit, along with other clues, will lead Maxi logically and correctly to locate the whereabouts of Fortunata and set in motion that train of events which will culminate in the presentation of Juanito's *bona fide* son to the Santa Cruz family. The demands of Madrid painters can thus be said to determine the most important conscious action of Fortunata's life.

Mauricia la Dura, Fortunata's companion during her stay in Las Micaelas, is another working-class girl whose natural beauty demands comparisons with figures from paintings. Her face resembles that of the Emperor Napoleon Bonaparte before he became First Consul. The comparison is accentuated when Mauricia lies dying, for some old reproductions of famous paintings of Napoleonic scenes by Vernet and Gros surround the mad alcoholic: "Who has not seen 'Napoleon in Eyleau' and in 'Jena', 'Bonaparte in Arcola', the 'Apotheosis of Austerlitz' and the 'Farewell of Fontainebleau?' . . . Mauricia completed that history exhibited on the walls: she was 'Napoleon in St. Helena'" (*OC*, V, 367).[21] The Napoleonic comparison becomes a reality, therefore, as Mauricia assumes the status of an art object, a historical painting. Also present at her death, however, are a number of traditional Spanish prints hung around the room; their subjects include Pope Pius IX, the famous Spanish ship, the *Numancia*, and a statue of Christ Crucified. The obvious antagonism between the two sets of prints representing the values of the two countries is intended to reflect the conflict between two opposite forces within this strange woman: on the one hand, her virile rebelliousness and opposition to all authority, a course she urges on Fortunata, and on the other hand, her conformity with traditional order and values, as her relationship with Guillermina demonstrates. The prints do no more, then, than graphically illustrate the conflict between natural impulses, a violent temperament, and the discipline of society, as dictated by her social superiors; the art work on display at her death could be said to represent the semi-successful attempt of the bourgeoisie and their aristocratic allies to exploit the native urges of Mauricia for their own ends, in the sense that their control of Mauricia's wilder impulses means greater security for the established order, in particular, that of the convent of Las Micaelas, and ultimately, of Fortunata's marriage to Maxi.

Fortunata, that block of beautiful human marble, first appears in the novel in the frame of a very considerable and imposing quarry: the fortress-like No. 11, Cava de San Miguel.[22] The staircase on which that explosive and emblematic first encounter between Juanito and Fortunata takes place has its own decorative art work scratched on the walls: graffiti by the children living in the building.[23] At the close of the novel, when Fortunata returns to No. 11, this plaster wall now has the appearance of an extended mural frieze with episodes from her life as panels: "From the doorway to the top of the stone staircase she saw her childhood painted in pictures like those in church on the Stations of Our Lord's Death and Passion" (*OC*, V,

[21] For reproductions of some of these paintings, see André Maurois, *Napoleon: a Pictorial Biography* (London: Thames and Hudson, 1963).

[22] See my "Fortunata and No. 11, Cava de San Miguel", *Hispanófila*, 59 (1976-77), 31-48, for an examination of the role of this building in the novel.

[23] See Stephen Gilman, "The Birth of Fortunata", *AG*, 1 (1966), 71-83.

477). These are Fortunata's own reflections, as recorded by the omniscient narrator; they are the product of a mind which has undergone a series of strenuous attempts to mould it to society's rules and expectations. Her artistic awareness at this stage is proof that she has absorbed some notions on aesthetics during her life's odyssey, amongst whose adventures are to be numbered affairs with two Catalan artists in Barcelona.[24] That burgeoning aesthetic sense manifests itself now in her desire to paint and decorate her new penthouse apartment: "It was necessary to whitewash the kitchen, plaster over some holes and enormous cracks to be found every-where, paper the room which was going to be her bedroom, and paint the doors" (*OC*, V, 478). This request, made to Estupiñá, agent and rent-collector for the new landlady of the building, Guillermina, elicits a catalogue of the merits of the building, not only in terms of its obvious architectural solidity (the stonemasons, the factotum re-ports, cannot make even a dent in the walls that seem made of diamonds), but also in terms of its cash value as real estate, currently at 35,000 duros, a not inconsiderable sum for Madrid in 1876. Estupiñá's retort reminds us that every art object, and especially this granite house, has its own price tag; even the art renovations Fortunata now wants to carry out within her own small apartment will have to be paid for by Guillermina, who has mortgaged the building to provide money for her orphanage. Once more the working class and works of art associated with it (here the castle-fortress of No. 11, Cava de San Miguel) are exploited by social superiors for their own ends.

In her self-imposed confinement in the top-floor apartment of this building Fortunata experiences some periods of happiness and is able to reassess her past life, putting its many incidents into the correct perspective, "in the light of reason, and from a distance which allows one to appreciate fully the size and shape of objects" (*OC*, V, 482). Below this perch of peace and tranquillity lie the equestrian statue of Philip III and the beautiful baroque façades of the Main Square. The picturesqueness of this area is enhanced one winter's day

---

[24] This is despite Juanito's disparaging remarks about her selection of paintings for their secret apartment (*OC*, V, 322), and her own modesty when apologizing to Feijoo for her inability to decorate chinaware like Villalonga's mistress (*OC*, V, 330). Stephen Gilman, *Galdós and the Art*, p. 374, laments that Fortunata's wedding party did not imitate the hilarious visit to the Louvre by Gervaise and her guests in Zola's *L'Assommoir*: "For surely Fortunata would have greatly enjoyed herself there." While that assumption is plausible, it could be argued that Fortunata had already been exposed in the period before her marriage to Maxi to the stultifying effects of third-rate paintings and architecture in Las Micaelas.

when a snowfall covers the square, emphasizing the horizontal lines of the four façades and the railings of the balconies. The statue of the monarch now has an ermine cloak and nightcap. A short while later, however, this "magic charm of the snow" (*OC*, V, 483) (and we recall this delight with similar scenes in the *Episodios nacionales*) has disappeared as a result of the dissolving effects of the municipal workers' hose-pipes clearing away the slush.[25] Picturesque snowfall soon gives way to the normal street contours, just as Fortunata's peace of mind immediately disappears when she catches sight of her estranged husband crossing the square amidst the puddles of melted snow.

Fortunata's susceptibility to Romantic escapism when gazing at picturesque landscapes is again evident when one day she watches the funeral procession of a Santa Cruz relative winding its way along, like other funeral processions, over the barren wastes of the city's outskirts towards the cemetery: "The sky, the horizon, the fantastic forms of the blue sierra [the Sierra de Guadarrama], mixed with the masses of clouds, suggested to her vague notions of an unknown world, perhaps better than the one in which we live; but surely different" (*OC*, V, 412). The procession-covered landscape matches the mood of Fortunata: she is disconsolate at the thought of Juanito ignoring her presence in the street when he returns to the city centre. Naturally, this is Romantic self-pity, much like Maxi's before the same majestic landscape and Las Micaelas convent, and immediately disappears when Juanito resumes contact with her. For a person whose physical figure is statuesque and whose most important dwelling in the novel is an architectural fortress, the appeal of the picturesque in natural landscape scenes is appropriate, yet at the same time it underlines her lack of a sense of reality when under the sway of love for Juanito.

This weakness appears strongly in her final action in the novel, the surrender of her baby to the Santa Cruzs, which is represented as the work of a great artist. Her "mischievous idea", to which she has previously made many cryptic allusions, now receives its concrete

[25] The use of the word "dissolve" here recalls a previous example of artistic consciousness on Fortunata's part: having been urged by Feijoo to return to the household of Maxi and his aunt, Fortunata has a nightmarish vision of her in-laws in which the lines and contours of one face slowly fade into another in the manner of the "cuadros disolventes" or "dissolving pictures" which, according to Ricardo Gullón, "Estructura y diseño en *Fortunata y Jacinta*", in his *Técnicas de Galdós* (Madrid: Taurus, 1970), p. 140, was a very popular visual art entertainment towards the end of the nineteenth century.

form and the language of the narrator becomes significantly plastic: "Into that idea, as if into a mould, she emptied all the good she could feel and think; in that idea she printed with an easy formula the most beautiful and perhaps least human profile of her character, in order to leave behind a clear and energetic impression of it" (*OC*, V, 536).

Yet once more, the metaphor suggests one thing and ignores another; it expresses the nobility, almost divinity, of the creation-cum-sacrifice, but fails to mention the mother's materialistic considerations: as a mother who is dying she is – naturally, of course – trying to assure the best future for her infant son, and that future will be one fully guaranteed by the Santa Cruz money when the baby is acknowledged as the family's heir. But by the same token the surrender of the baby means the removal of any chance for Fortunata's own family or class to benefit materially from the birth of the child, as Segunda had avidly hoped. As the situation finally resolves itself, not only do the Santa Cruzs obtain their heir scot-free, but Fortunata also donates her bank shares to Guillermina's orphanage, depriving the Izquierdos thereby of permanent economic support. The artistic body of Fortunata has indeed been used to the full advantage of the bourgeois Santa Cruzs, but also with the connivance of the human art work herself.

In closing his masterpiece Galdós chooses to remind the reader of his central argument about the commercial exploitation of art in a scene in which a visual art object is given prominence. Maxi and Segismundo Ballester, Fortunata's last admirer, pay a visit to the cemetery where she is buried. Both men gaze at the stone over her grave with its carved crown of roses and inscription, the final tribute of art to a statuesque beauty. The tablet is the gift of Ballester; had he more money he would have erected a marble statue to her memory. As at the beginning of the novel, when the Manila shawl had been exalted by the narrator, the question of the relative beauty of a work of art is intimately linked to money, its very existence dependent upon the availability of the latter. Art is a bourgeois pursuit; those of the working class who have any natural beauty are absorbed into the higher social circle and converted into art objects, fit for socially conscious eyes, and capable of financial evaluation and, consequently, of financial exploitation. This is a brutally frank statement on the economic realities behind the cultivation of a very seductive art form to which Galdós in real life had so often succumbed.

CHAPTER 10

PICTURESQUE LANDSCAPE

Doña Perfecta (1876), *Gloria* (1876-77)

In the novels of our first group (*La familia de León Roch, Lo prohibido* and the *Torquemada* tetralogy) visual art objects, mostly in the form of paintings and architecture, had been presented as a reflection of the idle vanity of bourgeois and aristocrats who filled their dwellings with these objects but who were, by and large, impervious to the relevance of the moral message the visual art objects projected. In the novels of the second group (*La desheredada, El amigo Manso, Tormento* and *Fortunata y Jacinta*) the visual art objects presented were of a slightly diverse nature (architectural friezes, coloured posters, colourful shawls, sculptures, as well as paintings and buildings). Furthermore, whilst their admonitory function was still directed in most cases to both fictional character (regrettably unheeding) and the real reader (hopefully more perceptive), very often this function was introduced in an initial sequence that appeared to suggest important ways in which the subsequent fiction could be interpreted. Now, in this our third group of novels we shall see how two novels of Galdós' earlier series, "the novels of the first epoch", (*Doña Perfecta* and *Gloria*) had pioneered this technique, but with natural picturesque landscapes rather than man-made art objects providing the initial art lesson for character and reader. Significantly, both of these novels were written at the same time as the Cantabrian travelogue, "Cuarenta leguas por Cantabria", for the *Revista de España* which, as we saw in Part I of this study, also preached relevant messages on the dangers of visual fascination with picturesque landscapes.

Doña Perfecta

The memorable scene in which the young protagonist, the civil engineer Pepe Rey, arrives at the railway station of Villahorrenda in the early hours one morning has often been considered as foreshadowing the effect his non-conformist actions and words will have on the people of the nearby community of Orbajosa and especially upon his aunt and future antagonist, Doña Perfecta.[1] Less critical attention has been focused on the careful attention Galdós pays to the pattern of colours and lines in this arrival scene and the subsequent horseback journey to Orbajosa.[2] The first words of greeting at Villahorrenda, from an abrupt station employee, are to the effect that no lodgings are to be found in this village. The employee is swinging a lantern as he walks down the platform "projecting geometric series of luminous undulations. The light fell on the ground of the platform forming a zigzag like that of water sprinkling from a garden watering-can" (*OC*, IV, 415). Two aspects of this description suggest that Galdós is probably wanting to compose a highly memorable verbal painting. First, the bright light of the lantern obviously stands out against the dark of the rest of the platform and produces a chiaroscuro effect which is continued at other points in the opening chapter: for example, after the employee with the lantern has walked off, Pepe turns around on the platform to see the shrivelled face of one of Perfecta's servants, Licurgo, sticking out of a black mass of clothes, and at the end of the chapter, as the train leaves Villahorrenda and enters a nearby tunnel, attention is focused on the black round mouth of the tunnel emitting a whitish exhalation. Consequently, this countryside landscape is seen in terms of black and white colours and geometric shapes. It might well be that as he fashioned this scene Galdós had in mind the famous picture of the English Pre-Raphaelite painter, William Holman Hunt, "The Light of the World" (1854), which shows Jesus with a lantern knocking at a door in the dark, an obvious allegorical painting of Jesus' call to each human soul. The Christ parallel is in fact suggested in the same chapter on other occasions: when the station employee retorts that there is no lodging in Villahorrenda,

[1] See J. E. Varey, *Pérez Galdós: Doña Perfecta* (London: Grant and Cutler, 1971).

[2] See Vernon A. Chamberlin, "*Doña Perfecta*: light and darkness, good and evil", in *Galdós (Papers Read at the Modern Foreign Language Department Symposium: Nineteenth-Century Spanish Literature: Benito Pérez Galdós, Mary Washington College of the University of Virginia, April 21-22, 1967* (Fredericksburg, Virginia, 1967), pp. 57-70.

which is an obvious echo of the greeting given to Mary and Joseph at the inn in Bethlehem, and when Licurgo tugs at Pepe's cloak, as Mary Magdalen did at Christ's as he passed through a crowd, an analogy, as we have seen, Galdós uses in *Torquemada en la hoguera*.[3]

The second factor in this station platform scene that suggests a pictorial effect is the emphasis on the geometric shape of the light projected by the lamp: the "geometric series" obviously refers to the glass divisions of the lantern, and as an image is projected onto the ground, these metal linear divisions become the miniature frames of the luminous painting, as it were. The comparison of the lantern to a watering-can also reinforces the geometrical pattern of light on the ground, through the vertical trajectory of the spray. Yet these luminous images are given an ominous character when it is reported that the lantern, as it swings to and fro with the gait of the employee on the platform, offers luminous undulations similar to the movement of a snake and also to the irregular pattern of drops on the ground produced by the watering-can, so different from the regular lines of the jets' vertical descent.[4] Neither light nor water falls on this Spanish soil with any reassuring warmth or regularity.

Galdós develops the artistic implications of this potent opening scene during Pepe's ride into town with Licurgo. What should have been a repeat of a traditional literary topos – a beautiful dawn breaking over a picturesque landscape with poetic names – becomes a visual Hell for the traveller: "... this countryside, which is Paradise to the tongue, is Hell for the eyes" (*OC*, IV, 417). The rays of the dawn sun intrude through "all the windows and skylights of the Hispanic horizon" (*OC*, IV, 418), just as the station lamp had projected its light through the square or rectangular frames of the panes of glass. The sun's rays do not fall on some lush, verdant pasture, but on a bleak, inhospitable land divided into a chiaroscuro patchwork of yellowish and blackish triangles and quadrilaterals, a

---

[3] Although Lily Litvak, *A Dream of Arcadia: Anti-Industrialism in Spanish Literature, 1895-1905* (Austin: Univ. of Texas Press, 1975), p. 16, refers only to a 1900 article by Joan Maragall that mentions Hunt's name, it is quite possible that Galdós saw lithographic reproductions of the famous picture years earlier in illustrated journals. The Christ analogy, of course, is ironic, in that Pepe is only a martyr to his obstinacy and sexual love for Rosario, not the spiritual saviour of mankind in Orbajosa. Furthermore, it is not Pepe but the station employee who is holding the lamp. This possible pictorial evocation is not mentioned either by J. B. Hall, "Galdós's use of the Christ-symbol in *Doña Perfecta*", *AG*, 8 (1973), 95-98, or Gustavo A. Alfaro, "Religious symbolism in Galdós's *Doña Perfecta*: Pepe Rey's passion", *Revista de Estudios Hispánicos*, 14 (1980), 75-83.

[4] See Jennifer Lowe, "Theme, imagery and dramatic irony in *Doña Perfecta*", *AG*, 4 (1969), 49-53, for other allusions to animal imagery.

beggar's cloak over which Moors and Christians had fought bloody battles for centuries and over which Pepe and Doña Perfecta will shortly do combat. If the lands surrounding Orbajosa are a beggar's cloak as the narrator suggests, then the city itself and its buildings are the beggars, and in this way the novel's major locale forms part of the harsh tableau that Galdós is anxious to paint. Aureliano de Beruete's real painting of the fictional city over twenty years after the novel first appeared is a tribute as much to Galdós' powers of pictorial suggestiveness in the landscape descriptions of these opening chapters as to the effect of the whole book.[5] The hallmarks of those descriptions, sinuous rigidity of geometrical lines and chiaroscuro colourings, anticipate and express the inhuman severity and antagonism Pepe will find in the people of Orbajosa.

The city's buildings are indeed architectural monstrosities: the castle has nearly fallen down, pieces of deformed walls form the base against which miserable hovels raise their frontispiece. The one exception is Doña Perfecta's mansion, whose five balconies looking onto the main street resemble five castles. A back garden, surely an oasis in the desert of the region, is where Pepe first catches sigh· of his cousin and eventual lover, Rosario, as she stands talking to a priest from the cathedral, Don Inocencio, who, with Perfecta, will be Pepe's chief enemy in the city. This garden encounter, with all its overtones of life and death, as Noël Valis has shown,[6] is woven into what we have established as the opening pattern of lines and light in two different ways. Firstly, the encounter between the two takes place at a distance, and as Pepe is riding by in the side street, he has to stand up in his stirrups and crane his neck to peep over the wall, a dangerous elongation, perhaps, of normal vertical lines that calls to mind those of the lantern's image on the Villahorrenda station platform and the angular division of the country fields. Secondly, Rosario is compared by Licurgo to the sun, which, when she sees Pepe, becomes a setting sun, as her cheeks turn red with embarrassment. An inevitable contrast arises here with the severe dawn sun bursting through the windows of the Spanish horizon that had greeted Pepe as he stepped into the Orbajosan countryside. Furthermore, there is a chiaroscuro effect: the glow of Rosario [the sun]

---

[5] See Hoar, "Galdós y Aureliano de Beruete", and Weber, "Galdós". Alfieri, "El arte pictórico", p. 79, reports that in a letter of 19 February 1880 Galdós' artist friend, Pellicer, announced he had made twenty drawings for a stage version of *Doña Perfecta*.

[6] "El significado del jardín en *Doña Perfecta* de Galdós", in *Actas del séptimo congreso de la Asociación Internacional de Hispanistas* (Rome: Bulzoni, 1982), pp. 1031-38.

against the black cloth of the priest's cassock. The incorporation of the two lovers within this web of sharply angular lines and chiaroscuro colouring bodes ill for their future survival.

These negative overtones are continued three chapters later when Rosario and Pepe, enjoying a rare moment of solitude in the drawing-room of Perfecta's castle-cum-house, are suddenly interrupted by the return of Don Inocencio from a walk in the same garden in which Pepe had espied him on his entry into the city. The priest's presence is felt in a visual art way: as a black shadow or silhouette standing before the frame of the French windows. For a moment the light from the garden is blocked out and, significantly, the sun's rays bounce off the dark glasses worn by this obscurantist priest. This strange silhouette of Don Inocencio is linked to art forms in the drawing-room: a collection of French prints depicting the conquest of Mexico by Hernán Cortés and whose prolix legends with references to a "Ferdinand Cortez" and a "Donna Marine" are "as improbable as the figures painted by the ignorant artist" (*OC*, IV, 428). The parrot, perched in his cage close to the French windows, receives the artistic designation of a caricature, comparable to the profile and silhouette of the priest, who finds the pet so delightful. Thus poet, priest and prints are linked by a common distorted shape that ridicules in turn those sharp acute angles of the opening light images.

The comic distortion of the priest's figure continues during the famous dream sequence in which Rosario relives a scene she had witnessed some time earlier. Vicente Gaos has correctly pointed out that this dream constitutes a second layer of distortion placed over the original scene (Doña Perfecta and her cronies huddled in secret confabulation), viewed by Rosario through the window of a downstairs room.[7] Inocencio now resembles a fantastic bird, the outline of his body taking the shape of a thick, ridiculous angular shadow (Caballuco, Perfecta's henchman, is likened to a fairground doll). These grotesque figures will later be responsible for the death of Pepe and the insanity of Rosario. Inocencio's continuing status as a grotesque art object in this nightmare points to his lack of humanity and consideration beneath the mask of civil humility. Nor is it inappropriate that he should be the spokesman of the opposition to the visual arts in Orbajosa. In a significant theoretical debate with

---

[7] "Sobre la técnica novelística de Galdós", in his *Temas y problemas de literatura española* (Madrid: Guadarrama, 1959), pp. 220-22.

Pepe after the latter's rather irreverent art inspection of the cathedral during a mass, Inocencio, whose face is now fittingly described as a cardboard box, sardonically pretends that artists, even though they concentrate solely on form, "deserve every respect. It is better to be an artist and be delighted with beauty, even though it is only represented by nude nymphs, than to be indifferent and unbelieving in everything" (*OC*, IV, 440). In response, Pepe, whilst savagely attacking the crude artistic forms to be found in the cathedral, does proclaim some important aesthetic principles:

> The great works of art, giving tangible form to ideas, dogmas, faith, mystical exaltation, realize a very noble mission. The aberrations of taste, the grotesque works with which a poorly understood piety fills the churches, also fulfil an aim, but that is a sad enough one: they foment superstition, cool enthusiasm, *force the eyes of the believer to shift from the altar, and with their eyes shift a soul which has a faith that is neither deep nor assured.* (my italics; *OC*, IV, 441)

If Pepe is arguing for the association of art and religion, it is interesting to note that Galdós had questioned this premise, albeit in passing, in his newspaper piece, "Las generaciones artísticas en la ciudad de Toledo", written six years before *Doña Perfecta*. Later, of course, he was to demolish the whole argument in *Angel Guerra*. But what is important about Pepe's words quoted above is that he states as a corollary to his main argument that bad – i.e. grotesque – art is a strong determining factor in the loss of a person's religious faith. In so arguing he is really showing how he attaches greater value to external artistic beauty than to spiritual faith.

The point is made with succinct humour in the chapel scene when Pepe, in attempting to seduce Rosario, bumps his head repeatedly against a statue of Christ! Finally, however, it will be the grotesque art shapes of Inocencio and other figures in Rosario's nightmare who will annihilate Pepe. The art-loving youth will be destroyed by the sinuous, grotesque caricatures just as the angular shapes of the fields in the countryside have led to the deaths of countless Moors and Christians in past centuries. The order for his execution comes from Doña Perfecta whose full portrait is strangely reserved until the antepenultimate chapter. For this otherwise unpardonable delay in presenting the physical figure of the main antagonist of the novel some justification might be sought in the structural parallel it forms with the lantern painting that had opened the novel. For when we do see Perfecta's body it is appropriately described as an art object and in a context of chiaroscuro illumination.

She is shown writing at her desk, her bust, face and hands brightly illuminated by the desk lamp. The rest of her body is covered in darkness. Surrounded by prints of saints or religious sculptures, Perfecta takes her place in the gallery of art objects. On her orders, Pepe's blood is now spilt in the luscious garden where the two lovers had tried to find happiness. This beautiful oasis is now assimilated to the rest of the parcels of land dotted around the Orbajosan landscape and which had offended Pepe's sense of aesthetic form.

Gloria

The opening landscape description in *Gloria* is presented directly and immediately to the reader, and is the antithesis of the barren, bleak landscape of *Doña Perfecta*. Here we have a truly magnificent picturesque landscape, one Galdós had personally enjoyed on his summer trips to Santander: that of the Cantabrian coastline. Yet our discussion of the non-fictionalized description of the same area he wrote (at the same time as *Gloria*) for the *Revista de España* ("Cuarenta leguas por Cantabria") noted the persistence with which he signalled out, not the picturesque, beautiful components of this landscape, but precisely its least appealing aesthetic features. The same technique is applied to some extent in this initial description in *Gloria*. But Galdós is now able to weave the topographical details into his fiction and at the same time to suggest important lessons for the reader's comprehension of the novel. However much Galdós excelled at landscape painting in words, he achieved much more when he was able to integrate that painting into the main matter of his fiction.

Gloria opens with the narrator travelling towards the town of Ficóbriga, whose location he fixes for the reader: it is situated on a flat coastline and surrounded by mountains in the distance. The odd cottages dotted around in the foreground suddenly bunch together, as it were, as if seeking mutual protection, and form "the most noble urban collectivity which history has called Ficóbriga" (*OC*, IV, 515). The note of apprehension sounded by the allusion to "mutual protection" grows when the narrator points to the most dominant feature of the urban skyline: a church tower whose unfinished structure is likened to a head without a hat, and two belfry windows compared to two observant eyes with metal tongues inside.[8] The severity of the simile suggests that the organization occupying this building, the Catholic Church, is a zealous watchdog of all it surveys, both of the faithful within the city and of the strangers who may come from afar, from over the sea and mountains, as Daniel Morton, the Jewish lover of Gloria, will come. The simile also expresses the importance given to physical eyesight in the contemplation of the surrounding landscape. It is a subtle self-referential device inserted into the narrator's own description of the Ficóbriga landscape in order to underline the fact that he is giving a description of the landscape as it first strikes his own eyes. Yet the simile also achieves something else: the belfry windows are not really eyes; if they are, they are empty sockets; does in fact the Church, whether as building or institutional organization, see what is before and around it? And, by extension, does the narrator see correctly or indeed at all what is really around and before him?

Coming closer to the town, the narrator again refers to the beautiful meadows and vegetation in the foreground, and in the background to the majestic sweep of the mountains, their crests wreathed with clouds that cover the deformed architectural patterns created by the sunlight on the sides. At this moment, the narrator suddenly turns his gaze away from this lovely panorama and stares at the urban scene which now is directly before him: it is a totally different landscape altogether: a rotting wooden bridge leads into the town over a river that is reduced at low tide to a trickle of water between mud flats. The houses at the edge of the town are even more wretched-looking: they are dirty and cramped, and it is a miracle that they are still standing. Ficóbriga seems as depressingly ugly and grotesque as Santillana del Mar and San Vicente de la Barquera in "Cuarenta leguas por Cantabria". Galdós has deliberately contrasted two very different landscapes: the picturesque, idyllic panorama of the surrounding countryside, and the ugly urban landscape located in the middle of that pretty rural landscape. Now the relevance of the eye simile applied to the belfry windows can be appreciated: a distant view of Ficóbriga in this picturesque landscape leads the viewer to believe that it is as beautiful as the surrounding countryside, but

---

[8] This reference did not appear in the earlier drafts of the novel. In the second version the phrase reads: "It is a head which lacks a hat; even so, it still raises itself proudly, observing and scrutinizing everything that comes before its gaze"; reproduced in Walter T. Pattison, *Benito Pérez Galdós: etapas preliminares de "Gloria"* (Madrid: Puvill, 1979), p. 207.

really the eye of the viewer cannot see the full picture from afar, and as in the case of San Vicente de la Barquera, the pretty landscape soon gives way to a countervailing ugliness. The lesson is obvious: physical eyesight is limited and cannot be trusted entirely, especially when confronted by picturesque landscapes, or, for that matter, any artistic surface.

This slow introit by the narrator is a pertinent preparatory lesson for a correct assessment of the opening scene of the novel proper, the contemplation of the distant horizon by the eponymous heroine. Gloria is gazing intently at the distant horizon of sea and mountains from the bedroom window. Her family house, like Doña Perfecta's, is an oasis of natural and architectural pleasantness amidst a desert of ugly structures. Thus, she is looking at one beautiful landscape from another; the ugly reality of the rest of the town does not interrupt her vision and she could be well forgiven for believing that the world and her world in particular is eternally beautiful. Yet she is not really looking at the picturesque landscape: her gaze, like that of the belfry windows, may be directed towards a focal point on the distant horizon, but she is not scrutinizing anything that is already located on that horizon. What she is doing is looking intently to see if a person, one particular person, will appear on that horizon: at this initial moment it is the figure of her beloved uncle, the Bishop, but one could also say that in general psychological terms she is scanning the horizon for the arrival of a lover. This impression, which will, of course, be ratified with Morton's subsequent arrival in a ship on the same horizon, is reinforced here by Galdós' initial concealment of the identity of the longed-for distant image. The narrator laconically hints at the danger in this intense viewing (probably a blasphemy in Christopher Fry's credo of optics[9]) when he remarks that Gloria's eyes must travel faster than light, for he can see only mountains on the horizon. And these are words of wisdom from a narrator whose own optical powers when confronted by a distant picturesque landscape have proved already to be somewhat faulty!

In the course of the novel picturesque landscapes become the Romantic backdrop against which the lovers visualize their ecstasy or despair, or in which their passionate or tearful scenes are enacted. For Morton, Gloria is beautiful nature personified:

---

[9] See his *Vision and Design* (London: Chatto and Windus, 1957), p. 47.

All the beauty of the afternoon, temperate and calm, had been concentrated in her person, as the eyes of a lover's affection perceived her; and she was blue sky, the sea, deep and full of poetic harmonies, the earth fresh and spotted with smiles; the gentle shade of the wood with its balsamic air, the light which at intervals entered through the openings in the trees, as through the windows of a cathedral. (*OC*, IV, 645)

Their secret trysts take place in a wood outside Ficóbriga which is characterized as a poetic Garden of Eden. When they have to separate and return to town, this action becomes a discordant disruption of nature's harmony. Like Gloria who had searched the Cantabrian coastline for the figure of her uncle, Morton, awaiting his beloved's return from a visit to their illegitimate son in Part II, stares fixedly at the horizon and although it is night believes that he can see her figure on the horizon:

Putting his whole soul into watching the horizon, he searched in the black immensity for a trace of the bird whose flight he had seen, and so great is the power of the spirit that he eventually found it. He did *not see anything with his eyes, but his curiosity, excited to the point of inspiration, was sure of the existence of a mysterious trail, traced by a heart running in search of its love.* (my italics; *OC*, IV, 645)

On her final trip to see her child in the country Gloria repeatedly believes that she sees his foster home on the horizon at each turn of the road. Thus both lovers are given to staring at objects without seeing them, their thoughts fixed on internal preoccupations. Just as Gloria stares at the Cantabrian horizon or at the bird-filled telegraph lines outside her window (with the birds staring back at her!), so Morton, racked by the problem of whether to become a Christian or not, stares at the waves of the ocean, which in turn stare back at him. Nature immobilized becomes the staring board for these lovers.

However, this picturesque panorama is utterly disturbed by the sudden apearance of Daniel Morton.[10] The traditionally immobile landscape painting loses its stasis, and its figures and components are animated by this infusion of dynamic energy. Morton's arrival will transform completely the life of Gloria, of the Lantigua family and of the town of Ficóbriga. The language of the lovers noted above shows how far what should have been a classical picturesque landscape to be gazed at for its beauty has eventually become a Romantic mirror

---

[10] Marie-Claire Petit, *Les Personnages féminins dans les romans de Benito Pérez Galdós* (Lyons: Université de Lyons, 1972), p. 374, brings out this pictorial contrast very well.

on which to write every hope or fear of the heart. Gloria, whose readiness for that development was evident in her initial horizon-gazing, illustrates the effect Morton has had on her life in terms of his position in this seascape, when, before her death and separation from her lover and her child, she dreams:

> Suddenly she saw the expanse of the heavens, the sea; but not the earth or place where she was. Everything was brightness, light, infinite day. Far away in the distance she finally discerned a kind of meagre bank, mountains, a tower and from that horizon advanced a man with the steps of a giant. As he approached he kept growing so big that when he reached her body [i.e. Gloria's] he touched the sky with his head. He passed by without seeing her and dashing into the sea he ran over her. He slipped by like a cloud. In his arms he carried a small human being, a boy whose eyes shone like black stars against the brightness of the day. (*OC*, IV, 688)

Morton has indeed disrupted the spatial dimensions of that beautiful landscape Gloria gazed at so often from her bedroom window, and the position of this harrowing dream in the antepenultimate chapter accentuates the disruption of the original image.

Daniel's arrival also has some disturbing effects on other art forms in the region: the unbalanced arches and windows of the town's old Romanesque, plaster-covered abbey where Gloria happens to be praying are shaken by the storm that brings Morton to Ficóbriga. Gloria takes refuge in the sacristy of Caifás where religious art objects provide a fitting setting for the comparison of Gloria to a statue of the Virgin Mary. When Gloria returns home later she sees Morton's body stretched out in a bed in the old wing of the house. On this, his first appearance in the novel, the Jew is also given an art-image identity; his face, as Caifás had foreseen, resembles that of Christ on the Cross:

> [It was] a livid, grief-stricken face, with some purple spots like bruises, with mouth half-open, eyes closed, the brow slightly knitted and the hair wet. The outline of that face was perfect, the forehead very handsome between dark, dishevelled locks of hair. Starting at the straight eyebrows, slightly arched towards the temple, stretched the sharp, aquiline nose, as if cut by a skilful chisel ... In that brief moment of observation, Gloria drew a rapid parallel between the head she was looking at and that of Our Lord in the abbey inside the glass urn covered by very white sheets of fine Dutch linen. (*OC*, IV, 542)

During the Holy Week ceremonies that take place in Part II, a great deal of attention is focused on the appearance of the abbey's statue of Christ: the head is a great work of art, superior to anything in Greek sculpture, but the most arresting features are its piercing eyes: "His black eyes looked at you with a gentle and deep seriousness . . . the huge pupil which sees everything and penetrates to the innermost part of human hearts could not have had a more suitable representation" (*OC*, IV, 609). Gloria, very much aware of the uncanny resemblance the statue has to her lover, cannot bear to look at it during the procession, whilst those citizens in the street below her balcony are transfixed by the beautiful face which seems to be smiling to His faithful followers in Ficóbriga.[11] There is, though, a number of ironic implications in this confrontation of statue and devoted admirers. Firstly, they fail to appreciate the resemblance between the statue and Morton; secondly, in their treatment of Morton the Jew they ignore the message of brotherly love preached by Christ, the figure represented by the statue; and thirdly, whilst staring intently at the Saviour's eyes, they make no attempt to interpret the meaning of that stare in any spiritual sense. Like the eyes of the abbey tower and those of Gloria and Morton themselves on various occasions, the eyes of the crowd are riveted on the artistic representation of that human optical instrument, without meditating on its significance. The eyes of the people are, ironically and paradoxically, immobilized by a simulacrum of that organ; art is superior to the natural eye and in turn assimilates those eyes of the crowd to its own substance. If Christ's eyes are full of intense human expression, those of the crowd are apparently devoid of insight or introspection. The point is proven beyond all doubt when the arrival of Morton and his servant on the scene causes a mêlée to ensue. The reverence the crowd had paid the religious icon is now contrasted with the fury directed towards the Jewish intruder, that human replica of the statue of the Saviour. Galdós brilliantly caps the whole sequence with an erudite comparison to a specific canvas by a famous painter:

> The picture by Goya, "The Procession Dispersed by the Rain", can give an idea of this scene. In one street, the processional cross was making for safety, without the help of the large candles. They were busily escaping down another street, carried on the shoulders of men, like guns by soldiers after dismissal from parade. The priest, waving

---

[11] Gustavo Adolfo Bécquer, *Obras completas*, 12th ed. (Madrid: Aguilar, 1966), p. 1223, in an article on Holy Week in Toledo noted that the statues standing on their floats resembled real people who look and see with their glass eyes.

his cape, as if he were going to swing it around his waist for an attack, shouted for the deacon. (*OC*, IV, 622)[12]

The visual art comparison serves to cast an aptly comic light on the whole procession and at the same time to emphasize that the cause of this scene and the antagonism between the crowd and Morton's party is an exaggerated respect for an art object. Excessive ocular attention on its shiny surface is at the cost of any inner spiritual insight or its application to the living replica of that art image. The human eye's fascination with beautiful appearances, whether of a statue or of a picturesque coastal landscape, causes the misreading of reality, that failure to penetrate the total reality before one's eyes. In the case of Gloria and Morton, their assimilability to art objects would seem to denote their own ocular shortcomings, albeit less reprehensible than those of the citizens of Ficóbriga. In short, in *Gloria*, as in *Doña Perfecta*, a landscape sequence serves to alert the attentive reader to the dangers inherent in the ocular appreciation of beautifully artistic surfaces, as well as to the importance of this theme in the subsequent narrative.

[12] According to Gassier and Wilson, *Goya*, Don Francisco did not complete any canvas under this title. There is one entitled "Village Procession" (1786-87), No. 253, p. 96, but there is no rain falling. Another canvas called "The Hurricane" (1808-12), No. 950, p. 265, shows a procession of people appearing to head for the shelter of a church. Galdós may have confused these two titles: he was not always absolutely precise in these matters!

CHAPTER 11

INITIAL ART FORMS, PICTURESQUE
LANDSCAPES AND LESSONS IN OPTICS

Marianela (1878), *El doctor Centeno* (1883), *La de Bringas* (1884)

The prominence given to the role of the human eye in the correct appreciation both of an artistic landscape at the beginning of *Gloria* and of a religious effigy in Part II of the same novel is expanded further in our Group IV novels with pertinent details about the organ's functioning. At the same time this optical discussion continues to be launched in the initial frame of a picturesque landscape or art object that, paradoxically, reinforces doubts about the validity of the ocular perception of reality.

Marianela

Like its predecessors in "the first epoch", *Marianela* opens with a description of a landscape that demands intense scrutiny on the part of the traveller. But whereas both *Gloria* and *Doña Perfecta* opened with landscapes that could be clearly seen by the eye, *Marianela* commences with a setting whose visibility soon disappears after sunset. An unnamed traveller is attempting to walk from the railway station at Villamojada across the hilly Cantabrian countryside to the zinc mines at Socartes. The scene could be described, then, as a fusion of the two that had respectively launched the previous novels. But what stands out in this description, as opposed to the other two, is the constant emphasis given to the function of the eyes in determining the advance of this gentleman's journey. It is learnt later that he is none other than the world's leading eye surgeon, or ophthalmologist, Teodoro Golfín. He is carrying binoculars and is forever scanning the horizon (like Gloria) for sight of the mine which, he believes, with all its plant machinery and buildings should stand out in the distance even at night. However, his eyes and binoculars (of even less use at this time) record nothing. When following the paths on the ground leads him to a complete impasse on a slag heap, he is forced to sit down, and petulantly blames the absence of the moon for his predicament. To show the complete uselessness of eyesight on this occasion, Galdós introduces a voice singing in the distance, which Golfín immediately associates with a fantasy creation of the imagination, and then the barks of a dog nearby. Hearing, not sight, will prove to be a more substantial source of help. For this famous eye surgeon there is additional irony in the fact that the master of the dog who sniffs his way towards the immobile doctor is a blind boy, Pablo Penáguilas, whose infirmity Teodoro has come expressly to the region to cure in an operation. Naturally, Pablo is looking forward to the possibility of seeing the physical world and praises eyesight as the most wonderful gift in the world. But in the circumstances of this nocturnal rescue of the immobilized ophthalmologist, such a viewpoint strikes a ridiculous note, and already suspicion arises about the advisability of the eye operation, a suspicion that will be confirmed by the novel's dénouement. Just as Pablo reaches Golfín sitting atop his slag heap, the moon appears in the sky, to the latter's relief, adding another ironic touch to underscore the limitations of the human eye in this nocturnal landscape.

The artistic dimensions of this landscape are strengthened when the party comprising the doctor, blind boy and guide (Marianela) makes its way through some exhausted mine shafts, which take on a pictorial chiaroscuro appearance in the moonlight. But the shapes of the first chamber, called "La Terrible", are not picturesque; quite the opposite, they offer the grotesque outlines of monsters frozen by death. In a second chamber rocks are aligned in a formation that recalls the shape of a shipwreck. In the moonlight, the illusion is complete. Pablo not only knows his way through this area without any guidance but he also likes it so much that he spends many hours wandering there; not an inappropriate place for a person whom Golfín had believed, on first seeing him, was a motionless, stone doll. These fantastic shapes are, then, not the result of careful artistic expression: they are the fortuitous result of man's mad scramble to extract the rich ore from the earth.[1] As the first manifestations of the activity of the Socartes mine these frenzied sculptures must cast a negative shadow on the value of this industrial work and the attitudes of mind of the person who directs it, Teodoro's brother. Both siblings are, therefore, identified with the scientific wonders of the modern world, but the value of those professional skills has been seriously questioned by these introductory artistic pictures. If one brother is an artist of the eye whose skills are rendered useless in a natural landscape, the other possesses skills that are directly responsible for producing grotesque art forms.

Pablo's status as guide to Teodoro in this journey through the mine excavations is the reversal of his normal passive role as a patient led around by Marianela. As the daughter of the town's former lamplighter, this young girl had, as a baby, been carried around with the glass tubes in her father's work-bag. Now she has a greater light to give: she illuminates the dark world of Pablo with her descriptive paintings of external physical reality: "He asks me what a star is like, and I paint it for him in such words that for him it is just the same as if he were seeing it ... *I tell him what is ugly and what is pretty, and that is how he finds out about everything*" (my italics; *OC*, IV, 711). This ability as a landscape painter is displayed for Teodoro's benefit when they reach the mining complex and she indicates the location and purpose of each building. But it must also be borne in mind that Marianela is physically deformed: an adult face is incongruously placed atop a child's puny body in what, according to one acquaintance, looks like an inverted image produced by a diminishing glass. The comparison suggests perhaps that Marianela's view of her own person may not be so accurate as her landscape painting, filled with topographical detail, was for Teodoro Golfín.

That early reference to Pablo as a stone doll is expanded in later chapters. He is now described as having a remarkably beautiful body; he is a living statue, the peer of any in Greek art, a blind Antinoüs. Like the statue of Christ in *Gloria*, he has beautiful eyes, put into relief by the ivory colour of his face. As Marie Wellington has demonstrated, there is some affinity, apart from just surname,

---

[1] See my "Egotism and charity in *Marianela*", *AG*, 7 (1972), 49-66. In his picture of the machines of the zinc factory processing the extracted ore, Galdós emphasizes the ferocity of their movements, despite the visual attractiveness of the kaleidoscopic interplay of light, water and earth. After the purification stage, the zinc is hammered into artistic forms by the large hammer; such is the sculpture carved by modern industrial machines.

between Pablo Penáguilas and Rafael del Aguila in the *Torquemada* tetralogy.[2] The comparison of both men's bodies to art objects reduces, to a certain extent, their status as human beings. They are beautiful figures whose value lies in their surface appeal to the eye of the beholder. When the blind man recovers his sight or has enjoyed it previously, then eyesight, "that gift which constitutes the nucleus of the human expression" (*OC*, IV, 718), may become a dangerous vehicle for the art object's narcissistic obsession with its own beauty. In Rafael's case, this stage had already been reached, as we saw in our first chapter of this Part III; but Pablo's egotism and narcissism are not yet much evident. Nonetheless, these artistic references constitute a clear danger signal that they might well appear very soon.

Our apprehensions about Pablo, and indeed Nela, strengthen in Chapters VI and VII, pertinently entitled "Stupidities" and "More Stupidities". Nela expounds some naïve, superstitious notions about the stars being the looks of the Blessed Souls who have ascended to Heaven, while the flowers on Earth represent the glances of those still in Purgatory. For his part, Pablo mutters sweet noises about his mate's extreme kindness, and following the line of thought generated by his father's occasional readings to him on aesthetics, he believes that the only true beauty is that of the soul. Yet at the same time he asks some alarming questions about Marianela's physical appearance. The two have gone on one of their walks into the countryside around Socartes and are standing before a beautiful natural landscape: nearby a wood with a reservoir, and in the distance lush meadows, green rolling hills and snatches of blue sea. This picturesque setting forms the frame for Nela's pathetic gazing at her figure in the reservoir surface and then in a small mirror. For the first time in her life she is tempted to feel some "presumption" about her figure against the visual evidence of the mirror image: " 'Me, pretty!', she said, *full of confusion and anxiety*, 'Well, the girl I see here on top of the pool is not as ugly as people say. The truth of the matter is that there are many people who cannot see properly*' " (my italics; *OC*, IV, 725). Her reluctance to face up to the truth of the aquatic picture causes her, contrary to her usual practice, to misrepresent the ocular reality in her verbalized description; she would really like to be as beautiful a picture (especially in such picturesque surroundings) as Pablo at this point believes her to be. Ashamed of her ugliness,

---

[2] "A symbolism linking *Marianela* and the *Torquemada* series", *Hispanófila*, 73 (1981), 21-27.

however, she cannot reject the suggestiveness of Pablo's vision.

Her ability to see external images correctly is proven in a strangely paradoxical way on another occasion when she is walking down a country lane. She catches sight of Florentina, cousin and future bride of Pablo, and believes she is the Virgin Mary, about whom she has dreamed the previous night. Of course Florentina is not the Virgin Mary, but Marianela is not mistaken in her visual appreciation of the figure before her, for, according to the narrator, Florentina is the living image of the Virgin Mary as her features have been transmitted by the great painters in world art from St. Luke to Dürer, Van Dyck and Murillo. But Galdós chooses one iconological representation in particular, Raphael's famous portrait of the Virgin, to fix the facial contours of his fictional character:

> The oval of her face was less narrow than that of the Seville Virgin [i.e. by Murillo], offering the pleasant roundness of the Italian one [i.e. by Raphael]. Her wonderfully proportioned eyes were serenity itself linked to grace, to harmony, with a glance as far removed from glacial indifference as from the exaggerated twinkling of Andalusian eyes. Her eyebrows were the delicate creation of the most subtle paintbrush, and traced a fine arch. (*OC*, IV, 745)

But then at this point Galdós chooses to pull the rug from underneath this serious-minded art study of Florentina, observing that she has a blemish (just like the three female Louvre portraits he had criticized in *La Nación* ten years previously): she has rather fat lips that conceal the finest teeth to have ever bitten Paradise's apple. Despite an immediate apology for this lapse, Galdós creates more havoc by saying that the picture of the Virgin by Raphael has been revered by both pious and impious generations. The point is obvious: the art work appeals to all mankind, not through the religious importance of the subject, but primarily through its artistic excellence. The implications for the aptly-named Florentina are obvious: she has only the surface appearance and not necessarily the holy virtues of the Mother of Jesus. Her kindness and acts of practical charity towards Nela are well-intentioned but lack a true appraisal of the girl's needs and really betray a do-goodism on Florentina's part.

As with her handsome husband-to-be, there is some aesthetic incongruity in her enjoyment of the grotesque art forms in the exhausted mine workings of La Terrible. Her comparisons, however, humanize the shapes and change the tone from grotesque to caricaturesque; for example, she describes one rock as having a toothpick in its mouth and smiling at the three onlookers. Pablo, still blind at this moment, makes some very sensible comments which in many ways sum up Galdós' opinions on the dangerous subjectivity at work in each individual's appraisal of a visual art reality:

> With the eyes you see a lot of stupid things, which just shows that that precious organ serves at times to present things in a disfigured way, changing objects from their natural form into another, false and artificial one, for in what you have before you ... there are no men or toothpicks ... but simply cretaceous rocks and masses of limestone earth, smeared with ferrous oxide. Out of the simplest of things your eyes have made a mess.

Florentina, rather perceptively, replies:

> You are right, cousin. That's why I say that our imagination is what sees and not our eyes. (*OC*, IV, 748)

Later, Pablo himself, once he has regained his eyesight, will be guilty of the same optical subjectivity. But for the moment this humorous banter between the couple hides a serious concern on Galdós' part: he is anxious to indicate that the imagination, that interference of the mind's uncontrolled eyes, subverts the retinal appraisal of reality.[3] Consequently, the doubts raised in the opening landscape description about the value of exclusive reliance on physical eyesight have increased in an alarming manner as the novel has progressed.

As the moment approaches for Golfín to remove a hard opaque crystallin, only the second operation of its kind that he has performed, Teodoro's enthusiastic forecasts about the merits of the operation (it will bring Pablo from the world of illusion to the realm of truth and reality) seem exaggerated. Likewise, the application of the metaphor of art – Teodoro's surgical knife now becomes the sculptor's chisel – seems to denote an audacious attempt to correct what is really a divinely created art object, the "compendium and abbreviated summary of the immense architecture of the universe"

---

[3] For eighteenth-century thinkers and writers, the imagination was an essentially visual faculty. Joseph Addison in his 1712 essay, "On the Pleasures of the Imagination", reproduced in *Eighteenth-Century Critical Essays*, ed. Scott Elledge (Ithaca: Cornell Univ. Press, 1961), I, 42, wrote: "We cannot indeed have a single image in the fancy that did not make its first entrance through the sight, but we have the power of retaining, altering and compounding those images." Galdós would not have disagreed, but the thrust of his argument in *Marianela* and the other novels of this fourth group is that the mental image is so disconnected from the retinal image that it bears no relation to reality. Moreover, Galdós would not have accepted Addison's other statement that "our sense of sight is the most perfect and most delightful of all our senses". The trouble was that the imagination often takes over the role of eyesight in people's appreciation of the physical world.

(*OC*, IV, 750).[4] Golfín is playing the role of God at a second Creation. The technical details evident in Teodoro's discussion of Pablo's eye problems with his father are omitted in the very brief reference to the operation, for Galdós is more concerned here in relating the all-important reactions of Pablo to the discovery of his new world of physical eyesight. The reader's earlier suspicions about the dangerous nature of Pablo's interest in the material and visual appearance of people, aroused by a number of classical art references, are now confirmed: once the bandages are removed and his spatial disordering has been corrected by the wearing of specially graduated glasses, he revels in the beauty of all he can see: " 'My inside,' Pablo said, 'is inundated with beauty, a beauty which I never knew before' " (*OC*, IV, 763). A very important cause of this excited reaction (and Galdós repeatedly brings attention to Pablo's nervous state) is his cousin Florentina, with her beautiful Raphaelite appearance. Pablo's remarks to her are significant: "I see you within my own eyes ... you merge with all my thoughts" (*OC*, IV, 764). In other words, he now erects the highly artistic beauty of Florentina into his criterion for judging visual reality. The world is now seen in terms of beauty or ugliness, as if objects and people were figures and objects on a canvas. He rejects an ink-pot as an ugly object, whilst a butterfly that flies in the window enchants him enormously. The serving girls of the village are ugly by comparison with his cousin. Appropriately for a character presented originally in terms of Greek sculpture, he prefers a print showing Galatea surrounded by tritons and nymphs to one of Jesus on the Cross. The concepts of utility, kindness and religion are completely ignored as he judges everything in terms of their approximation to the ideal of art beauty.

His reactions to his own beautiful, sculpturesque body are dangerously ecstatic: "They brought him a mirror and Pablo looked at himself: 'That is me', he said *with mad wonderment*, 'I cannot believe it ... Indeed, I am not ugly, am I, cousin?' " (my italics; *OC*, IV, 765). Dramatic tension now builds up as he searches vainly for Marianela, wanting to contemplate a person whom he has imagined beautiful in appearance because she is kind and considerate in nature. Pablo's fault is not only that he relates spiritual beauty to

---

[4] The remarks of Katherine Kuh, *The Open Eye ... In Pursuit of Art* (New York: Harper and Row, 1971), p. 152, are pertinent here: "As a universal iconographical symbol, the eye turns into both the observer and the observed. We not only see it in works of art; we see works of art with it. This duality makes for a provocative interchange, a constant dialogue."

physical beauty but also that he gives priority to the latter. At first this had occurred only in his imagination and only semi-consciously; now this priority is fomented by his physical eyes, both deliberately and consciously. Galdós captures this dangerous motivation during Pablo's troubled sleep one night after the operation and before he has been able to see Nela:

> Afterwards he managed to get to sleep quietly, but he was still tormented during his sleep by *images of all he had seen and by the ghosts of what he himself had imagined.* His sleep which began sweetly and peacefully later became disturbed and anguished, because in the deep bosom of his soul, *as in a cavern recently illuminated, the beauty and ugliness of the plastic world fought against each other arousing passions, burying memories and disturbing his whole soul.* (my italics; *OC*, IV, 767)

The references to the cavern of his soul remind the reader of La Terrible with all its grotesque shapes which, when blind, Pablo had found so comforting and pleasant. Clearly what emerges in this nocturnal scene is the exclusive domination of Pablo's mind by the dimensions and appearances of an art world. Even his memory of Nela, now fading, is represented in terms of a landscape detail, all the more fitting in view of their numerous idyllic visits to the countryside in happier times: "Until nightfall he did not fix his attention again on a point of his life [i.e. Marianela] which seemed to move away, diminish and erase itself like ships on a calm day disappearing on the horizon" (*OC*, IV, 766-67). As feared, the cataclysmic meeting between the two former playmates is an experience of stark disillusionment for Pablo and leads directly to Marianela's death. It is only Teodoro who, in the anguished exclamations of the penultimate chapter, realizes the folly of putting excessive reliance on physical eyesight in human relationships. The gift of eyesight to Pablo has destroyed a world of happy innocence that lived off the spirit, for the human eye, when directed by the imagination to concentrate on the beautiful, artistic appearances of people, scenes and objects, ignores and distorts the greater spiritual reality contained within.

Galdós reinforces this important point in his closing chapter where, as in *Fortunata y Jacinta*, he describes the tombstone erected to his eponymous heroine. As in the later masterpiece, this grandiose art object owes its existence to money: it is the generous gift of Florentina, partly to assuage her guilt feelings about Marianela's death and her own inability to foresee or prevent it. The money needed to pay for this stone comes from the Penáguilas estate, which, with Pablo's successful operation and subsequent marriage to Florentina, is assured of its continued prosperity. As with the grotesque sculptures of the mine excavation of La Terrible, financial considerations have played an important part in Pablo's operation and now in the erection of this tombstone for Marianela. With its beautifully carved wreath of flowers crowning the noble-sounding inscription ("María Manuela Téllez, who was reclaimed by Heaven on the 12th of October" [*OC*, IV, 774]), the magnificent stone slab stands majestically amidst the collection of rustic crosses in the Aldeacorba cemetery. Galdós' point is very obvious: this art work, erected by a person insistently compared to a pictorial image, distorts the reality of Marianela's existence for subsequent generations of townsfolk or visitors from other parts, as is all too evident in the account of the monument that is composed by some tourists for an English journal, very probably an illustrated one. The sight of the monument prompts them to concoct a wholly fictitious, romanticized article (entitled "Sketches from Cantabria") on the life of Marianela as if she were some aristocratic lady who had disguised herself, in good literary tradition, to frequent the company of popular types and is now immortalized in all sorts of poetry. The irony is, of course, firstly, that Marianela has been immortalized, not in popular poetry, but in the prose fiction of Galdós' novel; and secondly, that she is worthy of comparison with the daughters of the illustrious family whose name is engraved on her tombstone because of her charitable and noble character. If the plastic arts may deceive because of their strong appeal to the eye, the written word can expose that deceit and paint the truth, the point that Galdós was also going to make in the year after he wrote *Marianela* in the *episodio Los apóstolicos,* where in his picture of events at La Granja he had contrasted the external portraiture in the tradition of "ut pictura poesis" with the more probing, profound painting of human character required of literature. Thus, in one final superb flourish, Galdós is able to tie his novel and its literary format to the whole question of the correct or incorrect vision of reality when physical eyes are attracted by a visual art object of imposing appearance.

El doctor Centeno

Although written five years after *Marianela* and forming part of "the contemporary series", *El doctor Centeno* is linked to its predecessor in our fourth group by two important factors. First, the protagonist, Felipe Centeno, is a secondary character in *Marianela* who is selected by Galdós to close the novel as he promises to write the story of the youth in another novel. Galdós keeps his word and so *El doctor Centeno* can be considered the sequel to *Marianela*. But of greater importance is the fact that both in the closing lines of *Marianela* and the opening of *El doctor Centeno* Galdós pertinently employs the language of vision, thereby suggesting that both novels treat the same important theme – the correct appreciation of reality. This is also underlined by the use of the visual arts either in concrete objects or as components of similes and metaphors. Galdós enjoins his readers of *Marianela* to turn their eyes elsewhere, to search for another human being (i.e. after Marianela's story) who is so small that he can hardly be seen: ". . . he is an imperceptible insect, smaller on the face of the earth than the phylloxera on the brief extension of the vine. At last we see him, there he is, small, puny, atomistic" (*OC*, IV, 775). Lilliputian Felipe is still a problem for the eyes of the narrator-viewer at the beginning of *El doctor Centeno*: he is one of the heroes who "when looked at with the eyes which serve to see normal things, is confused with the first fly that goes by or with the silent, common, colourless insect that troubles no one" (*OC*, IV, 1312). Felipe is the reverse, both in physical stature and importance, of the normal hero; he is an anti-hero who is now presented to the reader standing on a hill and surveying a landscape, not the picturesque idyllic Cantabrian coastline of *Gloria*, nor even the majestic sweep of the Guadarrama mountains as in our Group II novels, but rather the mundane and prosaic picture of Madrid factories, railway stations, hospitals, the wastelands of Getafe and Leganés, and finally the dribble of a river called the Manzanares, its pools of water visible amidst the black poplar trees like pieces of a small mirror that has broken in the hands of some riverbank nymph. Felipe's excited reaction to the toy-like appearance of the trains in Atocha station, his expectorations and final fit of vomiting and fainting, occasioned by puffing at a cigar, complete the comic inversion of the normal picturesque landscape and its contemplation by enraptured beholders. To consolidate the image of a landscape painting Galdós observes that with the attack of giddiness Felipe sees the sky falling in on him like a stage curtain tumbling down once the ropes break.[5]

This canvas had also included as its last component before its dissolution the Madrid Observatory which stands at the top of the hill Felipe is climbing. Our first appreciation of this high temple of cosmic vision is thus mediated through the irreverent eyes of an ignorant youth of thirteen or fourteen just before he loses control of his faculties of normal vision and spatial proportions:

> Well, and what about that big house which is up there, with that wheel of *coluns* ... Ah, yes; now he remembered ... That's the house where they count the stars and *esamine* the sun to find out about that thing of the days which run and if there are thunder and water up above ... Paquito also told him that those gentlemen have some glasses as big as cannons with which ... another spit ...
> But, what is happening? Have the planets come unhinged and are rolling around in chaos? (*OC*, IV, 1314)

A few seconds later in his hallucinatory vision Felipe feels the Observatory on top of his head. This far from flattering introduction to the Observatory suggests that the science of astronomy is not so highly practised as the name of the institution would lead one to expect. Further doubts are raised during a more normal look at the building offered by the narrator: it resembles some ancient temple with its Greek-style vestibule. Its doorman, the loquacious Don Florencio Morales, stands at the entrance like some statue depicting the allegorical figure of Vigilance. Moreover, the astronomer's assistant, Ruiz, is an amateur playwright and it is this literary ability that the young students, who have carted the sick Felipe to the

---

[5] At the same time this disparaging aerial view of the city is part of another (literary) tradition: the satirical telescopic view of human life from an elevated position. Luis Vélez de Guevara's *El diablo cojuelo* (1641) is the first example in Spain. Early in his career Galdós had recommended that novelists select an aerial perspective from which they could capture all the gall "that seems necessary to season the bitter condiment of the modern novel" (*AN*, 190). One of Galdós' chief mentors, Mesonero Romanos, had also recommended at the beginning of his collection of articles on Madrid customs and types, in *Escenas matritenses*, p. 514, that those who wanted to know the inner truth about Madrid's social and human life should accompany him to his lofty perch in the Puerta del Sol. Judith Wechsler, *A Human Comedy: Physiognomy and Caricature in 19th-Century Paris* (London: Thames and Hudson, 1982), p. 20, maintains that the mid-nineteenth century in Paris is the period of the bird's-eye view, and she refers specifically to Victor Hugo's opening scene in *Notre-Dame de Paris* (1831) and Rastignac's view of the same metropolis in *Le Père Goriot* (1835). In the Spanish nineteenth-century novel, Leopoldo Alas' famous view of Vetusta from the cathedral tower in *La regenta* (1885) is the best example of this technique. In *El doctor Centeno* Galdós employs the device on a second occasion: when Felipe climbs up a lamp-post to watch the funeral procession of the political journalist, Calvo Asensio. Galdós manipulates the boy's excitement, as in the opening panoramic scene of the novel, to ridicule the vulgar appearance of the funeral cortège. (*OC*, IV, 1364).

Observatory, have come to appreciate. What is supposed to be the seat of the science of vision looks initially from the outside and from this preliminary conversation between the students like a literary meeting-house with some appealing classical architecture.[6] Felipe's introductory picture, which had appeared at first naïve, now seems incredible. Once inside the building, the narrator proceeds to deflate even more the status of the house of science. In reality it has all the appearance of an old Madrid apartment house:

> Those who enter that precinct with their spirits inflamed by faith in a science which truly and really scales the heavens believe they detect mysterious echoes of the lofty sidereal harmonies ... But those who enter as if they were entering some old government office where the Almanac is made ... see only poor and undistinguished architecture, the two staircases with the doors of the astronomer's rooms opening onto the landing, and the green night lamps with their curved hats that look like cuirassiers' helmets. (*OC*, IV, 1321-22)

It is true that the Observatory will soon be receiving some new equipment, but the premises are hardly conducive to the practice of astronomy. Ruiz is in fact bored by his job, preferring to use the eyes of his imagination: "A man of imagination, Ruiz turned his eyes, tired with scanning the sky, towards the showy art of the theatre, the only one to provide fame and fortune" (*OC*, IV, 1322). Indeed, Ruiz is no exception in Spain; even the director of the Observatory is a poet. The practice of the science of astronomy takes second place to the literary exercises of the individual imagination, for the latter promise quicker fame and rewards. The great irony is that Ruiz, like Golfín in *Marianela*, is an expert in a specialized branch of optics, but yet closes his eyes to the reality of social life happening around him, by living within the artificial, literary world of his imagination. We can now appreciate the relevance of Felipe's distorted tableau of the Madrid panorama: human beings, even those who specialize in the science and study of human vision, have difficulty in obtaining the correct perspective on life.

Ruiz's daily task of measuring a segment of the sky is not really conducive to a more balanced overview of the world reality around him. Moreover, the lens that allows this close-up of the firmament is

---

[6] In the number of the illustrated magazine *El Museo Universal* for 6 May 1860, pp. 150-51, which Galdós possessed in his library, there is an account by a writer who just signs himself "R" on the history and appearance of the Observatory, which Galdós might well have consulted for this novel. The anonymous writer concludes his piece by saying that the Greek-style building is one of the few in Madrid which, because of its site, and when seen from afar, gives a monumental appearance to the city.

something of a canvas: it is divided into four by the threads of cobwebs collected expressly from trees for this purpose. The pictorial analogy also suggests that the particular image of the sky has a stasis or immobility which emphasizes its distance and removal from the observer. But there is one more important aspect of this telescopic vision of the universe: the spider is an infinitesimally small animal which is indispensable to astronomy: "Who would have said it? [Spiders have] such a wise and useful application. Marvellous little animals they are!, unwitting weavers of almost invisible threads . . . with which the measurements of the billionary proportions of the firmament are taken" (*OC*, IV, 1360). There is an immediate contrast between the minuteness of the cobweb and the infinitude of the spheres in whose measurement it is of vital use. The contrast of size also recalls the opening description of the anti-hero, Felipe, as indistinguishable from a fly buzzing before the vast panorama of the capital. Is Galdós suggesting that in both instances the disparity of size between viewing agent and landscape viewed can only signify that the resultant picture will be circumscribed in scope or nature?

The incompleteness of Felipe's adolescent vision is again evident in his appraisal of scenes within the Observatory. The boy's view of a birthday party in the caretaker's apartment is obtained from the adjacent hallway and through a half-open door, so that he sees only some details and then from a distance. Otherwise, he has to rely entirely upon his hearing to reconstruct events happening inside the room. Eyesight, as Teodoro discovered in the opening pages of *Marianela*, is a distinct handicap at times, completely ineffective in some physical situations. Again Galdós reinforces this obvious point by the use of visual art material: a print of Christ on the Cross hanging in the vestibule intimidates Felipe so much that – absurdly – he feels himself as worthy of pity as the Lord. After some food is brought to him and his spirits have revived, he now believes he perceives a corresponding change in the picture of Christ: He no longer has a ferocious countenance! Felipe's eyes are dangerously susceptible to misinterpretations. The same weakness shows up in his visual appraisal of some of the characters present at the party and who will become the major actors in the novel's drama. They are presented as if they were figures in a painting: they come to the doorway of the dining-room to look at Felipe out of curiosity, and as they stand within this pictorial frame, the outlines of their bodies are illuminated from behind by the table lamps. The result is that Amparo Sánchez Emperador, who, as the protagonist of *Tormento*, will be consistently compared to figures depicted by the visual arts as we saw in Chapter 2 of this Part III, is now likened to a heavenly seraphim, albeit slightly rounder than the laws of aesthetics would permit, and who, if dressed in classical Greek dress, would pass for Diana or Cybele, as represented traditionally by the visual arts. Later Felipe will remark that he has seen Amparo's figure in the illustrations of his textbook on mythology and Christian doctrine. The image of the priest, Pedro Polo, who will be Felipe's first master, takes on the appearance of a bronze figure in the doorway. At the same time as the art analogies dehumanize the characters to a certain extent, they also reveal Felipe's ability to appreciate art; his creative urges surface slightly later in his desire to paint the outlines of different countries on a map and in his donning of the papier-mâché head of a very realistic bull – a strange companion to several Holy Week art objects in the moonlit attic of Polo's establishment where Felipe sleeps.[7]

With his next master, the amateur playwright Alejandro Miquis, Felipe's experiences are more with the literary world, but there are still occasions when the visual arts play an important role in the understanding of the novel. For example, Miquis takes Felipe to the Prado where the boy marvels, like Isidora Rufete in the company of Miquis' brother in *La desheredada*, at the display of such a wealth of artistic beauty. This lesson in aesthetics is hilariously brought to a close one Sunday morning when both master and servant are denied entrance to the gallery because of their shabby attire. Earlier, the two had also been ejected from the boarding-house of Doña Virginia where Miquis had desecrated the heraldic prints of her common-law husband because of their grotesque quality. Their new lodgings in Cervantes Street (not an inappropriately named street) also offer the comic inversion of the picturesque landscape usually enjoyed by penthouse tenants, according to the mysterious beautiful female friend of Miquis, La Tal, who had recommended this apartment. To reach this ethereal paradise the two characters have to climb their way up graffiti-covered staircases. The beautiful gardens that master

---

[7] Felipe's friend, Juanito, is an apprentice gilder whose account of his trade provides a grotesque slant on the world of official art, with Felipe's enthusiastic reactions increasing the ridicule: "Putting the smile of the sun on everything, clothing objects with light, deifying vulgar old wood, giving it the veneer of the purest and most valuable of metals ... The guy who had such a job was really lucky! ... He [Felipe] would give anything to be able to use the elements of that art and gild the bed, the books and even the boots of his master" (*OC*, IV, 1433). Ido del Sagrario, Polo's other employee, has achieved immortality as the subject of a street-long mural of caricatures with their appropriate captions.

and servant were supposed to gaze at are situated so low down the adjoining building that they appear to be at the bottom of a well. Alejandro's marvellous landscape thus consists of clouds and a whimsical jumble of roof-tops, cupolas, attics and chimneys; in other words, it would make a wonderful meteorological station. In many respects, this penthouse in Part II forms a pendant with the Observatory of Part I. Both buildings are located at great heights, ideally situated to observe the sky, yet both seem to encourage in their respective inhabitants a literary escapism through an unbridled imagination. Observation of the heavens is perfunctory in the case of Ruiz, accidental with Miquis. But the great advantage of these lofty perches, as Galdós had emphasized in other writings,[8] was that they could encourage a more probing, encompassing view of the world or human society below; but this is precisely the perspective shunned by both men as they lose themselves in the world of the imagination. For example, the unbearably hot, baked Madrid landscape which confronts Miquis' view all summer is replaced by the mental or imaginary picture of a beautiful Italian setting for his historical play. But, then, Miquis is the apologist for the imagination that embellishes reality: "Defects in human beings ... are errors of these optical instruments we call eyes ... He who sees things as they really are is more of a mirror than a man" (*OC*, IV, 1449). These are the declarations of an unrepentant playwright whose physical appearance is compared to Christ on the Cross or a charcoal-shaded etching (*OC*, IV, 1424). In short, there seems to be a comic discrepancy between the reality of Miquis' visual art experiences (ejection from the Prado and from Doña Virginia's boarding-house, and the panoramic view from his Cervantes Street penthouse) and what they should have been.

The escapism induced by the visual as well as the literary arts emerges conclusively in the closing sequences of the novel. As he lies dying in his garret, Alejandro Miquis is visited by his aunt, the testy and eccentric Doña Isabel Godoy[9] and La Tal, both likened to dolls. The two meet on the darkened stairway where a lamp provides a

---

[8] See note 5 above.

[9] She has the varnished face and black and white eyes of dolls to be found for sale in a children's toy shop. On an important mission for cash to her darkened apartment, Alejandro associates her with an absurdly Romantic old print which hangs on her living-room wall and depicts the abduction of Matilde, sister to King Richard the Lionheart, by the infidel Malek-Adhel, a scene taken from a very famous nineteenth-century novel by Vicomte d'Arlincourt widely read in Spain under the title of *Matilde, o las cruzadas*.

chiaroscuro illumination. Galdós is deliberately sketching an art scene where background lighting and characters have a strongly pictorial outline. The fact is that he wishes to expose the absurdity of this world of the imagination inhabited by Miquis as a disease of the mind that is completely lacking in depth of vision of human reality. On the one hand, Doña Isabel maintains that if Alejandro sets his eyes on La Tal's beautiful appearance, he will be saved from death: "Eyes kill [a very deliberate echo of the title of the penultimate chapter in *Marianela*], oh dear, but they also cure ... and revive people ... Let him see her ... He will get better immediately" (*OC*, IV, 1459). On the other hand, astronomer-cum-playwright Ruiz views La Tal as the person responsible for his friend's death, and stands light in hand in the stairway, ordering her expulsion from the penthouse like a "statue of public morality illuminating the world and expelling vice from the cenacle of good behaviour" (*OC*, IV, 1460). The pictorial mould of the whole scene emphasizes the fact that, though both Doña Isabel and Ruiz have exercised their physical eyesight, an over- or under-active imagination respectively controls the interpretation of the retinal image. The title-phrase from the *Marianela* chapter is an ironic reminder that it is not so much the gift of physical eyesight that destroys human relationships, but what often accompanies it and is inseparable from it: individual subjective ideas and wild imagination. Eyesight, "that precious organ" (as Galdós remarked in a letter of December 19, 1887, to his Catalan friend, the novelist Narciso Oller[10]), which should distinguish man from art object, really increases the similarity when eyesight becomes the handmaiden of imagination.

La de Bringas

The last novel in our Group IV presents this dangerous liaison between imagination and eyesight in a more subtle and complex form. Instead of a blind statuesque boy recovering sight, as in *Marianela*, a normal healthy person loses his eyesight precisely because of his fixation with the art object he is creating, which, moreover, is, in its configuration, an optical illusion of a picturesque

[10] Reproduced in William H. Shoemaker, "Una amistad literaria: la correspondencia epistolar entre Galdós y Narciso Oller", *Boletín de la Real Academia de Buenas Letras* (Barcelona), 30 (1963-64), p. 286.

landscape. Furthermore, this art object occupies that strategically important position of the novel's opening chapter. But *La de Bringas* surpasses its two companion novels in that this initial art form is the source from which the rest of the novel's matter derives, its verbal description even reflecting the optical illusions of the object itself.

The art work of Francisco Bringas, living replica of the journal illustration of Adolphe Thiers, as we know from our discussion of *Tormento*, is a minor manifestation, a hair picture. It is an art work composed in layers: on a wooden base are affixed various outlines of funeral objects cut from all sorts of picture books. Over this design is placed a glass to which are stuck the various threads of hair arranged according to the underlying drawings. Surmounting these layers is a convex covering glass. The result is that what initially appears as a landscape study of a cenotaph surrounded by funeral objects with distant moonlit palace and mountains is a composite work in three dimensions of a motley collection of art materials. In fact, the work deceives with its surface appearance: the layers of substance beneath its glass covering cannot be glimpsed at first viewing. The narrator has some difficulty in identifying the precise category of this art work: "Was it a wood carving, an etching, a steel plate, an engraving on boxwood or a work of patience executed with a sharp pencil point or with an Indian ink pen?" (*OC*, IV, 1587). Only at the end of the long description is this uncertainty dispelled: it is a hair picture, a miniature genre enjoying a certain popularity earlier in the nineteenth century and now only to be seen in the niches of cemeteries or in an old hairdressing shop. Moreover, to analyse correctly the composition of the art work, a microscope would be necessary; so, optics has to come to the aid of the visual arts if the viewer is not to be deceived by this small art object. Since we have already seen the limitations of optical instruments and operations in *Marianela* and *El doctor Centeno*, the proclaimed need of a microscope to view this art work correctly augurs ill for the ability of the artist to perceive human reality correctly. What is more, Francisco's great skill in splitting and amalgamating threads of hair of different hues is unequalled by fellow artists and the narrator hails him as an originator of a new technique. First and foremost, then, Francisco is categorized as a master artist.

Galdós not only shows us the artist Francisco bent over his painstaking work in his studio (a window area in one of the family rooms), but also records the prehistory of the work, its moment of artistic conception. The general idea springs from the distraught mind of a family friend, Carolina Pez, who wants to immortalize the memory of a recently deceased daughter in a work whose quality she unwittingly devalues when she orders that it must speak the same language as popular verses, artificial flowers, plaster, metallic paint or piano nocturnes! Bringas, elated with the commission from his patroness, immediately exclaims that he knows the precise art form and that he can see the completed object in his mind, and stumbles out of the Pez house in a state of feverish excitment. The melo-dramatic, exaggerated reactions of Francisco to his friend's request are in direct contrast to the artistic merit of this hair picture as described in the opening chapter, and which is now further devalued by the extreme cheapness of the materials that Francisco purchases for its construction. The artist's joy with the low costs of the artistic creation serves to remind the reader that the very first step in the chain of events leading to the finished art object, now so enthu-siastically envisioned by the artist, is in reality a kind of financial debt owed by Bringas to the Pez family; Carolina's husband has secured a position in the Civil Service for Bringas' eldest son, so he now feels obliged to repay the favour. As in most of the novels we have discussed so far, the possession of an art object is a sure sign of the owner's social and financial standing, but *La de Bringas* develops this important relationship in a way unequalled in the other novels by converting the art object into the indirect generator of the need for more money felt by the artist's wife.

If the essential nature of the hair picture is that of an optical illusion, this quality is captured by the narrator in his description of the object, for its extreme length and detailed style give the impression that the narrator is describing a real mausoleum and landscape:

> It was ... how shall I say it? ... a graceful sepulchral contrivance of extremely daring architecture, grandiose in design, rich in orna-mentation, on the one hand severe and rectilinear in the "viñolesca" manner, on the other, moving, undulating and fragile in the Gothic fashion, with certain Plateresque touches where they were least expected, and finally, crests like those in the Tyrolese style that prevails in kiosks. It had a pyramidal staircase, Greco-Roman socles and Gothic buttresses and faces, with pinnacles, gargoyles and small canopies. (*OC*, IV, 1587)

But this grandiloquent style, so appropriate for Galdós' architectural reviews of the Happy Outcome church in *La Nación* of 1867, as we saw in Part I, is entirely inapposite for the minute object he is describing here in *La de Bringas*. Moreover, it is invalidated by the degeneration in tone which leads at the end of this paragraph to the description of the purposefully elongated characters of the tomb inscription, reported to appear like drivel running across the stone. The same deterioration of tone is noticeable in the description of the background landscape: the weeping willow trees recede to the horizon snivelling all the way; in the sky the moon appears like a mass wafer. Confusion of architectural styles and perplexity about the artistic identity of this scene are accompanied by distortion of spatial perspective: for example, the foreground of this miniature composition is crowded with all sorts of small funeral objects and plants whilst the background is filled by the vague outlines of larger masses like a city, mountains, sky, river and moon. As I have shown elsewhere, this completely unaesthetic arrangement of objects in the hair picture is symbolic and anticipatory of other disordered spaces in the rest of the novel, like the Madrid Royal Palace where the Bringas family lives, their own apartment and that of Refugio Sánchez Emperador, another reappearing character from *Tormento*.[11]

There is one final layer of illusion created by this opening description of the hair picture: even though it is discovered at the end of the first section of the first chapter that the description corresponds to a work of miniature art and not a large architectural structure or picturesque landscape as first suggested, the reader still believes that the narrator is describing a hair picture that does exist in reality with the features he has patiently recorded. This certainty is gradually undermined in the remaining chapters of the novel, for it is learnt that Francisco never completes the hair picture to the degree it seems to have reached on the first page of the novel. The narrator could be transcribing the details of a picture that was near to completion or as outlined to him by his friend, artist Francisco. Whatever the reason for this unadmitted obfuscation of the reader by the narrator, the fact remains that the hair work is a picture that disorientates at many levels. It is an enigma, a puzzle for the eye of the observer and, by extension, of the reader. For the eye of its creator, the art object becomes an eventual agent of destruction: it not only ruins his eyesight (even though he recovers from the blindness, his vision remains impaired) but it also destroys his previously happy marriage,

---

[11] See my *Benito Pérez Galdós: La de Bringas* (London: Grant and Cutler, 1981), Chapter 2, for a further discussion of this point. For a photograph of a Spanish hair picture, see López Rubio, *Benito Pérez Galdós*, p. 114.

for the ultimate irony is that, in order to pay off the debts for clothes purchases she has incurred during Francisco's incapacitation, Rosalía is forced to commit adultery with Pez, whose wife had expressly forbidden Francisco to adulterate the hair work with hairs from people outside the Pez family. The artistic adultery imagined by Carolina is absurdly petty by comparison with the greater moral adultery committed by her own husband with the artist's wife.

Both adulterers, brought together, as it were, by a work of art, are suitably compared on occasion to figures in famous art works. We saw how in *Tormento* Rosalía's buxom figure had been compared to that of a Rubens goddess. This analogy almost becomes a reality in *La de Bringas* when at sunset she strolls with Pez on the terrace of the Madrid Royal Palace:

> The stroll through such a monumental site pleased the lady's fantasy, bringing back memories of those architectural backgrounds which Rubens, Veronese, Van Loo and other painters include in their paintings to magnify the figures and give them a very aristocratic air. Pez and Rosalía imagined that they stood out elegantly against the background of balustrades, mouldings, archivolts and urns, *an assumption that forced them unwittingly to harmonize their posture and even their gait with the majesty of the scene.*[12] (my italics; *OC*, IV, 1606)

The adjustment of body movements to the rigid art postures that befit the mammoth monument of the Palace is not only worthy of their iconographical status, but also expresses their commitment to the world of visual and artistic appearances at the expense of any inner spiritual values. One further aspect of the architectural assimilation deserves a mention: Pez, always immaculately dressed and with a svelte figure, bears a striking resemblance to the images of St. Joseph as painted by Murillo. Rosalía, we recall, is buxom and like a Rubens goddess. As the two stroll along the Palace terrace, fitting their postures into the architectural frame as in a painting, the juxtaposition of their bodies creates a completely caricatural effect because of the marked contrast of physical outlines. The noble Rubens and Murillo resemblances, when merged into one composite outline, create a totally comic effect: buxom pagan goddess beside phantasmal Christian saint; painting now becomes caricature. The contrasting cultural associations (goddess beside saint) also increases the comic effect. But disproportionate sizes were an outstanding

---

[12] Galdós' interest in the Prado's collection of Rubens canvases can be gauged by the many annotations against the Flemish painter's name and work in his copy of Viardot's *Les Musées*, pp. 94-100.

feature of Francisco's masterpiece. One might say that the eventual coupling of the discordant shapes of Rosalía and Manuel Pez is only another (albeit unsuspected) artistic creation by Francisco the miniaturist, now unwitting cartoonist, with the final laugh directed back by the caricatures towards his own eventual cuckoldom.

CHAPTER 12

VISUAL ART ENIGMAS

Miau (1888), *La incógnita* (1889), *Nazarín* (1895), *Halma* (1895), *Misericordia* (1897)

In many ways our fifth group of novels, all from "the contemporary series", is the exception in the pack. Written in what is generally termed the spiritual period of Galdós' career, when he was less and less concerned with the parameters of the normal physical world, none of them seems to project the clear visual art images that he had persistently fashioned to great effect in our previous four groups. The visual art material, whether in concrete objects or in metaphorical references, is now characterized by an ambiguity of meaning that sets the novels apart from the rest. Galdós still believes that a character's similarity to or preference for art objects signifies some degree of artificiality in his or her approach to life and reality, but now, perhaps because of the intensity of the inner spiritual lives of the main characters, not all the artistic references are unflattering or intended to be interpreted as shorthand signals of negative or ironic meaning. More often than not, the reader has extreme difficulty in interpreting these art similes or objects. The perplexity raised, again often at the strategic point of the novel's opening, continues through the work.

Miau

In introducing the Villaamil family, Galdós puts great stress on their resemblance to art images, but they are ambivalent images. Luisito imagines that his grandmother, great-aunt and aunt are three cats dressed up as human beings, like those he has seen in illustrations in the children's picture book, *Animals Painted By Themselves*. Galdós does not merely compare the females to three cats, but rather he mediates the analogy through the impressionable mind of the boy so as to raise doubts about their profile: are they human beings or cats or indeed picture-book illustrations? Similarly, in the portrait of Doña Pura, Villaamil's wife, Galdós compares her face to that of an old coin whose features a numismatist would have difficulty in deciphering. Yet in her youth she had been extolled by a provincial newspaper reporter (who was also responsible for the wheat report) as a heavenly beauty out of one of Fra Angelico's paintings. Which image does Galdós wish us to retain, or is it that both are valid? Her daughter, Abelarda, is likened one evening, as she sits by the kitchen table, to a sculpture of the muse Polimnia; yet she lacks the primary requisite for such a comparison, that of physical beauty! So she resembles the classical sculpture and yet she does not. Having made the pictorial analogy, Galdós instantly casts doubt upon it by a number of means.

The same confusing visual reverberations are generated by the initial description of the head of the Villaamil family, the unemployed civil servant, Don Ramón. As he paces up and down his small room, pondering means to regain his position in the Finance Ministry, and ultimately, after two months, pension entitlement, he is likened to an old tiger. But when he sighs over his misfortune and gazes up to the ceiling, the narrator is immediately reminded of the similar pose of a human body in Ribera's famous painting of St. Bartholomew being taken down from the cross. Instant confusion results as the reader is propelled from one image to a completely different one. The incongruity between the bestial and the saintly comparisons is arresting and forces the reader to wonder which image Galdós really wants one to accept. Or are both, despite the incongruous juxtaposition, representative of the ambiguous character of the protagonist? Certainly, in the recent polemic over Villaamil's character, sides have been rigidly taken for or against Galdós' portrayal of Don Ramón as a martyred victim of nineteenth-century Spanish bureaucracy.[1] Is it not more likely that Galdós wished both sides of Villaamil's character to be accepted for what they were: the old man does behave ridiculously and furiously at times; but yet his farsighted proposals for reform of Spain's fiscal system, as represented

---

[1] See especially volumes 4 (1969) and 6 (1971) of *Anales Galdosianos*.

by the anagram M.I.A.U., and the suffering he has to endure within his family and from former colleagues transform him into something more than a comic, circus character. Yet the Ribera comparison is not presented as a totally serious contrast to the tiger analogy. The narrator's familiar language manages to counteract the serious impression given earlier and at the same time subtly reminds us, through another comparison, of the tiger image: "... those rogues of Gentiles [St. Bartholomew's executioners] skin the saint as if he were a kid goat" (*OC*, V, 555). Does Galdós intend us to consider Villaamil like St. Bartholomew in the painting, or is he trying to withdraw this possibility with his completely irreligious tone and image at the end of the reference? The only plausible answer seems to be that Galdós intended both images: they are contradictory and the overall impression is enigmatic, but Galdós refuses to offer a crystal-clear definitive art image of his character. That unidimensional view is no longer possible, even in the use of art references.

The same conflicting impressions of the dismissed civil servant are created by a concrete art work of a kind completely different from the beautiful Ribera painting. Villaamil's life becomes the subject of an extended series of caricatures (with corresponding legends) drawn by the cripple Guillén, the satirist in the Ministry office. The whole work constitutes an example of the popular "aleluya", a visual art form that, as we saw above, Galdós had also grafted into the thematic structure and meaning of *La desheredada* in our Group II novels. Following his usual style, Galdós eschews a description of the graphic art work, although, as is natural, their forms are easily imaginable for the reader from the legends that Galdós itemizes. The humour of the captions and of their matching drawings lies in the substitution of the main points in Villaamil's financial plans for the more normal materials involved in a person's development as a human being: for example, instead of nappies or diapers, the infant Ramón is wrapped in Government credentials, his baby milk is a budget, and so forth. From our knowledge of Villaamil's personal suffering and attempts to regain his job against the indifference of his former colleagues and superiors, the life painted by the cartoonist is an exaggeration: but on the other hand, the caricatures are not total fabrications of untruths; Villaamil has obviously given high priority in his life (at the tragic expense of other values) to the elaboration of his financial plans. The narrator's comments on the "aleluyas" are also revealing in this regard: he refers to their poor-quality art work, and states that they are inaccurate in some biographical details and that there are blatant misspellings. It is noteworthy, though, that the narrator does not reject the whole "aleluya" out of hand. His stance is very important: it is equivocal, hovering between two positions, between condemnation and sympathy for the plight of Villaamil. It is this equivocation or ambivalence in the presentation of the pictorial referent that represents Galdós' major innovation in his use of visual art material in our fifth group of novels. The equivocation present in previous art pictures, like the configuration of the Leganés asylum at the beginning of *La desheredada* or the optical illusion of the hair picture at the beginning of *La de Bringas*, had caused initial bewilderment, but had been eventually resolved. But in *Miau* the confusion seems all the greater because the narrator is either unable or reluctant to *attempt* to clear up the contradictions himself, and thus he persists in contributing to the mystification of the reader.

The employment of another art image later in the novel reinforces the ambivalent presentation of Villaamil: as he walks down the Ministry corridor his figure is compared to a caricature of the traditional image of Dante, while his companion through the dark passageway is a caricature of the traditional image of Virgil. And yet, at the end of the same paragraph, the narrator categorically observes:

> Neither Dante nor Quevedo on their fantastic voyages dreamed of anything like this office labyrinth, with the discordant sound of bells ringing from all the confines of the vast mansion, with the constant opening and closing of doors, of screens, and the sound of shoes on the floor, or of the civil servants clearing their throats as they went to hang their coats and hats beside their desk. Neither Dante nor Quevedo had dreamed of anything like the sound of dusty papers or glasses of water being pulled out or put back, or of coal being shovelled into the fire; of anything like the smoke-filled atmosphere, the orders shouted from desk to desk: they had, in short, never dreamed of anything like the bustle and humming activity of these beehives where the bitter honeycomb of the administration is fashioned. (*OC*, V, 656)

The tone of this office description is bleak indeed, and there is every reason to believe that Galdós did intend the reader to conclude that, *mutatis mutandis*, Villaamil's torment in the Ministry was far worse than anything Dante had imagined in the rings of Hell, however outlandish that proposition first appears to the reader. Yet on the other hand, in delineating the caricatural outlines of the unemployed civil servant Galdós had seemed to commence on a humorous note. The reader remains in a state of perplexity as to the real intentions of the author, or as to the real focus he is being encouraged to adopt.

There is also another noteworthy difference between Galdós' use of visual art referents in *Miau* and the other novels of this Group V if compared to that of some of the novels discussed earlier. For example, when he had compared Francisco Bringas to the image of Adolphe Thiers as it appeared in newspaper illustrations, or Bailón to a sibylline fresco figure, Galdós had deliberately drawn a parallelism of external features that had rigorously excluded any transference of internal correspondences: these characters were in some ways empty dummies or "look-alikes" of the referent. In the case of Villaamil, Galdós goes beyond the ironic physical parallels to suggest some resemblance of an internal, spiritual nature as well. Villaamil will to some extent become a martyr like St. Bartholomew, and his vision of the Ministry will become as bleak, or bleaker than Dante's vision of Hell, but the irresoluble problem concerns the precise extent to which Galdós intends a serious dimension to be drawn from the art comparison. This judgement, it would seem, depends on each individual reader's reading of the novel.

Mendizábal, the concièrge of the tenement house where the Villaamils live, is another example of this bewildering contrast of external features and inner qualities, although the point of comparison is now a visual art form of an unusual kind: the concièrge has the appearance of a gorilla to be found on exhibition in an anthropological museum. The static pose of the taxidermist's creation converts the animal into an art-display item comparable to any other art object. Yet this outer analogy constitutes a disorientating guide to the quality of his inner character. One of the few people to appreciate the inner turmoil suffered by his neighbour, Mendizábal is also the soul of kindness to the infant Luisito, as befits the holder of a surname which recalls that of one of the most famous Liberal Finance Ministers in nineteenth-century Spain responsible for attempts to create a more equitable finance system.

Víctor, the flamboyant civil servant, father of Luisito and mortally detested by his envious father-in-law, presents another contribution to this series of contrasts between outer artistic appearances and inner spiritual realities. Víctor is not given any historically recognizable physiognomy from world art, but his portrait follows the proportions and shapes prescribed by the rules of aesthetics:

> Víctor was a perfect type of virile beauty, one of those specimens destined to preserve and transmit the elegance of forms in the human race. Disfigured by cross-breeding ... from time to time, the race

comes to reproduce the handsome model, as if to gaze at itself, to delight in its own mirror and to convince itself of the permanence of the archetypes of beauty, despite the infinite derivations of ugliness. The chiaroscuro produced by the light of the lamp on the kitchen table [at which he was sitting] modelled the features of the handsome man. His nose had a pure contour, his eyes were dark, the expression of their wide pupils varied at will from the tenderest to the most serious tone. His forehead, pale in colour, had the cut and shine that in sculpture serves to express nobility. This nobility is the result of the balance of cranial parts and perfect harmony of line. The robust neck, the somewhat dishevelled jet black hair, the short, black beard completed the beautiful engraving of that bust, more Italian than Spanish. His height was average; his body as well proportioned and elegant as his head. (*OC*, V, 578-79)

So Víctor is the supreme example of classical male beauty, but Galdós draws particular attention to the model's eyesight. Not only is it an instrument used, like that of all beautiful humans, to gaze narcissistically at his own body, but also, in its exceptional range of ocular expressions, it becomes a weapon of deceit and theatrical behaviour when directed towards other people, as his relationship with Abelarda amply demonstrates. But the grotesque visual art counterpoint to this image of archetypal beauty is painted in a nightmare Víctor experiences one night after his return to the Villaamil household. He dreams that he is chasing a lady through a gallery of unending mirrors which reflect his own beautiful, artistic image. The lady in this surrealistic picture has boots whose heels are made of eggshells and she is carrying a heavy chest of drawers which she refuses to hand over to Víctor. As John Crispin has recently shown, the nightmare picture reflects the grotesque use to which Víctor is putting his beautiful body: he is carrying on an affair with a wealthy but ugly old lady in order to obtain the financial support he needs and which his civil service job cannot provide.[2]

Another pictorial topos in the novels of the previous groups had been the picturesque landscape (in particular that of the Sierra de Guadarrama outside Madrid), often for ironic or parodic effect. Its function also undergoes some modification in the novels in our Group V and in *Miau* particularly.[3] In the dénouement of the novel, Ramón deposits his grandson with the boy's aunt and then heads for

---

[2] "The role of secondary plots and secondary characters in Galdós' *Miau*", *Hispania*, 65 (1982), 365-70.

[3] Federico Sopena Ibáñez, *Arte y sociedad en Galdós* (Madrid: Gredos, 1970), p. 45, reckons that only mad characters poeticize this landscape.

the city outskirts. He stands entranced by the sight of the beautiful mountains on this lovely spring day:

> The mountains were of a bright blue, with touches of snow, like a blob of watercolour spread out on the sheet of painting paper through the natural diffusion of the drop of paint; it was a work of chance more than of the artist's brush. "Oh, how beautiful this is! ... It seems as if I'm seeing it for the first time in my life, or as if this sierra, these trees and this sky have just been created. True, in my miserable life, full of trials and tribulations, I have not had time to look up or across at ... Always with my eyes down, looking at this wretched earth which is not worth a cent ... As I say: far more interesting is a bit of sky, however small, than the face of Pantoja [his departmental boss in the Ministry] ... Thank God I can taste this pleasure of looking at nature ... now I am another man; I know now what life is ... I am the happiest of men. So, to eat, and bravo, my girl." (*OC*, V, 675)

This extensive passage, far more complex than mere background landscape painting as William H. Shoemaker suggested,[4] captures the serious contradictions in Villaamil's thoughts and actions at this critical juncture. Unlike the other Guadarrama-gazers in our Group II novels (like Maxi, Fortunata and Ido del Sagrario) who see their respective moods reflected in the mountain scene, Villaamil is led to reappraise his past life, and to awaken to a new awareness of the meaning of human existence: he now sees that it has been a complete waste of time to worry about the reform of the country's tax system. He seems to forget himself now in a joyous contemplation of beautiful nature. Yet, the tone is deceptive; the change is too abrupt to be acceptable, for this panegyric of the beauty of the Guadarrama is soon followed by acts of vandalism to tree saplings and threats to shoot passing sparrows. The ultimate paradox, of course, will be Villaamil's suicide within sight of this beautiful landscape. But then, the description of the Guadarrama itself had been cast in terms of a landscape painting, as if Galdós were alerting the reader to the basic inauthenticity of Villaamil's change of attitude. The canvas comparison injects the required warning note of artificiality: the sight of the mountains does lead Villaamil to reject his past obsession with the Ministry and his claim for job reinstatement, but the abruptly announced renewal of zest for life strikes an excessively discordant note and masks the real new direction in Villaamil's life: his

---

4 *The Novelistic Art*, p. 310. Jennifer Lowe, "The function and presentation of the world of nature in three Galdosian novels", *AG*, 14 (1979), p. 10, also considers this landscape scene to be more than picturesque decoration, although she does not go as far as I have done in noting its paradox.

determination to kill himself and escape the world. The paradox, typical of all suicides, as Arthur Schopenhauer pointed out,[5] is manifest in the manner in which he curses the wretched earth after having just praised the beautiful mountains that lay before him. What exactly is Villaamil's attitude towards his surroundings at this point? All one can say with certainty is that it is an ambivalent attitude, which is reflected in his soliloquy; but the precise proportion of those conflicting attitudes is impossible to determine. Thus, art and artistic appearances are no longer a reliable guide to the full complexity of the inner human character for which they serve as an outer visual jacket. And that new application of the visual arts had been signalled by the initial pictorial description of Villaamil and his family.

La incógnita

The same ambiguity of pictorial appearance of characters is continued in Galdós' next novel, in epistolary form, and again, pertinently, the tone is set in the opening tableaux. Furthermore, the ambiguity is now extended to the question of the interpretation of works of art by these same enigmatic characters and is reinforced by the bewilderment of the politician-narrator, Manolo Infante, who encounters difficulty in fully and accurately explaining to his friend, Mr. X, who lives in the renowned Orbajosa, many of the strange incidents and people he meets in Madrid. Indeed, prominent amongst these experiences are his encounters with art works, the artistic appearances of people and the interpretations of the former by the latter.

Manolo Infante's uncle, Don Carlos María de Cisneros, is not likened to one pictorial figure in particular, but to a whole composite listing of Renaissance figures: Bishop Acuña, the Count of Tendilla, Torquemada and St. Peter Alcántara. Manolo recommends to his correspondent: "... reconstruct the stamp of the race and the type of Mother Castile and you will be able to say: 'There, that is him'" (*OC*, V, 690). Furthermore, all of these traditional portraits to which Manolo is referring his friend present impressions contrary to their supposed status: "Imagine those shaven warriors *who seemed like* priests, those lords *who resembled* farmers dressed in silk" (my italics;

---

[5] See *The World As Will and Idea*, trans. R. B. Haldane and J. Kemp (London: Trübner, 1883-86), I, 515 ff.

OC, V, 690). If it is hard to pin one particular pictorial image onto this character, it is even more so to determine exactly which are his proper features. This pictorial confusion is, of course, symptomatic of the much wider confusion Manolo experiences when he comes to examine the character of his uncle. It is significant that Mr. X protests that Manolo's picture of Don Carlos is an artistic creation and not a true likeness of the person. But Manolo responds: "Let not the strangeness of the silhouette move you to doubt its likeness and authenticity"(*OC*, V, 766). In the same way, Cisneros' beautiful daughter, Augusta, appears to be a perfect Greek goddess one moment, and then the next resembles the Virgin Mary.

To blame Manolo's relative inexperience of life in the capital for those confusing portraits is not only to diminish the degree of perplexity these people themselves generate, but also to ignore the narrator's own witting contribution to the mystification of the reader. For example, he believes that his uncle's art collection is not so perfect as he claims and that, beside the priceless gems, there are some pretty poor canvases, certainly not worthy of the gawping attention lavished on them by family visitors, nor comparable, as his uncle believes, to the collection in the Kensington Museum. This ambivalent opinion is not really the fruit of mature reflection or any deep knowledge of the subject, as we initially believe, but really the reaction of whim and ignorance. What is worse, Manolo suspects that his uncle has no real interest either in these old masters and that he is only playing the role of a great art collector.[6] There is no way to ascertain the truth of this suspicion as the whole narration is controlled by Manolo Infante as narrator-protagonist. Therefore, confusion abounds. Whose opinion is the most correct? That of owner Cisneros, even though it may be feigned, or that of the narrator who confesses his ignorance in the matter?

Manolo also intimates that Cisneros' assignation of the authorship of problematic canvases is far too hasty to be of any reliable accuracy: "If the painting in question has athletic and bouncy figures, it is by Rubens himself, or at least, Jordaens. If it is some squalid portrait with a feverish face, than it has to be an El Greco" (*OC*, V, 691). Cisneros' daughter also confounds the issue when she

---

[6] In an article for *La Prensa* of 30 May 1893 entitled "El coleccionista", Galdós gave a disturbingly contradictory evaluation of art collectors: at one moment he praises them for their great service to the decorative arts (*OI*, I, 199); at the next, he says that with their collections they satisfy their pride and are able to relax from their business cares (*OI*, I, 202).

denigrates by word and art form the work of her father's favourite painters, the Italian masters of the fifteenth century: ". . . she makes funny verbal and graphic caricatures of them, for when she is in the mood she gets a pencil and sketches with a few strokes a parody of these rigid saints, with their sad faces, hands like canes, impossible postures, hard fists, those architectural backgrounds with no perspective or proportions, those animals, coarse as the ones children paint" (*OC*, V, 713). Her own preference is for contemporary Spanish social art by artists like Jiménez Aranda, Arturo Mélida, Martín Rico, Emilio Sala, Beruete, Plasencia and others (many, as we know, personal friends of Galdós). Scenes of Madrid and Andalusian life and customs, gypsy and other exotic types and very pretty landscapes are her favourite subjects. There is, therefore, a total opposition in the areas of art preference between father and daughter, and although Augusta seems to champion the very subjects Galdós had recommended in his reviews of the triennial art exhibitions in *La Prensa* Galdós is not so much applauding these tastes as exposing the contrast in opinions between father and daughter as a reflection of their strange characters. Their respective preferences are so exaggerated and so firmly held that the rejection of the other's choice raises questions about their own understanding of the meaning of art and their ability to evaluate it. In other words, their respective positions in these art discussions have little to do with true evaluation of art and more with personal whims. As a consequence, the reader is even further disorientated about the artistic value of this collection, especially as the ignorant narrator is unable to clarify matters.

The same effect is produced by apparently more serious debates – between Don Carlos and another art collector, the cosmopolitan Malibrán – over the identity of certain tableaux or the differences between various schools of art. Malibrán is quite an expert: he is actively engaged in negotiating the sale of a Mantegna with the Louvre or Rothschilds of Paris, and on one occasion, when Manolo finds himself in his company, he proceeds to give the narrator a short history of the woodcuts and metal engravings by Dürer and Holbein. Like Cisneros, his physical appearance reminds the narrator, not of one particular painting figure, but of several: St. George, St. Francis, St. Jerome and St. Peter. These two "composite" icons, "saint" Malibrán and "count" Cisneros, now engage in a farcical debate over the authorship of a canvas Cisneros has recently acquired from a rural convent through the manipulations of his estate administrator.

Manolo's description of the canvas (on the baptism of Jesus) is laced with humour: its dimensions are very small – 50 centimetres by 40 centimetres – and the figures of Christ and John the Baptist are naked, yellow and stiff, standing out against a dark background; a pair of angels hover above, elegantly attired and holding a sign. The patient scrutiny of the composition and the frequent consultation of the work of such art authorities as Ceán Bermúdez undertaken by both connoisseurs seem to constitute an exaggerated reaction to the relative artistic merit of the small canvas. Even more absurd is the tenacious defence of their theses: Cisneros believes that the painter is Masaccio; Malibrán, that it is Pinturicchio. The enthusiastic support for these conflicting opinions given to Cisneros and Malibrán by Manolo and Augusta respectively adds a further layer of absurdity, because both supporters have no knowledge whatsoever of the period under discussion. Manolo denigrates the work of Raphael and Titian as childish and professes ignorance of Mantegna. These nonsensical remarks are prompted by his jealousy of what he believes is Malibrán's covert relationship with Augusta. Manolo even believes that the two are using the language of art as a secret code to carry on their affair. The overall effect of the scene is to sow utter confusion in the mind of the reader: what is really going on in this debate? Do the contestants believe, or even know, what they are saying, when their supporters are uttering nonsense? These are some of the questions raised and which can receive no answer because the narrator himself is unable to clarify the mysteries, and even deepens them with his irritatingly obfuscatory style, of which the following is a good example: "Declaring myself previously without any authority in this field and recognizing my ignorance, I declare to you [Mr. X, his correspondent] with all the crudity of an idiot, that the collection of my cousin [Augusta] pleased me more than that of Cisneros" (*OC*, V, 713). The purpose of this lengthy passage on the art tastes and collections of the Cisneros circle as well as of the earlier character portraits is surely to introduce the reader at this early stage (the first quarter of the narrative) to what will be the main point of the remaining three quarters of the novel: the impossibility of ever delving into the truth of the murder of Federico Viera, an impoverished aristocratic member of the Cisneros circle. By presenting a prologue, as it were, in which this impossibility is successively represented by the difficulty in interpreting visual arts and visual art resemblances, Galdós is alerting his readers to the more serious and more perplexing "incógnitas" or enigmas in the human tragedies and dramas that occur in that society.

Nazarín

The reader's initial bewilderment in the third novel of our Group V is not generated by character portraits, but, as in some of the novels of our earlier Group II, by a private building situated in the slums of Madrid: the boarding-house of Chanfaina. The narrator's opening designation of Madrid as "the city of the eternal joke, of sarcasm and malicious lies" (*OC*, V, 1679) is, however, an opportune admonishment that the visual interpretation of this private house might not be so easy to determine. Indeed, on the outside its portico gives the impression of an inn; its stucco has peeled away and left a thousand fantastic drawings. The inner structure of the patio is of an equally fantastic irregularity: it is a sort of architectural joke without any rhyme or reason, whose visual identity presents a baffling puzzle for the observer. There are sagging windows and elongated doors, twisted gutters, balustrades converted into partition walls, holes blocked up with pieces of metal nailed to rotten wood, angles and patches of whitewash, and rotten upright posts attempting to support a sagging gallery. This mess of contrasting, irregular lines, angles and shapes is covered with the artistic patina of chiaroscuro. Contributing to this visual disorientation are the narrator's colourful, bizarre thoughts on the possible uses of some of these features: the holes are big enough for tigers to jump through, if there were tigers in the area, whilst the glass crenellations on the walls would be to repel thieves. Yet both the narrator and the reader know full well that there are no tigers roaming loose in Madrid, and that buildings in these slum areas are the least likely to be burgled. Why, then, does the narrator bother to make the suggestions, unless his purpose is deliberately to confound the alert reader?

People are then seen emerging into the patio from openings that might be doors, rooms or caverns. What is more, these people are seen to be wearing Carnival masks, an art form that succeeds admirably in concealing the true identity of the wearer. In the case of one person, the mask is not superimposed, but sketched with black marks onto the physical face of the person, so that mask or art object and real face become one. What may be temporary in some groups becomes a permanent visual art persona in the prostitutes who enter Chanfaina's room. With their heavily powdered cheeks, reddened lips and darkened eyebrows, they are mistaken by the narrator for Carnival masks until he realizes that this particular facial mask or art adornment is the sign of their daily trade and the mask they always wear. Thus the inhabitants of this low-class tenement area present physiognomies that are confusing art pieces of three different kinds and match the disorder of the building in which they are first glimpsed by the narrator.

The optical confusion projected by the owner, Chanfaina, is also referred to an art base: on the one hand, she has a Herculean frame with the nose of a bull, but on the other, she also has the baroque beauty of a nymph painted on a ceiling fresco.[7] Furthermore, this painting is an optical challenge like the hair picture in *La de Bringas*: it is the type of painting intended to be viewed from afar, but Chanfaina's carnal replica is always viewed from a close position so that it is impossible for the viewer to get the gigantic figure in proper perspective.

The final canvas in this series of perplexing human art surfaces is the eponymous hero himself, who is first seen by the narrator and his friend as he leans out of his bedroom window onto the inner corridor of the boarding-house, as if he were indeed a figure in a canvas frame. At first sight he seems to be a woman, then a native of the Near East, although he was born in La Mancha. He also appears to be a lodger at Chanfaina's, whereas in actual fact his room is a structure that is independent of the main building described earlier in such puzzling detail. The undoubted purpose of these visual art puzzles is to create an appropriate prelude to the far more complex ambiguity surrounding the actions and motives of Nazarín in the main body of the novel as well as the nature and meaning of the whole work, as I have shown elsewhere.[8]

Picturesque landscapes, as in *Miau*, also reflect the same note of ambiguity. At the beginning of part II, when Nazarín sallies forth from Madrid into the countryside to imitate the works of Christ, it appears as if Galdós is continuing to deride the Romantic motif of

---

[7] Thomas R. Franz, *Remaking Reality in Galdós: a Writer's Interactions with his Context* (Athens, Ohio: Strathmore Press, 1982), p. 34, finds a resemblance between Chanfaina's portrait and that of the mistress of J. J. Rousseau, Madame de Warens, as painted in oils and words. Another character who appears later in the novel, Ujo, is the physical opposite to Chanfaina: he is a dwarf; but he is also related to a visual art base, for he is described as a devil who has escaped from an altar piece showing souls in Purgatory. Like Chanfaina, he presents an optical challenge to the viewer: a giant head sits atop his small body.

[8] "*Nazarín*: ¿enigma eterno o triunfo del arte galdosiano?", *CHA*, 124 (1981), 286-300.

the pathetic fallacy as he had done in the novels of our previous four groups. Nazarín is happy to be abandoning the bustle and vexations of the capital for what he expects to be the peace and solitude of the countryside: "*The imagination of the fugitive centuplicated the delights of earth and sky, and saw in them as in a mirror the image of his pleasure* at the liberty that he at last enjoyed with no other master but his God" (my italics; *OC*, V, 1707).[9] The preposterousness of this idealized view of Nature is soon exposed by a number of unexpected and unpleasant encounters that befall the priest on his trek through the countryside. Yet now in these later novels Galdós takes one step further the process he had used, for example, in *Gloria*: he not only ridicules the Romantic dreamer's reading of personal emotions into the picturesque landscape, but also adds the obvious corollary that two or more subjective readings of any landscape will tend to be different, if not contradictory. This point emerges very clearly from another landscape scene Nazarín gazes at. Now followed by his two female disciples, Andara and Beatriz, he comes at sunset to a knoll overlooking a beautiful valley. The passage could be cited as an example of Galdós' anticipation of the style of landscape painting to be practised by the Generation of 1898 writers.[10] Like Azorín in his view of the countryside surrounding Yecla in *La voluntad* (1902), Galdós refers now to more senses than sight: of course, he includes a

---

[9] See Christopher Hussey, *The Picturesque: Studies in a Point of View* (London: Frank Case, 1967), pp. 4-5, for the development of the Romantic landscape.

[10] Azorín perpetuated this belief in "El paisaje de España, visto por los españoles", in his *Obras completas*, ed. Angel Cruz Ruel (Madrid: Aguilar, 1961), III, 1188. See also Anthony H. Clarke, "Paisaje interior", and his *Pereda paisajista: el sentimiento de la naturaleza en la novela española del siglo XIX* (Santander: Instituto Cultural de Cantabria and Diputación Provincial, 1969), p. 46, where he demonstrates the difference between Galdós' attitude to landscape painting and that of Pereda: while the latter adores the natural landscape of his native La Montaña (near Santander) for its own sake, Galdós always relates Nature to its human occupant. This view does not really take into account Galdós' ironic use of the Romantic motif, both in the early and late novels.
Even in his fantasy novel of 1909, *El caballero encantado*, Galdós' painting of landscape still discharges an ironic function: the playboy aristocrat Tarsis discovers, in a second magical existence as the peasant Gil, that the Castilian landscape is a beautiful sight when seen close up instead of through a train window or from a hotel terrace as he was wont to view landscapes as a wealthy aristocrat. As labourer Gil, Tarsis comes to feel himself part of the natural landscape, to be a "brush-stroke of its painting" (*OC*, VI, 247). The quilt work of different-coloured crops is compared to a huge heraldic shield, with green dark-edged quarters, or gold quarters with gules lozenges (red poppies). The simile recalls the opening picture of the Castilian landscape that Pepe Rey had scrutinized as he made his way towards Orbajosa at the beginning of *Doña Perfecta*. Like the narrator of *Gloria*, Tarsis-Gil finds the interplay of clouds around the mountaintops a fascinating optical caprice. Yet this idyllic-landscape viewing is soon replaced by Tarsis-Gil's awareness of and own submission to the darker realities of human and social weaknesses in this rural area.

reference to the beautiful sunset reflections, but he also records the smell of smoke coming from the chimneys of village houses as well as the sound of bells (animal and ecclesiastical), all forming a mysterious language that speaks to the soul. But the most important aspect of this Modernist painting is its enigmatic meaning: the landscape proves to be an incomprehensible mystery for the mind of the viewer. The two disciples give conflicting interpretations: for Beatriz the scene expresses sadness, for Andara, joy. Nazarín is hard pressed to reconcile these opposing "readings", but in a neat exhibition of sophistry he is able to propose to the satisfaction of both "readers" that though the ending of one day is a cause for sadness, it also holds the promise of the happy birth of another day. Both "readers" are grateful for the acceptance of their respective versions, but as with the bedaubed faces-cum-masks of the people in the courtyard at Chanfaina's establishment at the beginning of the novel two divergently opposite readings of a picturesque surface are fused into coexistence simply because there is no objective means of testing the veracity of these subjective interpretations.

A short while after this landscape vision the trio of itinerants finds lodging in the ruins of an old hilltop castle. Nazarín, in his perch on the highest point, is likened to an overbaked ceramic standing out against the moonlit sky. While outwardly saying to his disciples that he has found an oasis of peace in which to come closer to God, inwardly Nazarín is really savouring the independence of solitude. But this simplistic Romantic "reading" has already been invalidated by that of his two disciples earlier and will shortly be shattered when the lover of Beatriz attempts to storm the castle retreat.

Even earlier, when standing directly in front of three sets of religious paintings in the mansion of the eccentric nobleman, Don Pedro de Belmonte, Nazarín had shown a marked inability to interpret pictorial surfaces. Of good quality, according to the narrator, the first series depicts scenes from the visit of John the Baptist to King Herod: the Evangelist is seen rebuking Herod in front of Herodias; Salome performs her dance of the seven veils in another canvas, and in the third she carries aloft the severed head of John. The paintings on the second wall are portraits of various saints (unidentified) of the Dominican Order. Alone on the third wall hangs a fine portrait of Pope Pius IX. After his rough welcome from Belmonte, Nazarín is, understandably, at a complete loss to explain the nobleman's interest in religious iconography. Ironically for a fictional character who will become in *Halma* even more of a visual art figure in his own right, Nazarín expresses no interest in deciphering the relevance of this collection of religious paintings. Had he possessed greater insight, he would not have failed to notice, as surely Galdós is urging the reader to notice, some ironic parallels between the subjects of these paintings and his own predicament at this juncture. He has marched resolutely into Belmonte's guarded estate in search of all sorts of trials and tribulations to compensate for all the pleasant and unwanted good fortune he has hitherto experienced in his wanderings. Belmonte's uncivilized treatment of his servants and all strangers has served as a sign that he too can expect some horrendous maltreatment, possibly death. The problem here is that Nazarín's vivid imagination exaggerates the nature and extent of those sacrifices and sufferings: he believes that Belmonte is going to decapitate him, much as John the Baptist had been beheaded by Herod. But the exact opposite occurs; when he is summoned from this room in which the paintings hang he finds, much to his astonishment, that Belmonte has prepared a lavish dinner for him, as befits the disguised itinerant Armenian patriarch that Belmonte firmly believes Nazarín to be. (Later, when Nazarín, Andara and Beatriz are expecting an attack on their lodging in a ruined castle from Beatriz's former lover, Pinto, Nazarín's imagination again leads him to expect a death similar to Herod's slaughter of the Innocents [*OC*, V, 174]). Consequently, the series of paintings on John the Baptist's tragic visit to Herod's palace would seem to offer an ironic visual art parallel to that of Nazarín to Belmonte's mansion, a parallel to which Nazarín is, regrettably, oblivious.

The second series of portraits confirms Nazarín's status as a preacher: he has already made an impassioned plea to Belmonte to change his ways, and during the subsequent dinner both will engage in an important review of the present state of Catholicism in the world. The irony, here, of course, is that despite Belmonte's enthusiastic agreement with the general diagnosis superbly outlined by Nazarín, the elderly nobleman resolutely refuses to reform his own personal ways by abandoning his wealth and luxury for a life of poverty. Even more frustrating for Nazarín is Belmonte's continuous refusal to believe that he is not the itinerant Armenian patriarch who is the gossip of the European press. In short, Nazarín is not as successful a preacher as the Dominican saints immortalized by the canvases on Belmonte's wall. And it is not without significance that in this passage Galdós refers to the Dominicans as the Order of Preachers, and not by the name of their founder.

The mention of the portrait of Pope Pius IX on the third wall is, again, not without its ironic shaft of relevance for Nazarín's story. In the dinner discussion with Belmonte, Nazarín apportions a great deal of the credit for the current revival of Catholicism throughout the world, and in which he is participating, to the liberal Pope Leo XIII (1878-1903), and not to Pius IX (1846-78), his dogmatic and conservative predecessor.

In other words, the art collection Nazarín is unexpectedly left to view in Belmonte's mansion presents a severe type of religious experience that his imagination encourages him to desire, when reality presents him with a more complicated and less extreme form. Furthermore, the severity of the paintings could be said to reflect the harsh outer personality of their owner. But in reality, as he shows during the dinner, he is not always the monster he initially and superficially appears. At heart he is a man of compassion, learning and generosity. Thus this mini art collection serves as a suitable guide to the complexity of both nobleman and priest, and of the novel as a whole.

Halma

In the sequel to *Nazarín* the rebellious priest, having been escorted back to Madrid by the Civil Guard and placed in a prison cell, now becomes the focal point of attention, the object of numerous visits by people who are intrigued by his doctrine, adventures and appearance and wish to probe deeper into these mysteries. His visitors include two famous contemporary artists, Sorolla and Moreno Carbonero. As he had done for Arturo Mélida in *Lo prohibido*, Galdós is here carving out a cameo appearance in fiction for his two painter friends. But the public acknowledgement of friendship (in Sorolla's case, Galdós was the recipient of a portrait in oils, which now hangs in the Casa-Museo Pérez Galdós in Las Palmas) is also dovetailed into the thematic use of visual art material in this novel, since both Sorolla and Carbonero are engaged in painting facial portraits of Nazarín in jail, as if by concentrating on his outward appearance in this way they can help solve for the general public the enigma of his personality.

Another visual art attempt to capture this strange spirit at the beginning of the novel is made by José Antonio de Urrea, maligned wastrel of the aristocratic Feramor family. Having taken a whole series of photographs of the priest and his two female disciples, he is going to print them in the first number of a new illustrated journal he wants to launch. Having studied zincography and heliography, and with a successful collection of photographs of old Andalusian buildings already to his credit, Urrea is optimistic about his new venture and its financial viability. His rich cousin, the Marquess of Feramor, is the logical target to canvas for financial backing and at an evening "tertulia" Urrea presses his case by claiming to the Marquess and his friends that his scoop story and photographs will supersede all other accounts of the eccentric priest. Another argument Urrea uses in order to persuade his listeners is that Nazarín will leave a deep impression on his age. At this point, Urrea does not realize how prophetic his words will prove to be in relation to his own life, for Nazarín will be responsible for counselling Urrea to marry his cousin Halma at the end of the novel and channel his undoubted spirituality in a way acceptable to society. Urrea's prophecy will not prove correct, however, as far as society in general is concerned, for its preoccupation is only with the surface man, Nazarín's identity, his relationship with the two women and his general physical appearance, all so neatly represented by society's fascination with the enigmatic artistic expression of his physiognomy. This point is expressed very clearly by the emphasis in this scene on the photographs of the three characters and their resemblance to universally known figures whose physical images have been transmitted down the ages by the visual arts. Beatriz recalls the image of the homonymic beloved of Dante, but there is even some resemblance to the great poet himself. However, other comparisons suggest the names of St. Clara and other biblical figures immortalized by religious art. Andara's confusing face is also a mixture of the twinkle of Heaven and Hell, whilst Nazarín's face defies exact iconographical affiliation: "But look carefully at Nazarín's face. Is it Job or Mohammed, or St. Francis, or Abelard, or Peter the Hermit, Isaiah or Shem, son of Noah? An immense enigma!" (*OC*, V, 1793). The visual art comparisons underline the visual enigma that these three characters present to the spectator, an enigma that is symptomatic of a greater spiritual confusion which the majority of society does not bother to probe. But in the case of Urrea, association with this visual art venture about Nazarín leads directly to a spiritual reawakening: his need for cash to finance the first issue of the illustrated journal eventually meets with a favourable response from Halma, much to the indignation of the Marquess of Feramor, her brother. The illustrated journal venture will be quickly forgotten as Urrea falls increasingly under the spell of his saintly cousin and eventually, forsaking all, joins her religious commune in the countryside at Pedralba. Again, visual art allusions are multiplied in an attempt to fix the iconographical affiliation of this modern-day saint: she recalls at various times the images of Doña Juana La Loca, Dante and Murillo's St. Isabel.[11] But it is as if the frantic attempt to find the right art image bespeaks the futility of the attempt itself when more important spiritual dimensions go unnoticed by the majority of the circle into which she was born.

Misericordia

Consistent with the pattern of most of the other novels in this and the preceding four groups, *Misericordia* opens with an arresting visual art picture – the two façades of the Madrid church of St. Sebastian – which, in the words of Diane Urey, "becomes the language of description, of the portrait of the heroine, of the Madrid of the novel, and of the novelesque structure as a totality".[12] This architectural prologue is characterized by a juxtaposition of opposites.[13] In the first instance, the solid ecclesiastical mass looks like a person: it has two faces, one of which, the tower, seems to be positioned atop a body that stands, legs apart, shouting abuse at the nearby Angel Square. Secondly, the statue of the patron saint in a niche above the entrance on the south side seems to be in the throes of a dancing session rather than in religious contemplation. The architectural and sculptural masses, therefore, appear to belie their status as art objects in two ways: the church and statue appear to be people, and furthermore, they both appear to be in a state of violent animation that ill accords with their religious purpose. These contradictions are increased by the narrator's assessment that the church's vulgar architecture and ornamentation constitute a source of aesthetic pleasure: "a pleasant ugliness" is the oxymoron that captures this art contradiction. Other art forms are enlisted to corroborate this contradictory impression: "aleluyas" and popular ballad sheets are kindred forms. The contradiction that we had noted in Part I in

---

[11] Urrea, when ploughing the fields at Pedralba, is ·compared to a terracotta allegorical figure of Agriculture.

[12] *Galdós and the Irony of Language* (Cambridge: Cambridge Univ. Press, 1982), p. 60.

[13] See John Kronik's "*Misericordia*'s two faces: the launching of a binary structure", forthcoming.

Galdós' liking for certain grotesque art forms in church decoration is now justified in aesthetic terms. It is a visual art paradox: the architectural monstrosities of the church (its double façade, the irregular roofs, the truncated walls, their cheap ochre colouring, the rusty work) are, if considered separately, ugly, but when viewed as a whole give aesthetic pleasure and should be preserved as an architectural caricature, "a pretty mess", like a ridiculous print (*OC*, V, 1877).[14] The reality of the architectural features is recognized by the narrator for its ugliness, but as a whole it has an artistic patina comparable to any grotesque face by Goya, for example, which transforms the ugliness, without destroying it, into something that is acceptable as beautiful. The aesthetic of the grotesque allows Galdós in this final novel of our Group V to reconcile those aspects of art forms that in his previous novels he had presented as visual engimas. Their resolution, however, is one which recognizes and maintains the coexistence of antithetical terms.

The same duality is continued in the physiognomical description of its perennial inhabitants, the army of beggars. For the most part they are a collection of grotesque faces (for example, Almudena, La Casiana and La Pitusa); but there is also the somewhat sweet, fine features of Benina: "Her dark face did not lack a certain interesting charm, which handled already by old age, was now a vague and hardly visible charm" (*OC*, V, 1882). Her expression of sweet sentimentality likens her to an image of St. Rita of Casia.[15] But another parallel might be drawn with the effeminate statue of St. Sebastian over the southern entrance to the church, for Benina does share some ugliness with her companions, and yet at the same time, like the architectural and sculptural surroundings of the church, she is also distinguished by a certain corporal charm. Physically, she fits into the aesthetic ambience of the church. On a spiritual level, of course, the duality is repeated, but with obviously enlarged proportions: her practical saintliness to others becomes her distinguishing feature, which dwarfs moral blemishes like cheating, lying, cursing or passing moments of vanity. It is not surprising either that an artistic "invention" by Benina should reflect the same mixture of ugliness

---

[14] Galdós in his "Guía espiritual de España", written in 1915 (*OC*, VI, 1508), refers again to the statue of the patron saint of the church as a friend who stands inviting the faithful to enter the church.

[15] Alfieri, "Images", p. 40, note 12, pertinently reminds us that a painting of this Italian saint, by Rafael Hidalgo de Caviedes, a contemporary of Galdós, hangs in the church of The Consolation in Madrid.

and beauty: the excuse she regularly gives her mistress, Doña Paca, to explain her absences from the house when she is begging at the church of St. Sebastian is that she is working at the house of a fictitious priest, Don Romualdo. To confound and upset her alibi, a real, live priest called Don Romualdo does appear in the novel, as the bearer of good news for Doña Paca – she has inherited some money from Andalusian relations. Benina's figment of the imagination has now become a reality: in other words, her initial invention of Don Romualdo has now become an artistic creation, analogous even to the creation of a novel, as Nicole Malaret has argued.[16] The portrait of Don Romualdo fits into the pattern of coexistent opposites that was established by the opening picture of the church of St. Sebastian: "His rough-hewn and bulky features did not lack beauty, because of their proportion and fine lines. It was a beauty one associates with a Michelangelo sculptural mask which decorates an impost, a corbel or the centre of a tablet, spewing forth garlands and flowers from its mouth" (*OC*, V, 1966)!

The Guadarrama landscape paintings in the novel also exhibit the same coexistence of picturesqueness and ugliness reconciled within an artistic frame. In the foreground of the mountain landscapes, Galdós now includes numerous details of vulgar urban reality (working-class houses and objects) in a manner that is reminiscent of the canvases painted by Galdós' good friend, Aureliano de Beruete.[17] Whether or not Galdós owed Beruete any particular debt for guiding him in this landscape painting of the area where urban vulgarities are contiguous with natural beauty, the fact remains that the painting accords perfectly with the pattern established by the edifice of the church of St. Sebastian. Ugly features are amazingly beautiful in their appeal to the viewer's eye:

> Benina found herself in a small square, bounded on the western side by a *vulgar* building, on the south by the parapet of the bridge's buttress, and on the other two sides by *uneven banks and sandy mounds where wild hawthorns, thistles and stunted weeds grow. The site is picturesque, breezy, and one could almost say, joyful, because from this position you overlook the green banks of the river, the washing places and the clothes-lines with clothes of a thousand colours.* To the west you can make out

[16] "*Misericordia*: théorie et pratique du roman", *Les Langues Néo-Latines*, 74 (1980), 64-74: see also John W. Kronik, "*Misericordia* as metafiction", in *Homenaje a Antonio Sánchez Barbudo: ensayos de literatura española moderna*, ed. Benito Brancaforte, Edward R. Mulvihill and Roberto G. Sánchez (Madison: Dept. of Spanish and Portuguese, Univ. of Wisconsin, 1981), pp. 37-50.

[17] See Bravo-Villasante, *Galdós*, p. 142.

the Sierra, and on the opposite side of the river the cemeteries of St. Isidro and St. Justo, *which offer a magnificent view* with so much crestwork of pantheons and so much dark green of cypress trees. *The inherent melancholy of the cemeteries do not deprive them of their decorative character in that panorama, like a good theatre curtain added by Man to those of Nature.* (my italics; *OC*, V, 1948)

The assumption underlying this landscape picture as well as that of the church of St. Sebastian is that conventional notions of beauty and ugliness are not mutually exclusive. The difficulty in determining the identity of the artistic form, so pronounced in the novels treated in the rest of this chapter, is now resolved by accepting the visual art enigma or paradox as it is. Furthermore, in the last analysis, the determination of visual art contours is irrelevant alongside the more important question of the spiritual values of Benina and the other characters. As we saw in Part II when discussing *España trágica*, the *episodio nacional* written twelve years after *Misericordia*, Galdós, after years of applying ridicule, now comes to reject the enigmatic, deceitful world of visual art objects and appearances as meaningless.

CHAPTER 13

VISUAL ART AS PRINCIPAL DETERMINANT OF NOVELISTIC ACTION

La sombra **(1871),** *Angel Guerra* **(1890-91) and** *Tristana* **(1892)**

Our final group of novels, written at different stages in Galdós' career, is constituted by those in which one can say that the central action is principally and directly determined by visual art material. This is to say that, besides continuing to have a very important thematic function often announced, as usual, at the important juncture of the novel's opening, art material is now responsible for creating in some manner or other the direction of the plot. It could be argued very forcefully and convincingly that this role was discharged by the hair picture in *La de Bringas* and therefore that that novel should be included in this final group. While recognizing the persuasiveness of this argument as yet another proof that the classifications I have made in Galdós' contemporary social novels are not meant to be rigidly hermetic, I believe that *La de Bringas* differs somewhat from the three novels I shall discuss in this chapter in that the visual art work of the hair picture is not perceived by the characters themselves as leading directly to the incidents of the plot, whereas in *La sombra, Angel Guerra* and *Tristana* there does exist this kind of a conscious perception, albeit in varying degrees, on the part of the characters.

La sombra

Galdós' first attempt at writing a short novel really set the pattern to which we have become accustomed from our discussion of his later novels: there is at the beginning of the novel a cluster of references to the visual arts that seem designed to alert the reader to the complexity of the subsequent narrative, whose interpretation he or she will have to ponder with care. Furthermore, this story of jealousy opens with a picture of the protagonist as an old man in his chemist's laboratory, or what at least seems to be a laboratory. With its mournful lamp it resembles those background scenes to be found in innumerable Dutch paintings. Harriet Turner has suggested that this description serves a comic purpose;[1] but of additional importance is the subsequent denial by the narrator that Anselmo's room has any such pictorial appearance: there are, in fact, no Gothic vaults, decorated windows, dark backgrounds or interplays of light. The room is just the ordinary type of enclosure to be found in almost all houses in Madrid. Similarly, in physical appearance Anselmo may give the impression of being a medieval sorcerer, but really he is an ordinary nineteenth-century Spaniard. From the outset we are made aware, then, of a confusing discrepancy between resemblances and reality: at the beginning it is between the artistic appearance of Anselmo and his setting, and the narrator's view of both; in the story proper, between Anselmo's hallucination that the rival for his wife's love is a figure in a painting that has taken human form, and the reality of his suspicions of his wife's cousin. And yet in this opening view of Anselmo in his room the narrator presents enough evidence for us to believe that his original impression is not without foundation, for the many objects strewn around the apartment (like a grotesque, disfigured statue of Christ or some animals suspended from the ceiling as in a Teniers study) are not found in ordinary dwellings. The narrator deliberately sows confusion, it seems, in the mind of the reader, but in the process he raises doubts about his own reliability.[2] How far can the reader accept his relation when in the first page of the novel he retracts a suggestion one minute after making it?

Anselmo's story unfolds in another strange location, the family home, and this is described in much greater art and architectural detail, but again the effect is one of confusion created by the surface

---

[1] "Rhetoric in *La sombra*: the author and his story", *AG*, 6 (1971), 5-19.

[2] See Eamonn Rodgers, *Pérez Galdós: Miau* (London: Grant and Cutler, 1978), p. 12, about this surprising twist offered by the narrator.

design of structures and decorations. From the outside the family home appears a typically nondescript eighteenth-century structure. But internally, it possesses all the visual art mysteries of a Moorish palace. According to Anselmo, erstwhile student of painting, the mansion can really be called a museum or art gallery because of its vast collection of art works.[3] The first feature Anselmo chooses to record is, curiously, the chiaroscuro lighting of an area with interconnected Moorish arches, the interplay of light and darkness giving the impression of the existence of some enormous, hidden mirrors. We have already noted in Part I how in the same year that *La sombra* was published Galdós showed a fascination for a similar optical effect in the Toledo hermitage of Christ of the Light in his article "Las generaciones artísticas en la ciudad de Toledo". In *La sombra* this interest is now woven into the fabric of the novel where it creates the appropriate texture of confusion for the remainder of the description of the house and the subsequent story. Furthermore, the reader is lulled into believing that Anselmo is describing a principal room of the mansion, when, in fact, he is only sketching the vestibule, so that we can state that not only the narrator's style of narration but also that of Anselmo contribute to the mystification of the reader. A succession of spaces in the classical Greek style leads the visitor further towards the centre of the house. There is also a progressive increase in pictorial ornamentation on the walls, and the figures chosen seem to have, in retrospect, some bearing on the story of Anselmo's jealousy: figures of centaurs, nymphs, Amazons, Greek heroes and gods suggest the prominence of sexual passion, jealousy and revenge that Anselmo's story will show. At this point, the narrator feels impelled to intervene to correct the impression created by Anselmo's long-winded vision of architectural splendour. The narrator now soberly states that the art collection of the family amounted to only one or two old canvases, jars, and bookshelves that Anselmo's father had bought in an auction. The narrator's rectification, consistent though it may be with his technique in the preliminary painting of old Anselmo's laboratory, is counter-productive, for Anselmo's description of the ancestral palace has been so replete with authoritative details and covers so much space on the printed page that the narrator's dismissal of the account as a fabrication of that architect of the imagination is unconvincing.

---

[3] Joaquín Casalduero, "*La sombra*", *AG*, 1 (1966), p. 34, maintains that this gallery reminds the reader of the Prado museum.

Anselmo continues to mystify the reader when he comes to the grand salon in the centre of the mansion. Having described, seemingly with approval, the regular architectural features of previous structures, he now appears to extol the attractiveness of this disordered space because it provides a welcome contrast and relief from the visual and mental demands of regular, classical architecture:

> Here the objects collected in a correct disorder, the infinite solutions of continuity, the complete absence of proportions, produced an immense pleasure, and erasing all starting points, avoided for the viewer the fatigue of that involuntary measurement the sight usually engages in when in the presence of architecture. Interiors, when they are beautiful, are like abysses: they fascinate the eyes and the viewer cannot avoid throwing a mental lead and tracing in the space the multiplied lines with which his imagination tries to sound the diameter of the arch, the height of the fust and the radius of the vault. In this involuntary mental labour produced by harmony, symmetry, proportions and gracefulness, the mind tires and weakens amidst fatigue and surprise. When there is no style and simply details, when there is no point of view or keystone, the eyesight does not tire; it spreads itself, swings back and forth, loses itself, but remains calm, because there is no question of measuring or comparing; it surrenders to the confusion of the sight and in losing its way, it saves itself. (*OC*, IV, 204)

It is hard not to believe that in this amazing passage Galdós is confessing some private thoughts on his attitude towards architecture in particular and the visual arts in general. It is as if at the start of his literary career Galdós is making an important theoretical justification of current and future lapses from a classical system of aesthetics, indeed of all those occasions in his subsequent work, both in his journalism and fiction, when he shows a taste for examples of unusual or popular art forms. Galdós evidently felt at times the strong urge to abandon the world of high art, classical beauty and symmetry, and to plunge into a completely different art world. He needed to swing to the opposite extreme and lose himself in architectural and art disorder; but as the opening words of the quotation make clear, that disorder was a *regulated* disorder, it was not a totally chaotic mess of designs and colours. There is an elementary order, but it is one which does not demand concentrated deciphering by the author's mind in conjunction with his eyes. Nonetheless, despite this disavowal of anarchy, one feels that Galdós is treading perilously close to the edge of visual art chaos in which the optical organ wallows in purely sensory ecstasy without the control of a guiding rational idea, as if he were going against the advice of his mentor, Federico Balart and, indeed, against the resounding message of his subsequent fiction where, as we have already seen, visual art objects lead characters away from a correct and deeper appreciation of phenomenal reality.

The salon of disordered perspectives also prepares the reader for the presentation of the art work that is the source of Anselmo's story of marital suffering: in a room adjoining the salon hangs a majestic painting of Paris and Helen in a cave on the island of Crannae. It is Anselmo's irrational belief that the figure of Paris steps out of the picture and becomes his wife's lover. This obsession with the painting differs from that of Christine Lantier in Emile Zola's *L'Oeuvre* (1886) or of Dorian Gray in Oscar Wilde's *The Picture of Dorian Gray* (1891), in that Anselmo's fixation is really the objective correlative for the jealousy he feels towards his wife's cousin, Alejandro. Anselmo has transferred his emotions to the visual art object and thereby confused the figure of Paris with that of Alejandro. This sequence of events is clarified by the narrator only at the novel's end after the reader has come to accept Anselmo's version as accurate: indeed the reader is forced to accept it, because it is the only one offered. Anselmo recognizes the truth of the narrator's diagnosis, but defends his inversion of the sequence of events by saying that his story thereby gained more veracity. The narrator's summing up of the process of mental distortion, conveniently aided by a painting, is put, appropriately, in optic terms: "His [Anselmo's] optic nerve underwent an appreciable alteration, producing retinal images by a process that was the reverse of the normal, with the first sensation coming from the brain and then the external impression being verified later" (*OC*, IV, 229). In other words, Anselmo's imagination controls his retinal vision of external reality.

Notwithstanding the narrator's unravelling of the logic of events in the case, the reader's assurance of his reliability is severely jolted in the closing lines of the novelette when the narrator, on his way out of Anselmo's modest apartment, wonders whether he should go back to check one detail that has slipped his mind: did the figure of Paris return to the canvas after the death of Helen? Although he immediately overcomes this impulse, declaring that really neither he nor the reader should be interested in such a detail, the narrator betrays himself: he has, in fact, succumbed to the illogical sequence of narration established by Anselmo; at second remove he too has been fascinated by the figure of Paris on the canvas, coming to believe in his reality as a human being. The visual arts transmitted by the verbal artifice of Anselmo have succeeded in subverting the narrator's reason too.

Angel Guerra

Parts II and III of the second longest novel by Galdós are located in Toledo and could be said to represent the culmination of his previous writings on the city-cum-art-museum ("Las generaciones artísticas en la ciudad de Toledo" and the conclusion of *El audaz*), a culmination in which the setting and artistic ambience are fully adapted to the psychological development of the protagonist. However, amidst all the praise these sections have elicited from critics,[4] it is often forgotten that the opening portion of the novel, like those so far discussed located in Madrid, also contains some visual art material of considerable importance for an understanding of how the magnificent art of Toledo will later affect Angel.

The extensive section on the architectural appearance of the Guerra family home in the centre of Madrid emphasizes the restoration carried out on this old seventeenth-century house:

> Its architectural character was very typical of Madrid: it was made completely of brick except for the wide rectangular main door with its enormous jambs, projecting wall stones and voussoirs ... The modern restoration of this building agrees in its picturesque character with the old severe structure. The surfaces have been painted red to imitate open brick and in the windows and buttresses at the top they have also simulated, with a sufficiently clever coat of paint, a stone projection similar to that of the door. (*OC*, V, 1228)

Galdós opines that this restored façade is preferable to the modern gaudy exteriors of stucco, which he had also bitterly described in his review of Madrid churches in his *La Nación* articles and then in *Fortunata y Jacinta* when discussing the Las Micaelas convent. And like Fortunata when she returns to her home in the Cava de San Miguel, Angel reads into this architectural mass scenes from his life: "The house in which he had been born, those noble walls with which his childhood and youth seemed to form an indivisible whole, spoke to him that very tender language with which the inanimate tells us all it knows and can tell us" (*OC*, V, 1230). It is legitimate, I think, to find a correspondence between the main feature of this architecture

---

[4] See Sopeña Ibáñez, *Arte*, p. 162, and "Juicio de Menéndez y Pelayo acerca de las obras de Galdós", reproduced in Antón del Olmet and García Carrafa, *Los grandes españoles*, pp. 193-97.

(namely, its restored exterior) and the change in Angel's life when at this point he returns to the family home. The army plot in which he had been a leading conspirator has failed, and with his pride hurt and disillusioned with radical politics, he feels the need to return to a life of order and stability. This need will be compounded subsequently by the death of his mother and his inheritance of the family estate as well as by the attraction exerted on him by the beautiful Leré, governess to his daughter. Angel's way of life is refurbished and restored to its former order, or so it seems.

It is of considerable significance that on this return to the family fold he should suffer one of his two recurrent or "constitutive" nightmares, as Galdós calls them. This frightening vision is pertinently related to an architectural form: Angel dreams that he falls through the timber scaffolding of a house under construction and crashes to the ground. Only in retrospect can the hallucination be fully appreciated: in Toledo he will undergo a spiritual reawakening that will kindle a desire within him to found a religious order. This ambition collapses, just as quickly as Angel falls through the scaffolding of his dream, when he is murdered by two enemies. Angel really cannot build a new religious order, as he cannot build a new character: he will inevitably crash through the scaffolding of his dreams because he cannot erase his former tempestuous character. His attempts to become another person are really a surface coating, like the red paint on the top part of his old family home. Beneath the surface appearance of a new persona, as beneath the red paint, there remains the solid character of the original structure. So, architectural reality and architectural dream in this opening section seem to suggest important aspects of Angel's character.

His second recurring nightmare when under stress reproduces a historical event, the 1866 execution of the sergeants of the San Gil barracks in Madrid who had unsuccessfully tried to revolt against the government of General O'Donnell. The dominant image in this re-created tableau is always the contorted, frenzied expression, like that of a Greek mask, on the face of an unknown witness of the event. José María Jover Zamora maintains that this picture is a verbal transcription of the figure with outstretched hands in Goya's famous canvas, "Execution of the Defenders of Madrid".[5]

Prior to these hallucinations in the ancestral home, Angel had

---

[5] "Benito Pérez Galdós: *La de los tristes destinos* (caps. I y II)", in *El comentario de textos 2: De Galdós a García Márquez*, ed. Andrés Amorós (Madrid: Castalia, 1974), p. 39.

one day rediscovered the portraits of his family in the drawing-room. He does not see their painted surfaces because there is no light in the room; he resees them in his memory and his imagination. Are the readers not entitled to see in this scene an important anticipation of Angel's later approach towards the art treasures of Toledo when his vision of particular art objects is heavily influenced by other personal considerations, especially his high opinion of his self-appointed role in founding a religious order? Here, in the darkness of the family drawing-room, Angel is spared some embarrassment at the visual confrontation with an unpleasant past reality preserved by Art.

Another aspect of the same tendency to subjective observation is revealed towards the end of Part I when his daughter, Encarnación, is near death. Angel finds consolation in some worthless religious paintings his mother had bought. Included in the group are two large oil paintings, copies of Ribera anchorites. Both are realistic studies whose chiaroscuro accentuates the squalor of the naked bodies. The subjects are, of course, a subtle iconographical anticipation of the role that Angel will later try to play in his residence in the Toledo countryside. This role, however, can only be appreciated later in the novel, but for the moment it is clear that the prayers for Encarnación's recovery which he addresses to these paintings are not wholly spontaneous or sincere. In exchange for his daughter's health he promises to sacrifice his love for Dulcenombre, his erstwhile revolutionary aide; but this is a meaningless offer, for he has already considered ways of breaking off the relationship, and anyway, he is now more attracted to the ample-bosomed Leré. In many ways, the scene summarizes in miniature the entire course of Angel's Toledan experience: his religious activities will be an attempt to sublimate his sexual desires for Leré and this act of self-deception will be fostered to a great extent by the abundance of beautiful art works that his eye will admiringly contemplate throughout the city.

Leré is the first of a series of characters in the novel who are insistently likened to art objects or associated in some way with the visual arts. She suffers an optical defect, a vibration of the optic nerve called rotating nystagmus, which, with her marble white skin and contrasting jet black hair, makes her the image of a clock doll. Dulcenombre and other members of the Babel family are always compared to sculpted figures: Dulce, to an alabaster bas-relief, and Arístides, a brother, to the figure of a herald on a shield or a Gothic portico. Two other siblings, Fausto and Policarpo, engage in the printing of political "aleluyas" and a lottery scheme. All of these characters, like Angel, are seen both in Toledo and in Madrid; one cannot say, therefore, that their iconographical resemblance is deliberately created or programmed for Angel's Toledan sojourn. Far more to the point is their status as art objects, wherever they are located. Whether pretty or grotesque, the members of the Babel family do not appeal to Angel as proper human beings; but then his view of the world and of people is through the glasses of art.[6]

The people of Toledo are associated with the visual arts in more direct ways, as is to be expected. Some are avid collectors of relics and artefacts. Typical is the array of figurines, dolls, pictures, photographs, pieces of wooden bas-reliefs that adorn the drawing-room of Felisita, the spinster sister of the priest Casado: the jumble of art objects is a veritable optical danger as the eye of the viewer is attracted from all angles by diverse colours and outlines. The same disordered perspective is associated with Felisita's lofty "tertulia" in the gallery adjoining the Cathedral belfry where she gossips to friends about Angel's latest activities: the grotesquely enlarged vision of the carved figures on the Cathedral façade adds a pertinent commentary on the distorted nature of Felisita's tales. The point is surely that Felisita collects an inordinate mass of bric-à-brac without rhyme or reason, just as she collects any odd scurrilous tale about Angel. Though a native of Toledo, she has no real artistic sense, just as she has no true appreciation of the reality of Angel's life.

The same lack of artistic awareness is shown by other local inhabitants as they try to sell old pieces of stone, wood or earthenware found in the city to gullible tourists. Leré's father had profited considerably from this trade, but it is in the example of the entrepreneurial abilities of Anchuras, a relative of the sickly priest and Angel's fellow lodger, Don Tomé, that Galdós pokes most fun at this absurd racket. Anchuras naïvely believes that more artists will come to paint the Moorish arches and Gothic windows of his patio if he splashes bright paint over the whole structure. Here Galdós may have had in mind his own visits to Toledan patios and alleys in the company of an artist friend, the locally born Ricardo Arredondo,

---

[6] Emilia Pardo Bazán in her review of the novel in *Obras completas*, III, 1102, declares that there is a profusion of characters whose faces are scrupulously studied and which recall those in Rembrandt's famous canvas "The Night Watch". There is an especially large number in Toledo: the priest, Juan Pintado, has a figure like a carved door-knocker. A nun, Sor Expectación, is like a sculptured alabaster negress. Mateo, one of the retainers on Angel's commune, resembles the portrait of "Maestro Juan de Avila" by El Greco, whilst the nephew of another inhabitant, Virones, has the beautiful figure of Murillo's Christ-Child.

precisely to gather material for this novel.[7]

Two patios in particular – those of Angel's relations, Teresa Pantoja and Don José Suárez de Monegro – receive extensive attention and again for the purpose of exposing the unaesthetic jumble of objects, albeit commercially unexploited. Crowded with art works and built at a number of different levels, both areas present a grotesque appearance. For example, the socle in Teresa's patio is covered with "broken tiles of a thousand different shapes and designs, as they came from demolished palaces and monasteries, some with grotesque figures, others with bits of border, many showing pieces of decorative stone, the quarter of a shield or syllables of a sign" (*OC*, V, 1309). Don José's patio is covered with collections of poor-quality religious paintings; for example, one canvas of some souls in Purgatory looks like a dish of cod dressed in the Biscayan manner! Further incongruities abound in inner rooms with prints and engravings of horse-races positioned alongside art objects from convents and monasteries. The wonderful plateresque façade of the mansion has been buried beneath coats of bright paint so as to suggest the surface appearance of other construction materials – hardly an encouraging sign of the aesthetic sense of a man who would like to modernize the street plan of the city by demolishing a number of old buildings. Galdós seems deliberately to have selected areas and structures that reflect badly on the visual appeal of this supposed art treasure-house of a city. But surely Galdós' greater aim is to build up a comic backcloth for Angel's own aesthetic experiences within the city, experiences which will lead directly to his spiritual reawakening.[8]

His first activity after calling on his relations is to familiarize himself with the lay-out of the labyrinth of streets and buildings. The experience is clearly a pleasant one, for he enjoys himself in "the odour of artistic, religious and noble sanctity which emanated from those venerable bricks" (*OC*, V, 1314). From the outset, then,

---

[7] See Marañón, "Galdós en Toledo" and Galdós' own account, "*Angel Guerra* y Toledo" and "Visita a una catedral" in his "Memorias de un desmemoriado" (*OC*, VI, 1693-99). Enrique Lafuente Ferrari, "El pintor de Toledo, Ricardo Arredondo (1850-1911)", *AE*, 26 (1969), p. 42, suggests that Arredondo's paintings may have influenced the selection of scenes by Galdós. But from the photographic reproductions given in Santiago Sebastián, "Arredondo y otros paisajistas toledanos", *AE*, 17 (1960), 113-27, it is obvious that these pictorial records were, if anything, only an external stimulus for Galdós' far more purposeful verbal descriptions.

[8] Francisco Ruiz Ramón, *Tres personajes galdosianos* (Madrid: Revista de Occidente, 1964), p. 69, contrasts Galdós' "realistic" picture of Toledo with Bécquer's romanticized vision in some of his *Leyendas*, but fails to note the ironic tone of the former's architectural descriptions.

Angel's religious arousal is based on an aesthetic response to the physical architecture of the city's buildings, some of which (the more private ones) have already been ridiculed for their grotesque appearance. Moreover, the reaction of Angel to what he thinks is beautiful is coloured with literary reminiscences: in other words, as we saw in his observation of the family portraits in Part I of the novel, these architectural masses trigger instant impressions that appeal to his imagination. The precise observation of the architectural features is soon replaced by the creations of his imagination:

> The doors bristling with nails; the infinite unevenness of grazing levels and hollows; the façades with innumerable folds; the balcony railings; the statues inside their wire-covered and lamp-illuminated niches; the narrow passageways between walls that want to come together; the covered arcades and steep cross-streets; the solitude; the shade distributed in capricious masses; all aroused in the spirit of the wanderer the impression of a dramatic legend or of historical lyricism.
> (*OC*, V, 1314)

Indeed, the sight of the different angles, levels and junctures of buildings from the promontory beside the church of St. Andrew suggests to Angel that he is in some exotic oriental city like Tamerlane's Samarkand. But Galdós punctures the Romantic delight Angel feels when on one midnight sally the newcomer to Toledo hears a voice in a darkened square. Angel is immediately reminded of one of the legends composed by the Romantic poet, Zorrilla. Just when he is expecting to see a knight in doublet step forward and challenge him to a duel, he is waylaid by the ex-mariner uncle of Dulcenombre Babel, Don Pito, who in one of his usual drunken stupors curses the chaotic arrangement of the city streets. It is as if Angel's Romantic escapism is not being allowed to go unquestioned as the ground for his important religious conversion is prepared.[9] Pito as a member of that grotesque family, the Babels, represents a reality of violence and evil (albeit in its least pernicious forms) that later in the persons of his two nephews will sweep away both Angel's dreams of a religious commune and his own life.

Naturally, the famous religious buildings of Toledo play an important role in this awakening of Angel's religious spirit, but again Galdós stresses that it is the artistic features, not the religious aura, of the locales which, at least in the first few days, appeal to Angel's

---

[9] Like other characters in our other previous groups of novels, Pito had enjoyed (again when in a drunken stupor) the beautiful landscape of the Guadarrama when living in Madrid, finding it an escape from the depressing turmoil of the capital.

senses. Even the nuns singing in a convent appear to his eye as if they were figures in a painting of some kind: "You could see through the iron screen the black and white silhouettes of the Lord's spouses bathed in a bluish, mysterious light" (*OC*, V, 1314). Really, though, this appreciation of beautiful art forms conceals the true motivating force in his life at this moment, his passion for Leré. All three levels of experience – the religious, the aesthetic and the erotic – are here fused into one. The same point is effectively made when, after another chance encounter with Leré, Angel finds himself during mass the following morning "looking for a deep and clandestine communication with the ultrasensorial world" (*OC*, V, 1321). He is so overcome by the beauty of the artistic appearance of the church that he feels love for "things which before seemed false to him, and, what is stranger, still seemed false to him. He did not know whether his urge to try the delights of piety was a phenomenon of aesthetic or religious emotion" (*OC*, V, 1321). What should have been the primary response in this religious building takes third place to the stronger emotions of sexual passion and art appreciation. Art thus becomes the mediator between two antithetical, yet closely related experiences: the erotic and the mystical. Later at the church where his fellow lodger, Don Tomé, says mass, Angel needs to fix his gaze on a statue of the Virgin Mary in order to pray. Staring at a statue of Christ on the Cross does not achieve the same results. Angel's religious feelings clearly have to be prompted by art, but art of a kind that recalls the female form of Leré.

The focal point of Angel's religious experience will, of course, be the city's magnificent cathedral with its incomparable art treasures. Here again Galdós engineers some scenes to show that Angel's dominating preoccupation is aesthetic and sexual, not religious. But before we see Angel in the precincts of the cathedral we see him first enjoying the spectacle of the outer structure from his room window. As he reclines on his bed reading a book on Spanish history he gazes through the artistic frame of the lead windows and their heavy, whitewashed wooden shutters. The picture he is looking at is the skyline (similar to that enjoyed by the Count of Cerezuelo from outside Alcalá de Henares in *El audaz*). The relevant features of the ecclesiastical structures, reinforced by the artistic frame, are skilfully chosen by Galdós so as to suggest and encourage the art base to Angel's religious aspirations. The humorous counterpoint to the sky-gazing of Angel is, of course, the subterranean burrowings of another lodger in the house, the archaeologist priest, Don Palomeque, who succeeds in discovering the remains of an ancient wall underneath the rooms of the house!

So as not to let the point go unnoticed, Galdós gives another even more attractive picture of the cathedral spire, when it is covered in snow. As we noted earlier in our discussion of some *Episodios* and of *Fortunata y Jacinta*, this particular example of a picturesque landscape appealed to Galdós' eyes and mind:

> The Cathedral, with its crests streaked by very fine reeds of snow, and its variety of projections and angular outlines, presented to one's eyes the appearance of a Chinese phantasmagoria. The tower stood out almost clean, dark and freckled, amidst so much whiteness, against the ethereal sky, with some touches of cascarilla on the helmet of the Cathedral and the tops of the three crowns; it stood out larger, dreamier, more slender amidst the desolation inherent to the boreal landscape. (*OC*, V, 1348)

This exotically beautiful picture is immediately counterbalanced by the scenes outside in the street where the frozen paths occasion fantastic gymnastic postures by pedestrians as they slip and slide. Galdós is always anxious to juxtapose human reality and pictorial escapism.

With hesitant steps Angel gradually comes to embrace religion with enthusiasm. The culmination of his preparation, now for leadership of his own religious order to be housed on his estate in the Toledan countryside, takes place within the confines of the cathedral and in front of its artistic splendours. It is true to say that Angel is overawed by the beauty of religious art and its great contribution to the propagation of religious, spiritual ideas. Yet because of the previous emphasis on the sexual motivation behind Angel's aesthetic response to religious and other places, our suspicions of the validity of this religious vocation are aroused.[10] They are confirmed very forcefully on one occasion when Angel learns of the imminent transfer of Leré to a convent in Gerona, near the French border. Angel flies into a rage, venting his anger on those art treasures of the cathedral that he had formerly found so attractive:

> The retable, which forms a complete doctrine of dogma translated by means of the engraver's chisel, gold and paint, from the language of ideas to that of form, always made him feel giddy with wonderment. But that day the retable *rose to the roof like a sublime display of human pride*. The extraordinary gratings usually gave him the idea of the

---

[10] See Scanlon, "Religion and art", p. 104.

Celestial Gates, which, if they are closed for sinners, open for the select few. *That day they seemed to him the frontispieces of magnificent cages for those madmen seized with the delirium of art and religion.* The Virgin on the prime altar in the choir reminded him, apart from its black colour, of his relative Doña Mayor, and in the lower choir stalls, the grotesque figures of carved walnut imitated the gestures and expressions of Arístides and Fausto Babel. The figure of Don Diego López de Haro had been transformed into Don José Suárez and one of the large masks on the organ with a Turkish turban was Don Simón Babel himself. (my italics; *OC*, V, 1414)

The passage superbly illustrates the main point Galdós has been making in all of his fiction: the human retina can indeed transform the appearance of beautiful (or ugly) art objects when it is subject to strong emotional pressure felt by the viewer. Yet Angel's amazing insight here into his own seduction by the visual arts proves too transitory, for when he discovers that Leré is not, in fact, going to be moved from Toledo, he resumes his customary reverence towards ecclesiastical art:

He had never seen the Cathedral so attractive, or heard singing so beautiful or inspired, or found the chancel so terribly sumptuous and elegant. All of the figures on the outside wall of the main chapel – angel musicians in various poses, some with a trumpet in their hand, others with a zither or a violin – joined their voices and those of their delicate instruments to the pathetic psalmody, a triumphal praise of the Lord and trust in His mercies. The huge church seemed to him to be of extreme artistic beauty, like a gigantic shrine of ivory carved by the hands of angels. (*OC*, V, 1419)

Angel's move to the country estate does not sever his links with the art-museum-cum-city of Toledo. The picturesque views of the city across the Tagus which he, Pito and others so much enjoy on their promenades, the reproduction of the Toledan style of architecture in the design of the new buildings for his own religious order, his instruction in church liturgy, all ensure that the last phase of his life is still held within the frame of the enchantment of religion and aesthetics. To his credit Angel wonders at times about the sincerity of his religious vocation, whether his adoration of the Eucharist is really a cover for an aesthetic dilettantism in which he wants to play the role of artist of the mass. The artistic base of his religious vocation is again exposed by two contrasting scenes. He is enthralled by the magnificent services in the cathedral on Maundy Thursday which he views from the proximity of the chancel: the setting encourages mysticism, communion with God. Yet the popular procession of images through the city streets later that day nauseates him beyond measure.

The essential conflict between Angel's striving for a religious vocation and his deep-seated desire for Leré is summed up in a nightmarish sequence later the same day when he returns to his country estate. Jesús, the son of one of his followers, has been instructed to bring his kid goat along the road to meet Angel. Unfortunately, the animal runs away from the boy into the countryside and Angel is forced to hunt for it during a thunderstorm at night. Naturally, he loses his way and comes to a halt in a cave on whose walls the lightning traces chiaroscuro outlines of fantastic animals. In an apparition the beautiful Leré ignores Angel's pleas for help and, instead, throws pieces of her ample breasts to the kid goat. Geraldine M. Scanlon has suggested that this scene derives from a number of traditional Christian iconographical sources, although there is no overt or indirect allusion to a visual art source.[11] The artistic patina would, indeed, be appropriate for this emblematic representation of the struggle between the spirit and the flesh within Angel's mind, for Toledo's art works have been instrumental in fomenting the belief that he has overcome his lust for Leré and developed a religious vocation. Art has been the medium for this struggle between the flesh and the spirit. It is highly appropriate that the verbal evocation of traditional iconography now eternalizes this dilemma in the reader's imagination with a highly memorable tableau.

Tristana

By comparison with the French novel of the nineteenth-century the Spanish novel of the same period shows a decided lack of interest in the role of the painter as fictional protagonist, one of those most likely areas for parallels between the visual arts and the novel that we noted in our introduction.[12] *Tristana* is Galdós' only attempt at this type of novel, though he had made passing references to the profession of the painter in *Torquemada en la hoguera* and *Fortunata y Jacinta*. Nevertheless, Horacio, the painter lover of the eponymous

---

[11] "Religion and art", p. 103; Hieronymus Bosch's visions of Hell and Joachim Patenier's painting (also in the Prado) on the temptation of St. Anthony theme are cited.

[12] See Theodore Robert Bowie, *The Painter in French Fiction: a Critical Essay* (Chapel Hill: Univ. of North Carolina Press, 1950).

heroine, is not the main character of the novel as Lantier is in Zola's *L'Oeuvre*, which is essentially a study of the life and work of the painter *manqué*. But on the other hand, Horacio is not merely the third member of the lovers' triangle, complement to Tristana and Don Lope, a role which Pardo Bazán found an unwarranted complication of the feminist theme with which the novel seemed to open.[13] By propelling the dreams and illusions of Tristana into the world of art, Horacio ensures that the theme of art has a far more prominent function in the elaboration of the novel's theme than that of merely adding a few Sorolla-like touches of light and colour to the narration, as Carmen Bravo-Villasante quaintly imagined.[14] By making Tristana's lover an artist by profession, Galdós is able to shift his preoccupation with the vulnerability of the human eye to the attractions of the visual arts to centre stage, as it were, where it becomes the main matter of his fiction, and also in a fascinatingly clever way that is still consonant with his aim to expose the inability of people to see reality correctly. Hence *Tristana* can be considered the ultimate development of all the previous novels we have discussed and in which various threads of visual art material have been intertwined in differing degrees; paintings, picturesque land-scapes, art metaphors and a discussion of the value of eyesight, all are now, perforce, filtered directly into the main story of painter Horacio's love affair with Tristana.

The art tone of the novel is set well before Horacio arrives on the scene. In filling in the background details to the cohabitation of chivalresque Don Lope and his ward-cum-lover, Tristana, Galdós fixes both with a visual art affiliation. Lope resembles a figure taken from "The Lances" by Velázquez, one of Galdós' favourite canvases. The comparison, repeated at other points later in the novel, is not inappropriate in view of Lope's antiquated code of chivalry (except in sexual matters). And yet this knight of yore is not housed in baronial splendour, but in a modest apartment room in the Madrid suburb of Chamberí close to taverns and stores! This impoverished state is the outcome of his efforts to aid the financially-troubled parents of Tristana by selling off his collections of paintings and armour. The only art objects remaining in his possession are a series of portraits of former female conquests, ranging from painted miniatures to photographs. So, Lope is an iconographical figure who

[13] See *"Tristana"*, in her *Obras completas*, III, 1119-23.
[14] *Galdós*, p. 142.

secures indirectly the gratitude and then sexual favours of Tristana through the sale of art objects. Art becomes the means, however indirectly and unwittingly it is engineered, by which the subservience of Tristana to her eventual guardian and lover is assured. Once more, as we saw in the novels of the previous groups, especially in *Fortunata y Jacinta* and *La de Bringas*, art is often the surreptitious or unrecognized means to a financial end.

Tristana too is cast in the mould of an art object, but the die is completely different from that of Velázquan Lope: she is likened to a figure from a Japanese painting with incredibly white alabaster skin that is always in a perfect state of pulchritude like the coat of an ermine. With her arched eyebrows (the work, it seems, of a painter's brush), her boots and a comb in her hair, she is the exact likeness of a Japanese lady. The texture of her skin is even like that of the warm plastic paper which Japanese artists use to represent the comedy and tragedy of life. The comparison suggests first that Tristana is a somewhat cold, dehumanized figure, proud of her own exotic beauty, and that she is more like an art object than a real person. Yet at the same time her svelte oriental appearance takes on a comic outline when placed alongside the contrasting full-blooded figure of a Golden-Age Spanish soldier, in a manner somewhat reminiscent of the composite caricature formed by Pez and Rosalía Bringas in *La de Bringas*. Furthermore, the reference to the Japanese use of a paper similar in texture to Tristana's face in order to convey the tragedy and comedy of life suggests that her own story will contain those ingredients, and conversely, at the same time, that Tristana's story will also have the texture of a Japanese print.

The narrator develops this oriental analogue in a very important way: in the seduction of his ward, Lope had played upon her tendency, quite natural in a young woman, to idealize and romanticize reality, to see reality not as it was, but as it suited her. With time Tristana comes to realize the true nature of her relationship with Lope, and the narrator casts this awakening of her conscience in terms of the visual appreciation and recognition of an art form:

> Her eyes did not know how to look at the future, and if they did, they saw nothing. But one day she noticed the shadow that the present cast on the spaces of the future, and that image of herself, elongated by distance, with such an ill-proportioned and truncated silhouette, occupied her attention for a long while, suggesting a thousand thoughts that mortified and confused her. (*OC*, V, 1543)

The metaphor of the art form captures brilliantly the extent to which a Romantic imagination activated by an association with a man with the mien of a Velázquez figure has led another art-object person to fail to see the moral implications of that relationship.

Failure to see reality is evident, for example, in her naïve belief, as expounded to her servant Saturna, that there are great financial rewards to be gained from painting landscape canvases; but, more importantly, it is also the dominant feature of her relationship with Horacio. The chance encounter that is responsible for launching this relationship occurs one Sunday afternoon, the only occasion Don Lope allows his mistress to leave the house with Saturna. The two women have taken their usual stroll to the nearby area of Cuatro Caminos and stand watching a party of blind and deaf-mute boys, also allowed out from their institution for an afternoon stroll. Tristana is amazed at the different means of communication between the two sets of disadvantaged youths: the faces of the deaf-mutes are full of expression and movement, whilst the eyes of the blind are empty and vacant with the pupil like a glass ball. Instead, their hands and fingers are their mode of expression, their medium of communication. Tristana is so upset by the appearance of the blind boys that she finds it difficult to look at them. The confrontation is slightly reminiscent of Galdós' own encounter with a skeleton in the cloisters of the Colegiata of Santillana del Mar, as recorded in his article, "Cuarenta leguas por Cantabria" (1876). As we noted in Part I of this study, the confrontation with the empty sockets of the skeleton propped up against the socle of the cloister wall had led to some bleak meditation on the transitoriness of architectural and human forms. The meditation prompted by Tristana's contemplation of the blind boys is not so profound. After averting her gaze, out of compassion for their plight, she muses, somewhat ironically, that the blind are incomplete people because "they lack the faculty of awareness, and what a job having to discover everything with the mind!" (*OC*, V, 1554). Like Teodoro Golfín in *Marianela* and Francisco Bringas in *La de Bringas*, those other artists of the human eye blessed with an even stronger imagination, Tristana extols eyesight as the supreme faculty possessed by human beings, without realizing that the value of eyesight is naught when controlled by the more potent force of the human imagination which can subvert and transform those retinal images.

This sequence of the blind boys, therefore, forms a kind of prelude to the first contact of Tristana and Horacio, one an artist, the other, an art object and then an eventual artist *manquée*. This first contact between the two lovers is made – importantly – through the medium of the eye and at some distance. Horacio is talking with the teacher accompanying the party of blind boys, and at one moment he lifts his eyes which, in good Romantic fashion, cross with those of Tristana which are gazing at the scene: it is love at first sight with the usual accompaniment of a *frisson* of the senses: "... in both, seeing and looking at each other was a single action: Tristana felt a shudder inside, like the instant suspension of the blood's flow" (*OC*, V, 1554). She averts her gaze, but is soon tempted to look at him again and this time his eyes are searching for her. Tristana is convinced that she has seen Horacio before, but she cannot remember the place. She makes a rapid evaluation of his masculine features, paying especial attention to his eyes, which at first she mistakenly believes are covered with glasses. This eye language is replaced the next day by a verbal intimacy which allows Tristana to see Horacio at a closer range. Not surprisingly, she has to correct a few of the impressions she had formed the previous day through her distant ocular appreciation: in particular, Horacio now appears younger than at first sight. This first contact of the lovers is nurtured by another medium of distancing: the exchange of letters (in the case of Tristana, full of cloying sentimentality) for which Saturna is the obliging messenger.[15] The emphasis given to the original and subsequent distancing of the lovers suggests that their relationship is founded essentially on a physical distancing which encourages a mental distancing of the two, as if they had the wrong images of each other. The irony of Tristana's sympathy for the blind boys now becomes clear: the physical faculty for which she professed so much concern is decidedly inoperative in the most important relationship of her life, for for her it will be love at a distance, which is the only way the imagination of the lover or beloved can function. And Tristana lives only off her imagination.

This initial distancing of the lovers is also reflected in the views offered of Horacio's art studio, surprisingly the only detailed view Galdós offers us in his fiction of a locale with which he was extremely familiar. Saturna is once more the intermediary for this picture, which is consequently ridiculed by her naïvety and ignorance of what

---

[15] Gilbert Smith, "Galdós' *Tristana* and letters from Concha-Ruth Morell", *AG*, 10 (1975), 91-120, and Carmen Bravo-Villasante, in her edition of Emilia Pardo Bazán, *Cartas a Benito Pérez Galdós (1889-1890)* (Madrid: Turner, 1975), both suggest that Galdós was drawing on his own love-letters, albeit to different women (!), for this novel.

she sees in the studio. Most of the art work consists of anatomical studies on canvas or in plaster and at various stages of completion and whose nudity shocks the servant. She lists all the props used by the models and her own conclusion is that the art profession is a great laugh! She reports that Horacio is always engrossed in writing his love-letters to Tristana; we never see him at work, painting. When Tristana discovers that Horacio is a painter by profession she is wildly enthusiastic, but the degree of elation seems hardly appropriate for the level of artistic talent he seems to possess, according to Saturna.

The idyll develops on trips to areas situated on the outskirts of the city and close to the surrounding countryside: Fuencarral, El Pardo and the Chamartín Hill, where the two towers of the Jesuit school resemble another Japanese visual art object, the pagoda. Sunsets over the Guadarrama are a particular source of enjoyment for these two artists and they exchange impressions as their eyes scan the horizon:

> At dusk they would gaze at the grandiose horizon of the Sierra with its rich turquoise hues, uneven touches and transparencies, as if the very pure blue had been poured over ice panes of glass. The curves of the bare earth, creeping and disappearing like lines that want to copy the calm waves, kept repeating to them that "more, always more", the inextinguishable anxiety of their thirsty souls ... To the west they would see the sky ablaze, that splendid trace of the setting sun. Against that strip, the cypress trees of the cemetery of St. Ildefonso, intersected by mournful gateways in the Greek style, more elegant in the half light, stood out like a black crest of sharp points. (*OC*, V, 1560-61)

Lest the reader be beguiled by the transcription of this beautiful canvas, Galdós now explicitly states that the lovers' delight with all they behold is only a projection of their own feelings. Other realistic elements of this landscape-gazing do, in fact, reduce its idyllic status: the two lovers often dally around the inactive amusement rides of a fairground near the city reservoir. The various immobilized, extravagant shapes of the rides, especially of the wooden horses, add a comic commentary to the lovers' sentimental mutterings as well as anticipating the artificial and sterile relationship Horacio and Tristana will come to experience after the amputation of Tristana's leg and its replacement by a wooden member have reduced her to a status semi-comparable to that of the fairground figures.

Perhaps even more disillusioning is the account Horacio gives to Tristana on these countryside walks of his career as a painter. It might be said that he served his apprenticeship when he made surreptitious caricatures in the business ledgers of his grandfather, who, sworn enemy of all artists, considered them as falsifiers of Nature and usurpers of God's gifts to man. Later Horacio had pursued his artistic bent by going to Italy but a period of moral dissipation in the flesh-pots of Venice had preceded a more settled period when he had studied painting very diligently and managed to overcome that great defect of all Spanish artists, as Galdós had diagnosed it in his *La Prensa* articles: the inability to reproduce lines on canvas. In the light of this career record and his current inactivity, his ambition to become a great painter and his belief that he possesses a great talent (". . . a part, not very big perhaps, but a part, in short, of the divine essence that God has given to humanity" [*OC*, V, 1560]) sound absurdly pretentious!

More seriously, it is this profession of Horacio that sows disturbing ambitions in Tristana's mind. Finally daring to visit Horacio in his studio, Tristana is captivated by the painted canvases; but Galdós makes it clear that it is not really Tristana's interest in the skill of painting that is aroused, but rather her potent imagination: the paintings "inflamed her fantasy and enchanted her eyes" (*OC*, V, 1569). It is Tristana's imagination, like that of Isidora Rufete in *La desheredada* or Rosalía Bringas in *La de Bringas*, which is her greatest enemy, controlling her view of reality. She does demonstrate some aptitude and skill in mixing colours on the palette and blending them into the canvas, yet her imagination, even here, outstrips her manual dexterity: ". . . if her hand did not help her, her mind proceeded ahead very arrogantly, knowing how things were to be done, although she could not physically do it" (*OC*, V, 1569). "Hurling herself into the free spaces of the mind and demonstrating the most audacious aspirations" (*OC*, V, 1569), Tristana imagines that she will even surpass Horacio as a painter.[16] Whilst this ambition leads Tristana to copy frenetically at the kitchen table figures from engravings or still-life compositions, Horacio becomes increasingly concerned, for he realizes that Tristana will not settle for the traditional role of a wife as housekeeper. As a result, his affection cools and he takes less interest in art. Proximity and normal human intimacy, it might be said, lead to mutual disillusionment, whereas both need to live at a distance so that their idealized views of each other can flourish unthreatened by reality, as the narrator makes

[16] See Noël M. Valis, "Art, memory and the human in Galdós' *Tristana*", *KRQ*, 31 (1984), 207-20.

very clear: "Distance became a voluptuousness of that subtle love, which was struggling to untie itself from all influence of the senses" (*OC*, V, 1604).

At this point their romance is saved and prolonged for a while by the opportune removal of Horacio, at the instigation of his aunt, to the family estates on the east coast. A flood of correspondence ensues, with the lovers rivalling each other in the expression of exaggerated affection. Horacio now – significantly – resumes painting and describes in a large number of words some of the magnificent land- and sea-scapes he has been doing. He assumes, confidently and correctly, given his "novia's" vivid imagination, that Tristana's artist's eyes can visualize the scenes he is painting. Indeed, his canvases are all too real for his beloved, who now believes that as a painter he will surpass Velázquez and Raphael when he has completed the masterpiece "The Embarcation of the Expelled Moriscos". As we know Galdós repeatedly ridiculed this type of historical painting in his articles for *La Prensa*, the fact that here Tristana extols Horacio's canvas would suggest that the author is again disparaging his protagonist's ability to discern good art. At the same time she substitutes for her fading mental picture of her lover's real features an image that is completely idealized, a product of violent twists of her imagination. In a sense this is her happiest period, for she can live entirely off her imagination, still be in communion with Horacio, and at the same time continue to paint her still-life compositions or touch up her copy of Velázquez's "The Spinners". Life, despite the rhetoric used by parted lovers, proceeds swimmingly for her. The nasty jolt of reality comes, however, with the amputation of her leg: Horacio returns to Madrid to see her and, of course, his physical appearance does not correspond to her idealized image of him. His attempts to give her art lessons after her recovery soon fail and with his departure for an arranged marriage in the East, invalid Tristana eventually settles down to domestic married life with Don Lope. Tristana's life of the imagination, fuelled by her relationship with artist Horacio and the subsequent interest in painting, now gives way to prosaic domesticity. Lope can enjoy the subservience of a human art object that he had bought earlier by selling off plastic art objects. For Tristana, on the other hand, the price is that her eyes are now firmly fixed on the physical infirmity of her wooden leg and her mind on the moral scar of her relationship with Lope. The irony of her observations on the blind boys surrounding Horacio òn that first fateful encounter is now redoubled: had she practised what she preached, by fixing her eyes on observable reality, then her moral insight might have been developed. But her strong imagination is depraved, as it were, by her discovery of the world of art. She has to be brought back to reality by the violent shock of her amputation. What could have been Galdós' praise of the life of the professional painter, had he followed the example of Zola in *L'Oeuvre*, becomes his most complete indictment of the collusion of art and imagination in deceiving the human eye in its attempt to appreciate phenomenal reality.

CONCLUSION

At its most elementary level, the age-old relationship between the sister arts of art and literature was limited to painting and poetry, as immortalized in Horace's catch-phrase, "ut pictura poesis": painting took its subjects from poetry, while poetry tried to imitate painting in its descriptions of external visual phenomena. If the nineteenth century saw a break in this tradition, with increasing importance now being given to senses other than sight in the appreciation of reality and with poetry losing its pre-eminence as a literary genre, there was, on the other hand, a countervailing revitalization of the tradition with the use of the visual arts in the popular new genre of the realist novel. The principal link, the description of a painting in words, was now strengthened by a number of other interart intersections: the protagonist could be connected with painting as a practitioner, art dealer or critic and this role could lead to a very dense incorporation of visual art material into a novel. But in a genre which often attempted to give a faithful reproduction of the physical world that was, by definition, an artistic immobilization of people and scenery, specific references to plastic models were not obligatory. The verbal transcription of the scene necessarily implied the roving movement of the narrator's eye over the chosen space, real or imagined, just like an artist copying that scene onto a canvas. Yet by far the most important employment of the visual arts in the nineteenth century was the figurative one: the metaphor of art becomes a convenient tool to clarify or to summarize the direction of the plot or theme.

If the use of traditional branches of the visual arts like painting, sculpture and architecture added a cultured, aristocratic or bourgeois leaven to the fiction, a wider definition of the visual arts that included popular prints, engravings, illustrated books or magazines, photographs, mural graffiti and cartoons, to cite a few examples, ensured that the interart parallels were not limited to the most sublime and learned manifestations, favoured by the more affluent social classes, precisely those most able to purchase the higher forms of the arts. If the novelist himself was also a practitioner of the visual arts, had contacts with artists, was a regular visitor to exhibitions and wrote publicly about them, then the presence of the visual arts in his fiction took on an added dimension of relevance. Yet whatever the points of intersection at which the parallels between the visual arts and the novel could occasionally be made, the greater justification for the marriage lay in the contribution it made to the successful elaboration of theme, character or plot. Otherwise, the references risked being labelled examples of name-dropping or intellectual snobbery. Benito Pérez Galdós participated fully in the construction of the nineteenth-century Realist novel and it can be said that he made as significant a contribution to the revitalized tradition of "ut pictura poesis" as those of more universally known novelists such as Zola, Proust, James and Eliot.

Galdós' interest in the visual arts, first aroused during his childhood in Las Palmas, manifested itself in a precocious talent for drawing and painting which soon achieved recognition. The size and quality of this art work, both in early and later years, are far superior to anything Balzac did, for example.[1] Had he applied himself more consistently, Galdós could well have excelled as an exponent of the visual arts. An additional value of his extant art work lies in the fact that its two dominant characteristics – caricature and classical linear composition – are also reflected in the preferences expounded in his art journalism and in the use of the visual art material in his fiction.

His move to Madrid in 1862 consolidated this interest in the visual arts, for he now had the opportunity to visit regularly the Prado and other permanent or occasional exhibitions, especially the triennial competitions of new art work. Regular attendance at the Ateneo and work on several newspapers allowed him to make contacts and friends with artists and critics. One friendship which was to have important repercussions on the determination of his life-long literary and artistic tastes was that with the satirist and art critic, Federico Balart. Frequent visits to galleries and artistic sites abroad,

---

[1] See Wingfried Mary Scott, "Art and Artists in Balzac's *Comédie Humaine*", Diss. Chicago, 1936.

especially during the 1880s, deepened and widened his already impressive knowledge of the history and techniques of the visual arts.

Galdós' first public writings, for such Madrid newspapers as *La Nación* and the *Revista del Movimiento Intelectual de Europa*, had included limited but perceptive discussions on the visual arts. By the 1880s, when he was writing another regular column for *La Prensa* of Buenos Aires, coverage of the visual arts had increased and deepened. But running through all of Galdós' art journalism is a certain pattern of aesthetic judgements: though the classical criteria of order, symmetry and balance are upheld, with condemnation of any deviations, at certain times Galdós shows a sneaking regard for irregular works of a revolutionary nature that somehow manage to express human reality, despite their exceptional and unusual forms. Realism, verisimilitude are also the criteria he applies to the innumerable works of ancient history that flooded the national exhibitions until 1890, when to his great satisfaction the tide turned and genre studies became popular. He criticized the inability of contemporary artists to take their subjects from contemporary history, or, at least, to modernize their figures, as the revered Velázquez and Rembrandt had done in their paintings of ancient or biblical history. Despite Galdós' strictures against this dominant genre, he was again forced to recognize from time to time the merit of some exceptional examples. Verisimilitude, realism, and the abhorrence of their opposites, artificiality and deceit, also led him to utter harsh words on the use of plaster for surface covering in many Madrid churches, precisely because it pretended to appear like other constructional materials. In all of this art appreciation the appeal to the eyes has to be controlled by the thinking mind which looks for the accompanying idea. But if the retina, the pivotal organ in all contemplation of art and indeed reality, is to be given a fair chance, it must be activated in areas of space properly illuminated for the exercise in hand. In his early articles for *La Nación* Galdós fulminated that these physical conditions did not often obtain in Spain.

The most outstanding art journalism Galdós wrote are two special pieces published by the Madrid learned journal, the *Revista de España* in the 1870s. Yet at the same time, because of their careful, almost literary, composition, both "Las generaciones artísticas en la ciudad de Toledo" and "Cuarenta leguas por Cantabria" can be said to form a bridge between Galdós' journalism and fiction. Both blend examples of the visual arts (paintings, sculptures and architecture) with landscapes (urban and rural). Yet the surprising dominant feature of what one would expect to be pleasant travelogues is the narrator's fascination with ugly, grotesque, abnormal works of art or landscape. Naturally, due obeisance is made to works of great beauty, but the persistence with which Galdós' eye spotlights the out-of-the-way and the strange raises questions about the entire reliability of the human eye in appreciating art forms, and the essential deceit practised by the beautiful art form in lulling the viewer into a false awareness of what is reality.

Galdós' first efforts at fiction were mostly in the historical novel, for which ample pictorial evidence could have been used as a source and recognized in the text as such. But by and large Galdós eschews direct presentation of famous art works, preferring a more subtle approach to the question of pictorial affinities. Even when he does mention famous canvases (detailed descriptions of the subject-matter and techniques employed rarely go beyond the title-phrase), their inclusion is tied to the theme of the narrative. This is particularly true of the extended series of iconographical references to Napoleon Bonaparte and Ferdinand VII in the first two series of *Episodios nacionales*, where the form of the art work representing these historical characters is always chosen for the purpose of demythicizing their legendary status. Remembrance of famous pictures is always subordinated to the dictates of his general thematic purpose in the series.

Even in the illustrated edition of the first two series which was published in 1881-1885 the natural tendency for the illustration to dominate the printed text is held in check, although Galdós, justifiably proud of the typographical achievements, felt that the illustrations contributed to a deeper appreciation of the text. Nevertheless, the skilful and imaginative designs of his principal illustrator, Arturo Mélida, with their extraordinary appeal to the eyes, must have made him ponder the advisability of allowing the visual arts to accompany fiction in this most immediate and most spontaneous of interart relationships. It is perhaps noteworthy that Galdós never ventured into any more illustrated editions, either of the historical or the social novels, despite the odd sign of interest from time to time, probably due to a desire for financial returns.

In the contemporary social novels of both "the first epoch" and "the contemporary series" Galdós could not be accused of airing his knowledge, for references to artists, while considerable in number as the list appended to this study indicates, do not add up to any concerted attempt to transmit a corpus of art knowledge to the reader. It is possible for the reader to determine from the texts Galdós' preferences for Velázquez, Raphael, Rembrandt, Goya and Murillo, but there is no attempt by Galdós to filter his own private opinions of great works of art into the text, as Eliot and James sometimes did.

By dividing the contemporary social novels into sub-groups, not according to chronology of publication, but rather according to communality of techniques used in the presentation of the visual arts (although some classifications might be arguable), I have attempted to show how this motif regularly included in the Galdosian novel does contribute to an understanding of each individual novel. In our first group (*La familia de León Roch, Lo prohibido*, the *Torquemada* tetralogy) Galdós details the valuable art collections to be found in the homes of wealthy bourgeois or aristocrats. The description of these paintings is interwoven into the action of the novel to form an ironic commentary on the behaviour and attitudes of the characters, who are indifferent to the visual message put before their eyes. In the following group (*La desheredada, El amigo Manso, Tormento, Fortunata y Jacinta*) the visual art lesson is now presented for the reader's (as well as the fictional character's) guidance, generally in the opening sections of the novel, so that the ensuing narrative can be interpreted in the light of this visual art instruction. In our Group III novels (*Doña Perfecta, Gloria*), this instructional role is discharged by landscape description, not a visual art object or an art comparison. In Group IV (*Marianela, El doctor Centeno, La de Bringas*) there is a fusion of elements used in the previous two groups when picturesque landscape, initial visual art image or comparison are welded together with a new element: the discussion of the problems of physical eyesight, hitherto implicitly a factor of importance in the appreciation of any visual art material whether by the fictional character before concrete art objects or by the reader in his reconstruction of mentioned art objects in his own imagination. Group V includes novels (*Miau, La incógnita, Nazarín, Halma, Misericordia*) drawn mostly from the later so-called spiritualist period of Galdós' fiction. They present an ambivalent initial visual art form which, in turn, alerts the reader to the more enigmatic meaning of the subsequent narration. The final group (*La sombra, Angel Guerra, Tristana*) represents Galdós' most elaborate treatment of the visual arts in his fiction, for now they have become an important factor determining the direction of the narrative. Nonetheless, Galdós' conclusions in all three novels remain the same as those he had made in the preceding groups, as well as in the historical novels: the cultivation and appreciation of the visual arts represent, for the individual fictional character or viewer, a strong temptation to ignore surrounding human or social reality, or to avoid relating the subject of the art object or art form to that reality. The human eye is so bedazzled by the physical appearance of the art form that mental reflection is forgone. What the art object in its glossy surface does incite and activate is the viewer's impressions, his imagination, that rival to insight in man's mind that the Spanish language humorously calls "la loca de la casa" or "the mad woman of the house", a phrase that often appears in Galdós' novels and which constitutes the title of one of his dialogued novels, published in 1892, the same year as *Tristana*.

In conclusion, then, there can be no doubt that the theme of the visual arts constitutes a central preoccupation in Galdós' oeuvre, and that Eugenio d'Ors's statement nearly half a century ago to the opposite effect can now be entirely discounted.[2] What is most startling – and perhaps most controversial! – about his treatment of this theme in his fiction and best journalism (by which I mean the two articles in the 1870s for the *Revista de España*), is the degree of distrust and suspicion he shows generally towards a mode of human expression that he himself cultivated and apparently prized in his own life. As Brian Dendle has suggested in another context, it may be that Galdós' attitudes in his fiction to various aspects of reality were far more radical than he ostensibly professed in real life.[3] Literature might have given him the opportunity to apply some mental self-therapy, to exorcize some misgivings he may have harboured in a private subconscious about the threat of the visual arts to man's ability to perceive human reality correctly. Galdós the novelist, indeed, might well have agreed with Ladislaw in George Eliot's *Middlemarch*, who, when discussing art with the German artist Naumann in the Vatican, declared: "Your painting and Plastik are poor stuff after all. They perturb and dull conceptions instead of raising them. Language is a finer medium."[4]

    [2] *Nuevo glosario* (Madrid: Aguilar, 1947), p. 380.
    [3] *Galdós: the Mature Thought* (Lexington: Univ. of Kentucky Press, 1980), pp. 182-86.
    [4] *Middlemarch: a Study of Provincial Life* (New York: The New American Library, 1964), p. 188.

LIST OF ARTISTS

BIBLIOGRAPHY

LIST OF ARTISTS MENTIONED

The aim of the following is to provide a check-list of the artists' names appearing in this study. Though most are taken from Galdós' writings, they comprise only a fraction of the total number of artists' names to be found in his work. For the more universally known names I have relied on encyclopaedias; for the lesser known Spanish names I have consulted M. Ossorio y Bernard, *Galería biográfica de artistas españoles del siglo XIX*, 2nd ed. (Madrid, 1883-84; facsimile reprint, Barcelona, 1975).

Angelico (Fra Angelico) (1400?-1455), Italian religious painter
Arredondo, Ricardo (1850-1911), Spanish landscape and genre painter
Bandinelli, Baccio (1493?-1560), Italian sculptor
Benlliure, Mariano (1866-1947), Spanish sculptor and painter
Bernini, Giovanni Lorenzo (1598-1680), Italian sculptor
Berruguete, Alonso (1480-1559), Spanish sculptor
Beruete, Aureliano de (1846-1912), Spanish landscape painter
Bosch, Hieronymus (1450?-1516), Dutch painter
Brueghel, Pieter (1525?-1569), Flemish painter
Casado del Alisal, José (1832-1886), Spanish historical painter
Castelló, Vicente (1787-1860), Spanish painter
Ceán Bermúdez, Juan Agustín (1749-1829), Spanish painter and art critic
Channel, French nineteenth-century painter
Checa, Ulpiano (1860-1916), Spanish historical, portrait and genre painter
Constable, John (1776-1837), English landscape painter
Cruzada Villaamil, Gregorio (1832-1884), Spanish art critic
Degas, Edgar (1834-1917), French Impressionist painter
Domingo, Francisco (1842-1920), Spanish historical and genre painter

Doré, Gustave (1832-1883), French illustrator
Dürer, Albrecht (1471-1528), German Renaissance painter and engraver
Egas, Enrique, sixteenth-century Spanish architect
Esquivel, Antonio María (1806-1857), Spanish portrait painter
Fenollera, José (1850-?), Spanish historical painter
Fillol, Antonio (1870-?), Spanish genre painter
Fortuny, Mariano (1838-1874), Spanish genre painter
Géricault, Jean Louis André Théodore (1791-1824), French painter
Goya, Francisco (1746-1828), Spanish painter and engraver
Greco, El (1541-1614), Spanish painter
Gros, Antoine Jean (1771-1835), French historical painter
Hidalgo y Gutiérrez de Caviedes, Rafael (1864-?), Spanish genre painter
Holbein, Hans, The Younger (1497?-1543), German painter and portraitist
Hunt, William Holman (1827-1910), English Pre-Raphaelite painter
Jiménez Aranda, José (1837-1903), Spanish genre painter
Jordaens, Jacob (1593-1678), Flemish Baroque painter
Leonardo da Vinci (1451-1519), Florentine practitioner and theorist of the visual arts
Lhardy, Agustín (1852-?), Spanish landscape painter
Lizcano, Angel (1846-?), Spanish historical painter
López, Vicente (1772-1850), Spanish portrait painter
Luna, Juan (1857-1899), Philippine historical painter
Madrazo, Federico (1815-1894), Spanish portrait and genre painter
Madrazo, Raimundo de (1841-1920), Spanish portrait painter
Maella, Mariano Salvador de (1739-1819), Spanish painter
Manet, Edouard (1832-1883), French painter
Mantegna, Andrea (1431-1506), Italian fresco painter
Masaccio (1401-1428), Florentine painter
Massys, Quentin (1466?-1530), Flemish painter
Mélida, Arturo (1849-1902), Spanish painter and sculptor
Mélida, Enrique (1838-1892), Spanish painter
Mestres, Apeles (1854-1899), Spanish cartoonist
Michelangelo (1475-1564), Italian painter
Morales, Luis (1509-1586), Spanish religious painter
Moreno Carbonero, José (1860-1942), Spanish historical and genre painter

Muñoz y Degrain, Antonio (1841-1924), Spanish landscape and
 genre painter
Murillo, Bartolomé Esteban (1617-1682), Spanish religious
 painter
Oms, Manuel (1842-1889), Spanish sculptor
Ortiz de Villajos, Agustín (?-1902), Spanish architect
Palmaroli, Vicente (1834-1896), Spanish historical painter
Pantoja, Juan de la Cruz (1545?-1610?), Spanish religious and
 portrait painter
Pasternak, Leonid (1862-1945), Russian illustrator
Patenier, Joachim (1472?-1524), Flemish landscape painter
Pedrero, Mariano (1865-?), Spanish illustrator and landscape
 painter
Pellicer, José Luis (1842-1901), Spanish genre painter and
 illustrator
Pinturicchio (1454?-1513), Italian painter
Plasencia, Casto (1848-1890), Spanish historical and genre painter
Poussin, Nicolas (1594-1665), French painter
Raphael (1483-1520), Italian painter
Rembrandt (Rembrandt Harmensz Van Rijn) (1606-1669), Dutch
 painter
Ribera, José de (1591-1652), Spanish painter and engraver
Ribera, Román (1849-1935), Spanish genre painter
Rico, Martín (1833-1908), Spanish landscape painter
Rosales, Eduardo (1836-1873), Spanish historical painter
Rubens, Peter Paul (1577-1640), Flemish painter
Sala, Emilio (1850-1910), historical and genre painter
Sánchez Coello, Alonso (1531?-1588), Spanish portrait painter
Sarto, Andrea del (1486-1530), Florentine painter
Sorolla, Joaquín (1863-1923), Spanish painter
Susillo, Antonio (1857-1896), Spanish sculptor
Teniers, David, The Younger (1610-1690), Flemish genre painter
Thorwaldsen, Bertel (1768?-1844), Danish neo-classic sculptor
Titian (1487?-1576), Venetian painter
Turner, William (1775-1851), English landscape painter
Van Dyck, Sir Anthony (1599-1641), Flemish portraitist
Van Eyck, Jan (active 1422-1441), Flemish painter
Van Loo, Charles André (1705-1765), French Rococo painter
Velázquez, Diego (1599-1660), Spanish painter
Vermeer, Jan (1632-1675), Dutch interior genre painter
Vernet, Horace (1789-1863), French historical painter
Veronese, Paolo (1528-1588), Venetian painter

Villegas, José (1848-1921), Spanish historical painter
Villodas, Ricardo (1846-1904), Spanish historical painter
Vos, Paul de (1596-1678), Flemish painter of animals
Watteau, Antoine (1684-1721), French painter
Zurbarán, Francisco de (1598-1664), Spanish religious painter

BIBLIOGRAPHY

1. GENERAL

Abrams, M. H., *The Mirror and the Lamp* (New York: Oxford Univ. Press, 1953)

Alas, Leopoldo, *La regenta* (Barcelona: Biblioteca "Arte y Letras", 1885)

Alcalá Galiano, Antonio, *Recuerdos de un anciano* (Madrid: Austral, 1951)

Alfonso, Luis, "La pintura contemporánea", *RE*, 29 (28 November 1872), 169-86

Alonso, Amado, and Lida, Raimundo, *El impresionismo en el lenguaje* (Buenos Aires: Univ. de Buenos Aires, 1936)

Alpers, Svetlana and Paul, "*Ut pictura noesis?*: criticism in literary studies and art history", *NLH*, 3 (1972), 433-58

Amador de los Ríos, José, *Toledo pintoresca, o descripción de sus más célebres monumentos* (Madrid: Ignacio Boix, 1845)

Arenal, Concepción, "El realismo y la realidad en las bellas artes y la poesía: IV: la pintura", *RE*, 74 (13 June 1880), 304-21

Artigas-Sanz, María Carmen de, *El libro romántico en España* (Madrid: Consejo Superior de Investigaciones Científicas, 1953)

Azorín [José Martínez Ruiz], *Obras completas*, Vol. III, ed. Angel Cruz Ruel (Madrid: Aguilar, 1961)

—, *La voluntad* (Barcelona: Heinrich, 1902)

Bacon, J., *Theory of Colouring* (London: George Rowney, n.d.)

Balart, Federico, *Impresiones: literatura y arte* (Madrid: Librería de Fernando Fe, 1894)

Balzac, Honoré de, *Le Père Goriot* (Paris: George Barrie, n.d.)

—, *Les Contes drolatiques* (Paris: George Barrie, n.d.)

Bayley, John, "The art of Russianness", *TLS*, 3 December 1982, p. 1329

Bécquer, Gustavo Adolfo, *Obras completas* (Madrid: Aguilar, 1966)

Berenguer, Pedro A., *La guerra y el arte* (Barcelona: Revista Científico-Militar, 1890)

Beruete y Moret, Aureliano de, *Historia de la pintura española en el siglo XIX: elementos nacionales y extranjeros que han influido en ella* (Madrid: Ruiz Hermanos, 1926)

Blanquat, Josette, and Botrel, Jean-François, *Clarín y sus editores: 65 cartas inéditas de Leopoldo Alas a Fernando Fe y Manuel Fernández Lasanata 1884-1893* (Rennes: Université de Haute-Bretagne, 1981)

Bowering, Peter, " 'The sources of light': pictorial imagery and symbolism in *Point Counter Point*", *Studies in the Novel*, 9 (1977), 389-405

Bowie, Theodore Robert, *The Painter in French Fiction: a Critical Essay* (Chapel Hill: Univ. of North Carolina Press, 1950)

Bravo y Moltó, Emilio, and Sancho del Castillo, Vicente, *Recuerdo de un baile de trajes. Reseña del verificado la noche del 25 de febrero de 1884 en el palacio de los excelentísimos señores Duques de Fernán-Núñez* (Madrid: El Liberal, 1884)

Brookner, Anita, *Watteau* (London: Hamlyn, 1967)

Bucknall, Barbara J., *The Religion of Art in Proust* (Urbana: Univ. of Illinois Press, 1970)

Canham, Stephen, "Art and the illustrations of *Vanity Fair* and *The Newcomes*", *Modern Language Quarterly*, 43 (1982), 43-66.

Caro Baroja, Julio, *Ensayos sobre la literatura de cordel* (Madrid: Revista de Occidente, 1969)

Cervantes Saavedra, Miguel de, *Obras completas*, ed. Angel Valbuena Prat (Madrid: Aguilar, 1967)

Clark, Kenneth, in *Aldous Huxley, 1894-1963: a Memorial Volume*, ed. Julian Huxley (London: Chatto and Windus, 1965), pp. 15-18

Clarke, Anthony H., *Pereda paisajista: el sentimiento de la naturaleza en la novela española del siglo XIX* (Santander: Institución Cultural de Cantabria and Diputación Provincial, 1969)

Colonge, Chantal, "Les Voyageurs espagnols du XIXème siècle et la peinture", in *Naturalisme et cosmopolitisme dans les littératures ibériques au XIXème siècle* (Lille: Université de Lille, 1975), pp. 79-102

Crankshaw, Edward, *Tolstoy: the Making of a Novelist* (New York: Viking, 1974)

Da Cal, Margarita Ucelay, *Los españoles pintados por sí mismos (1843-1844); estudio de un género costumbrista* (Mexico City:

El Colegio de México, 1951)

D'Ors, Eugenio, *Nuevo glosario* (Madrid: Aguilar, 1947)

Durán-Sanpere, Agustí, *Grabados populares españoles* (Barcelona: Gustavo Gili, 1971)

Eliot, George, *Middlemarch: a Study of Provincial Life* (Edinburgh: Blackwood, 1871-72; New York: The New American Library, 1964)

Elledge, Scott, ed., *Eighteenth-Century Critical Essays* (Ithaca: Cornell Univ. Press, 1961)

Esteve Botey, Francisco, *El grabado en la ilustración del libro* (Madrid: Consejo Superior de Investigaciones Científicas, 1948)

Festa-McCormick, Diana, "Proustian canvases in itinerant frames", *Symposium*, 36 (1982), 14-29

Fontanella, Lee, "The fashion and styles of Spain's 'costumbrismo'", *RCEH*, 6 (1982), 175-89

Fowler, Alastair, "Periodization and interart analogies", *NLH*, 3 (1972), 487-509

Frank, Joseph, *The Widening Gyre: Crisis and Mastery in Modern Literature* (New Brunswick, New Jersey: Rutgers Univ. Press, 1963)

Fry, Roger, *Vision and Design* (London: Chatto and Windus, 1957)

Gaither, Mary, "Literature and the arts", in *Comparative Literature: Method and Perspective*, ed. Newton P. Stallknecht and Horst Frenz, 2nd ed. (Carbondale: Southern Illinois Univ. Press, 1971), pp. 183-200

Gassier, Pierre and Wilson, Juliet, *Goya: His Life and Work* (London: Thames and Hudson, 1971)

Gaya Nuño, Juan Antonio, *Arte del siglo XIX*, Vol. XIX of *Ars Hispaniae: historia universal del arte hispánico* (Madrid: Plus Ultra, 1966)

Giner de Los Ríos, Francisco, *Educación y enseñanza*, Vol. XII of *Obras completas*, 2nd ed. (Madrid: Espasa Calpe, 1933)

Giovannini, G., "Method in the study of literature in its relations to the other fine arts", *JAAC*, 8 (1949-50), 185-95

Glendinning, Nigel, *Goya and His Critics* (New Haven: Yale Univ. Press, 1977)

Gómez de la Serna, Gaspar, *Goya y su España* (Madrid: Alianza, 1969)

Grabar, Oleg, "History of art and history of literature: some random thoughts", *NLH*, 3 (1972), 559-68

Hagstrum, Jean H., "The sister arts: from neoclassic to romantic", in *Comparatists at Work*, ed. Stephen G. Nicholls, Jr., and Richard B. Vowles (Waltham, Massachusetts: Blaisdell, 1968), pp. 169-94

—, *The Sister Arts: The Tradition of Literary Pictorialism in English Poetry from Dryden to Gray* (Chicago: Univ. of Chicago Press, 1958)

Harvey, J. R., *Victorian Novelists and Their Illustrators* (New York: New York Univ. Press, 1971)

Hatzfeld, Helmut A., "Literary criticism through art and art criticism through literature", *JAAC*, 6 (1947-48), 1-21

Horace, *The Complete Works of Horace*, ed. Casper J. Kramer (New York: Modern Library, 1936)

Hugo, Victor, *Notre-Dame de Paris* (Paris: Fasquelle, n.d.)

Hussey, Christopher, *The Picturesque: Studies in a Point of View* (London: Frank Cass, 1967)

Ilie, Paul, "Bécquer and the romantic grotesque", *Publications of the Modern Language Association of America*, 83 (1968), 312-31

James, Henry, *The Art of Fiction and Other Essays* (New York: Oxford Univ. Press, 1948)

King, Edmund L., *Gustavo Adolfo Bécquer: From Painter to Poet. Together With a Concordance of the "Rimas"* (Mexico City: Porrúa, 1953)

Krawitz, Henry, *Writers on Painting: a Study of the Theory and Criticism of the Visual Arts in Zola, Wilde, James and Proust and Its Relevance to Their Fiction* (Ann Arbor: Xerox University Microfilms, 1980)

Kuh, Katharine, *The Open Eye ... in Pursuit of Art* (New York: Harper and Row, 1971)

Lafuente Ferrari, Enrique, *El libro de Santillana* (Santander: Diputación Provincial, 1955)

—, "El pintor de Toledo, Ricardo Arredondo (1850-1911)", *AE*, 26 (1969), 37-79

Laubriet, Pierre, *L'Intelligence de l'art chez Balzac* (Paris: Didier, 1961)

Laude, Jean, "On the analysis of poems and paintings", *NLH*, 3 (1972), 471-86

Lessing, Gotthold Ephraim, *Laocoön*, ed. William A. Steel (London: Dent, 1949)

Litvak, Lily, *A Dream of Arcadia: Anti-Industrialism in Spanish Literature, 1895-1905* (Austin: Univ. of Texas Press, 1975)

Lozoya, El marqués de, *Historia del arte hispánico*, 5 vols. (Barcelona: Salvat, 1931-49)

Machado, Antonio, *Obras: poesía y prosa*, ed. Aurora de Albornoz and Guillermo de Torre, 2nd ed. (Buenos Aires: Losada, 1973)

Maurois, André, *Napoleon: a Pictorial Biography* (London: Thames and Hudson, 1963)

Mélida, Julia, *Biografía de Arturo Mélida* (unpublished manuscript)

Mendoza, Francisco de, *Manual del pintor de historia* (Madrid: Fortanet, 1870)

Merriman, James D., "The parallel of arts: some misgivings and a faint affirmation", *JAAC*, 31 (1972-73), 153-64, 309-21

Mesonero Romanos, Ramón de, *Escenas matritenses*, ed. Federico Carlos Sainz de Robles (Madrid: Aguilar, 1956)

—, "Prospecto", *Semanario Pintoresco Español* (Madrid: 1936)

Meyers, Jeffrey, *Painting and the Novel* (New York: Barnes and Noble, 1975)

Navascués Palacio, Pedro, *Arquitectura y arquitectos madrileños del siglo XIX* (Madrid: Instituto de Estudios Madrileños, 1973)

Osborne, Harold, *The Oxford Companion to Art* (Oxford: Clarendon Press, 1970)

Ossorio y Bernard, M., *Galería biográfica de artistas españoles del siglo XIX*, 2nd. ed. (Madrid: 1883-84; facsimile reprint, Barcelona: Gaudí, 1975)

Park, Roy, *Hazlitt and the Spirit of the Age: Abstraction and Critical Theory* (Oxford: Clarendon Press, 1971)

Pérez de Anaya, Francisco, "Estado que presenta la industria tipográfica; causas que impiden sus progresos con perjuicio de los operarios, ruina de considerables capitales, y medios que pueden emplearse para que se ponga al nivel de los países más adelantados", *Revista de España, de Indias y del Extranjero*, 13 (1848), 5-15; 113-37

Praz, Mario, *Mnemosyne: the Parallels Between Literature and the Visual Arts* (Princeton: Princeton Univ. Press, 1970)

Proudhon, P. J., *Du Principe de l'art et de sa destination sociale* (Paris: Garnier, 1865)

Proust, Marcel, *A la recherche du temps perdu* (Paris: Nouvelle Revue Française, 1913-27)

R., "Observatorio de Madrid", *El museo universal*, 6 May 1860, pp. 150-51

Regoyos y Valdés, Darío de, *La España negra de Verhaeren* (Madrid: La Lectura, 1924)

Riley, E.C., *Cervantes's Theory of the Novel* (Oxford: Clarendon Press, 1964)

Robert, Roberto, ed., *Las españolas pintadas por los españoles*, 2 vols. (Madrid: J. E. Morete, 1871-72)

Ruskin, John, *The Seven Lamps of Architecture* (London: Smith, Elder and Company, 1849)

Sartre, Jean-Paul, "What is writing?", *Partisan Review*, 15 (1948), 9-31

Schopenhauer, Arthur, *The World as Will and Idea*, trans.
R. B. Haldane and J. Kemp, 3 vols. (London: Trübner,
1883-86)

Scott, Wingfried Mary, "Art and Artists in Balzac's *Comédie
Humaine*", Diss. Univ. of Chicago, 1936

Sebastián, Santiago, "Arredondo y otros paisajistas toledanos",
AE, 17 (1960), 113-27

Seznec, Jean, "Art and literature: a plea for humility", *NLH*, 3
(1972) 569-74

Sinclair, Alison, *Valle-Inclán's "Ruedo ibérico": a Popular View of
Revolution* (London: Tamesis, 1977)

Skard, Sigmund, "The use of color in literature", *Proceedings of
the American Philosophical Society*, 90 (1946), 163-249

Teesing, H.P.H., "Literature and the other arts: some remarks",
Yearbook of Comparative and General Literature, 12 (1963),
27-35

Torre, Guillermo de, " 'Ut pictura poesis' ", *Papeles de son
Armadans*, 82 (1963), 9-44

Torres, David, "Del archivo epistolar de Palacio Valdés", *Revista
de Literatura*, 86 (1981), 263-78

Tubino, F.M., *El arte y los artistas contemporáneos en la península*
(Madrid: Durán, 1871)

Valle-Inclán, Ramón del, *Luces de Bohemia*, Vol. XIX of *Opera
omnia* (Madrid: Rivadeneyra, 1924)

Vélez de Guevara, Luis, *El diablo cojuelo* (Madrid: Alonso Pérez,
1641)

Viardot, Louis, *Les Musées d'Espagne*, 3rd ed. (Paris: Hachette,
1860)

Vicuña, R.L. de, "La exposición de bellas artes de 1876", *RE*, 50
(13 May 1876), 133-42

Wechsler, Judith, *A Human Comedy: Physiognomy and Caricature
in 19th-Century Paris* (London: Thames and Hudson, 1982)

Weisstein, Ulrich, "Comparing literature and art: current trends
and prospects in critical theory and methodology", in *Proceedings of the IXth Congress of the International Comparative
Literature Association, Innsbruck 1979*, ed. Zoran Konstantinović, Steven P. Scher and Ulrich Weisstein (Innsbruck:
Vlg des Inst. für Sprachwissenschaft der Univ. Innsbruck,
1981), III, 19-30

Wellek, René, "The parallelism between literature and the arts",
English Institute Annual for 1941 (New York: Columbia Univ.
Press, 1942), pp. 29-63

Wilde, Oscar, *The Picture of Dorian Gray* (London: Ward, Lock
and Bowden, 1891)

Witemeyer, Hugh, *George Eliot and the Visual Arts* (New Haven:
Yale Univ. Press, 1979)

Zola, Emile, *L'Assommoir* (Paris: Fasquelle, n.d.)

—, *L'Oeuvre* (Paris: Charpentier, 1886), in his *Oeuvres complètes* (Paris: Fasquelle, 1967), V, 423-747

2. GALDOS

Alfaro, Gustavo A., "Religious symbolism in Galdós' *Doña Perfecta*: Pepe Rey's passion", *Revista de Estudios Hispánicos*, 14 (1980), 75-83

Alfieri, J.J., "El arte pictórico en las novelas de Galdós", *AG*, 3 (1968), 79-86

—, "Images of the 'Sacra familia' in Galdós' novels", *Hispanófila*, 74 (1982), 25-40

Antón del Olmet, Luis, and García Carrafa, Arturo, *Los grandes españoles: Galdós* (Madrid: Alrededor del Mundo, 1912)

Bello, Luis, *Ensayos e imaginaciones sobre Madrid* (Madrid: Calleja, 1919)

Berkowitz, H. Chonon, *La biblioteca de Benito Pérez Galdós* (Las Palmas: El Museo Canario, 1951)

—, *Pérez Galdós: Spanish Liberal Crusader* (Madison: Univ. of Wisconsin Press, 1948)

Beyrie, Jacques, *Galdós et son mythe* (Lille: Université de Lille III, 1980)

Blanquat, Josette, "Les Annotations marginales des livres de Galdós", in *Etudes ibériques et latino-américaines* (Paris: Presses Universitaires de France, 1968), pp. 23-43

Bly, Peter A., *Benito Pérez Galdós: La de Bringas* (London: Grant and Cutler, 1981)

—, *Galdós's Novel of the Historical Imagination: a Study of the Contemporary Novels* (Liverpool: Francis Cairns, 1983)

—, "Egotism and charity in *Marianela*", *AG*, 7 (1972), 49-66

—, "Fortunata and No. 11, Cava de San Miguel", *Hispanófila*, 59 (1976-77), 31-48

—, "Galdós, the Madrid Royal Palace and the September 1868 Revolution", *RCEH*, 5 (1980), 1-17

—, "*Nazarín*: ¿enigma eterno o triunfo del arte galdosiano?", *CHA*, 124 (1981), 286-300

—, "Sallies and encounters in *Torquemada en la hoguera*: patterns of significance", *AG*, 13 (1978), 23-31

Bravo-Villasante, Carmen, *Galdós visto por sí mismo* (Madrid: Magisterio Español, 1970)

—, "El naturalismo de Galdós y el mundo de *La desheredada*", *CHA*, 77 (1969), 479-86

—, "28 cartas de Galdós a Pereda", *CHA*, 84 (1970-71), 9-51

Carretero, José María [El Caballero Audaz], "La figura de la semana", *Nuevo Mundo*, 9 January 1920

Casalduero, Joaquín, "*La sombra*", *AG*, 1 (1966), 33-38

Chamberlin, Vernon A., "*Doña Perfecta*: light and darkness, good and evil", in *Galdós: Papers Read at the Modern Foreign Language Department Symposium: Nineteenth-Century Spanish Literature: Benito Pérez Galdós. Mary Washington College of the University of Virginia, April 21-22, 1967* (Fredericksburg: Univ. of Virginia, 1967), pp. 57-70

—, "Galdós' chromatic symbolism key in *Lo prohibido*", *HR*, 32 (1964), 109-17

—, "Poor man's windmill: aquatic symbolism in *Fortunata y Jacinta*", *HR*, 50 (1982), 417-37

Clarke, A.H., "Paisaje interior y paisaje exterior: aspectos de la técnica descriptiva de Galdós", *Actas del primer congreso internacional de estudios galdosianos* (Las Palmas: Excmo Cabildo Insular, 1977), pp. 245-52

Cossío, Manuel B., "Galdós y Giner: una carta de Galdós", *LL*, 20 (1920), 254-58

Crispin, John, "The role of secondary plots and secondary characters in Galdós' *Miau*", *Hispania*, 65 (1982), 365-70

Cuesta, Leonel-Antonio de la, *El audaz: análisis integral* (Montevideo: I.E.S., 1973)

Dendle, Brian J., *Galdós: the Mature Thought* (Lexington: Univ. of Kentucky Press, 1980)

—, "A note on the genesis of the *Episodios nacionales*", *AG*, 15 (1980), 137-40

Franz, Thomas R., *Remaking Reality in Galdós: a Writer's Interactions with his Context* (Athens, Ohio: Strathmore Press, 1982)

Gaos, Vicente, *Temas y problemas de literatura española* (Madrid: Guadarrama, 1959)

Gilman, Stephen, *Galdós and the Art of the European Novel 1867-1887* (Princeton: Princeton Univ. Press, 1981)

—, "The birth of Fortunata", *AG*, 1 (1966), 71-83

Gimeno Casalduero, Joaquín, "La caracterización plástica del personaje en la obra de Pérez Galdós: del tipo al individuo", *AG*, 7 (1972), 19-25

Guimerá Peraza, Marcos, *Maura y Galdós* (Las Palmas: Excmo Cabildo Insular, 1967)

Gullón, Ricardo, *Psicologías del autor y lógicas del personaje* (Madrid: Taurus, 1979)

—, *Técnicas de Galdós* (Madrid: Taurus, 1970)

Hall, J. B., "Galdós's use of the Christ-symbol in *Doña Perfecta*", *AG*, 8 (1973), 95-98

Hinterhäuser, Hans, *Los "Episodios nacionales" de Benito Pérez Galdós*, trans. José Escobar (Madrid: Gredos, 1963)

Hoar, Leo J., Jr., "Galdós' counter-attack on his critics: the lost short story, 'El pórtico de la gloria'", *Symposium*, 30 (1976), 277-307

—, "Galdós y Aureliano de Beruete: visión renovada de Orbajosa", *AEA*, 20 (1974), 693-707

Johnson, Carroll B., "The café in Galdós's *La Fontana de Oro*", *BHS*, 42 (1965), 112-17

Jover Zamora, José María, "Benito Pérez Galdós: *La de los tristes destinos* (caps. I y II)", in *El comentario de textos 2: de Galdós a García Márquez*, ed. Andrés Amorós (Madrid: Castalia, 1974), pp. 15-110

Kronik, John W., "Galdós and the grotesque", *AG*, anejo (1978), 39-54

—, "*Misericordia* as metafiction", in *Homenaje a Antonio Sánchez Barbudo: ensayos de literatura española moderna*, ed. Benito Brancaforte, Edward R. Mulvihill and Robert G. Sánchez (Madison: Dept. of Spanish and Portuguese, Univ. of Wisconsin, 1981), pp. 37-50

López Rubio, José, *et al*, *Benito Pérez Galdós* (Madrid: Prensa Española, 1972)

Lowe, Jennifer, "The function and presentation of the world of nature in three Galdosian novels", *AG*, 14 (1979), 7-12

—, "Theme, imagery and dramatic irony in *Doña Perfecta*", *AG*, 4 (1969), 49-53

Madariaga, Benito, *Pérez Galdós: biografía santanderina* (Santander: Institución Cultural de Cantabria and Instituto de Literatura José María de Pereda, 1979)

Malaret, Nicole, "*Misericordia*: théorie et pratique du roman", *Les Langues Néo-Latines*, 74 (1980), 64-74

Marañón, Gregorio, *Obras completas*, Vol. IV (Madrid: Espasa-Calpe, 1968)

Mesa, Rafael de, "Galdós, dibujante", *Hispania* (Buenos Aires), 11 (1943), 18-19

Millares Cubas, Luis y Agustín, "Don Benito Pérez Galdós: recuerdos de su infancia en Las Palmas", *LL*, 20 (1920), 333-52

Montes Huidobro, Matías, "*El audaz*: desdoblamiento de un ritual sexo-revolucionario", *Hispania*, 63 (1980), 487-97

Nuez, Sebastián de la, and Schraibman, José, eds., *Cartas del archivo de Galdós* (Madrid: Taurus, 1967)

Orozco Díaz, Emilio, "El concepto y la palabra 'barroco' en los novelistas españoles del siglo XIX: unas notas sueltas centradas en Alarcón, Galdós y Clarín", in *Homenaje a Gonzalo Torrente Ballester* (Salamanca: Biblioteca de la Caja de Ahorros y Monte de Piedad, 1981), pp. 583-613

Ortega, Soledad, *Cartas a Galdós* (Madrid: Revista de Occidente, 1964)

Ortega Munilla, José, "Los *Episodios nacionales* ilustrados", *La Ilustración Española y Americana*, 2 (1881), 375-78

Ortiz Armengol, Pedro, "El convento de las Micaelas en *Fortunata y Jacinta*", *Estafeta Literaria*, 550 (1974), 4-7

Palencia Tubau, C., "Galdós, dibujante, pintor y crítico", *LL*, 20 (1920), 29-40, 134-45

Pardo Bazán, Emilia, *Obras completas*, Vol. III, ed. Harry L. Kirby, Jr. (Madrid: Aguilar, 1973)

—, *Cartas a Benito Pérez Galdós* (1889-1890), ed. Carmen Bravo-Villasante (Madrid: Turner, 1975)

Pattison, Walter T., *Benito Pérez Galdós: etapas preliminares de "Gloria"* (Madrid: Puvill, 1975)

Pérez Vidal, José, *Canarias en Galdós* (Las Palmas: Excmo Cabildo Insular, 1979)

—, "Pérez Galdós y la noche de San Daniel", *Revista Hispánica Moderna*, 17 (1951), 94-110

Petit, Marie-Claire, *Galdós et "La Fontana de Oro": génèse de l'oeuvre d'un romancier et les sources balzaciennes de "Fortunata y Jacinta"* (Paris: Ediciones Hispano-Americanas, 1972)

—, *Les Personnages féminins dans les romans de Benito Pérez Galdós* (Lyons: Université de Lyons, 1972)

Price, R.M., "The five 'padrotes' in Pérez Galdós' *El amigo Manso*", *Philological Quarterly*, 48 (1969), 234-46

Raphaël, Suzanne, "Un extraño viaje de novios", *AG*, 3 (1968), 35-49

Rodgers, Eamonn, *Pérez Galdós: Miau* (London: Grant and Cutler, 1978)

Rodríguez Batllori, Francisco, "La adolescencia de Galdós: su afición al dibujo, y sus primeras obras literarias", *Semana*, 610 (30 October 1951)

—, *Galdós y su tiempo: estampas de una vida*, 2nd ed. (Madrid: Augustinus, 1969)

Ruiz de la Serna, Enrique, and Cruz Quintana, Sebastián, *Prehistoria y protohistoria de Benito Pérez Galdós: contribución a una biografía* (Las Palmas: Excmo Cabildo Insular, 1973)

Ruiz Ramón, Francisco, *Tres personajes galdosianos* (Madrid: Revista de Occidente, 1964)

Scanlon, Geraldine M., "Religion and art in *Angel Guerra*", *AG*, 8 (1973), 99-105

Shoemaker, William H., *The Novelistic Art of Galdós* (Valencia: Albatros/Hispanófila, 1980)

—, "Una amistad literaria: la correspondencia epistolar entre

Galdós y Narciso Oller", *Boletín de la Real Academia de Buenas Letras* (Barcelona), 30 (1963-64), 247-306

Smith, Gilbert, "La elaboración del mito de Prometeo en las novelas de Torquemada", *Actas del segundo congreso internacional de estudios galdosianos* (Las Palmas: Excmo Cabildo Insular, 1977), II, 361-68

—, "Galdós' *Tristana* and letters from Concha-Ruth Morell", *AG*, 10 (1975), 91-120

Smith, V.A., and Varey, J.E., " 'Esperpento': some early usages in the novels of Galdós", in *Galdós Studies*, ed. J. E. Varey (London: Tamesis, 1970), pp. 195-204

Sopeña Ibáñez, Federico, *Arte y sociedad en Galdós* (Madrid: Gredos, 1970)

Terry, Arthur, "*Lo prohibido*: unreliable narrator and untruthful narrative", in *Galdós Studies*, ed. J. E. Varey (London: Tamesis, 1970), pp. 62-89

Turner, Harriet S., "Rhetoric in *La sombra*: the author and his story", *AG*, 6 (1971), 5-19

Urey, Diane F., *Galdós and the Irony of Language* (Cambridge: Cambridge Univ. Press, 1982)

Valis, Noël M., "El significado del jardín en *Doña Perfecta* de Galdós", in *Actas del séptimo congreso de la Asociación Internacional de Hispanistas* (Rome: Bulzoni, 1982), pp. 1031-38

—, "Art, memory and the human in Galdós' *Tristana*", *KRQ*, 31 (1984), 207-20.

Varela Hervías, E., *Cartas de Pérez Galdós a Mesonero Romanos* (Madrid: Excmo Ayuntamiento de Madrid, 1943)

Varey, J. E., *Pérez Galdós: Doña Perfecta* (London: Tamesis, 1971)

Vega, José, "Galdós, dibujante", *ABC*, 20 December 1955

Weber, Robert J., "Galdós y Orbajosa", *HR*, 31 (1963), 348-49

Wellington, Marie A., "A symbolism linking *Marianela* and the Torquemada series", *Hispanófila*, 73 (1981), 21-27

Wright, Chad C., "Artifacts and effigies: the Porreño household revisited", *AG*, 14 (1979), 13-26

Ynduráin, Francisco, *Galdós entre la novela y el folletín* (Madrid: Taurus, 1970)

3. BIBLIOGRAPHIES ON GALDOS

García Lorenzo, Luciano, "Bibliografía galdosiana", *CHA*, 84 (1970-71), 758-97

Hernández Suárez, Manuel, *Bibliografía de Galdós*, Vol. I (Las Palmas: Excmo Cabildo Insular, 1972)

—, "Bibliografía", *AG*, 3 (1968), 191-212; 4 (1969), 127-52; 6 (1971), 139-63; 7 (1972), 145-65; 9 (1974), 175-206

Sackett, Theodore A., *Pérez Galdós: an Annotated Bibliography* (Albuquerque: Univ. of New Mexico Press, 1968)

Woodbridge, Hensley C., *Benito Pérez Galdós: a Selective Annotated Bibliography* (Metuchen, New Jersey: Scarecrow, 1975)

—, *Benito Pérez Galdós: an Annotated Bibliography for 1975-1980* (Watertown, Massachusetts: General Microfilm, 1981)

LIVERPOOL MONOGRAPHS IN HISPANIC STUDIES

(ISSN 0261-1538)

General Editor: James Higgins. Assistant Editors: Ann Mackenzie, Roger Wright

Liverpool Monographs in Hispanic Studies consists of academic monographs covering a wide range of Hispanic subjects, and gives equal weight to Spain and to Latin America. Its tendency is towards modern and literary studies, but its scope is not confined to these areas. The editorial board operates from the Department of Hispanic Studies, University of Liverpool.

LMHS 1
THE POET IN PERU Alienation and the Quest for a Super-reality
JAMES HIGGINS   0 905205 10 3   x+166 pp.   1982

LMHS 2
GALDÓS'S NOVEL OF THE HISTORICAL IMAGINATION
A Study of the Contemporary Novels
PETER A. BLY   0 905205 14 6   xii+195 pp.   1983

LMHS 3
THE DECEPTIVE REALISM OF MACHADO DE ASSIS
A Dissenting Interpretation of *Dom Casmurro*
JOHN GLEDSON   0 905205 19 7   viii+215 pp.   1984

LMHS 4
THE STRUCTURED WORLD OF JORGE GUILLÉN
A Study of *Cántico* and *Clamor*
ELIZABETH MATTHEWS   0 905205 23 5   x+326 pp.   1985

LMHS 5
READING ONETTI Language, Narrative and the Subject
MARK MILLINGTON   0 905205 26 x   vi+345 pp.   1985

LMHS 6
VISION AND THE VISUAL ARTS IN GALDOS
A Study of the Novels and Newspaper Articles
PETER A. BLY   0 905205 30 8   x+242 pp.   1986

FORTHCOMING

LMHS 7
A HISTORY OF PERUVIAN LITERATURE
JAMES HIGGINS   around 400 pp.   1986

FURTHER VOLUMES IN PREPARATION